Praise for *Lean-Agile Software Devel*

"This book is a timely addition to our Agile body of knowledge. Very little has been said to date about how we scale Agile software projects beyond the single team. The authors do an excellent job of explaining the foundations of Lean thinking and how these concepts can be applied across the enterprise. Lean is the key to scaling Agile projects, and this book provides the foundational knowledge you need to make it happen."

—**Mike Cottmeyer,** *product consultant and
Agile evangelist, VersionOne*

"The book brings a pragmatic approach to the difficult transition from early adoption of Agile practices to enabling product development. It is thought provoking in the context of the teams I am currently coaching, and it highlights a number of areas for improvement. I would recommend this book to anyone who is coaching an enterprise-wide Lean-Agile transformation."

—**Kay Johnson,** *PMP, Agile development consultant
and project manager*

"The ideas from the Toyota Production System and Lean manufacturing in general are gradually making their way into the world of software development, and this book provides both a gentle introduction to those unfamiliar with Agile/Lean as well as more advanced material for those who are already practitioners in this area. Worth reading."

—**Mark Needham,** *application developer,
ThoughtWorks*

"For a good few years, when asking why Agile approaches work, we got the response 'It's empirical. We tried things and kept the ones that worked.' Now people have applied theory from the Lean body of knowledge, and it tells us why Agile approaches work. Using this theory, we can make well-reasoned choices about what changes to our ways of working would be improvements, overall. This book is about this synergy between Lean and Agile. For those who believe in magic, find an empirical guru to believe. For the rationalists among us, here's a good book for you."

—**Paul Oldfield,** *Capgemini*

"This book is a worthy roadmap to a successful adoption of Lean-Agile development and management. You can see in every detail the authors have on-the-job experience. The way they write shows their enthusiasm for Lean, and this motivates the reader to follow the principles and practices in the book. I had a great time reading this book and I am using it daily as a reference."

—**Domingo Chabalgoit** , *independent IT consultant*

"There are many sources of information for Agile software development and Lean systems thinking. Until now, attempts to merge the two have often resulted in frustration, delays, quality issues, and budget overruns. Lean-Agile Software Development is the roadmap to achieving success using Lean-Agile techniques and applying them throughout the enterprise and product-development life cycle."

—**Bob Bogetti,** *lead system designer,*
Baxter Healthcare

Lean-Agile Software Development

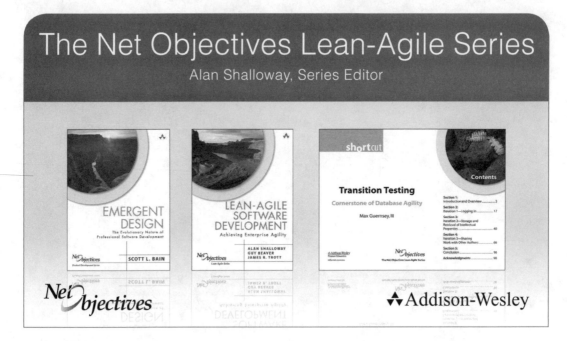

The Net Objectives Lean-Agile Series

Alan Shalloway, Series Editor

Visit **informit.com/netobjectives** for a complete list of available publications.

The **Net Objectives Lean-Agile Series** provides fully integrated Lean-Agile training, consulting, and coaching solutions for businesses, management, teams, and individuals. Series editor Alan Shalloway and the Net Objectives team strongly believe that it is not the software, but rather the value that software contributes—to the business, to the consumer, to the user—that is most important.

The best—and perhaps only—way to achieve effective product development across an organization is a well-thought-out combination of Lean principles to guide the enterprise, agile practices to manage teams, and core technical skills. The goal of **The Net Objectives Lean-Agile Series** is to establish software development as a true profession while helping unite management and individuals in work efforts that "optimize the whole," including

- The whole organization: Unifying enterprises, teams, and individuals to best work together
- The whole product: Not just its development, but also its maintenance and integration
- The whole of time: Not just now, but in the future—resulting in a sustainable return on investment

The books included in this series are written by expert members of Net Objectives. These books are designed to help practitioners understand and implement the key concepts and principles that drive the development of valuable software.

✦Addison-Wesley **Cisco Press** EXAM/**CRAM**

Lean-Agile Software Development

Achieving Enterprise Agility

Alan Shalloway
Guy Beaver
James R. Trott

✦✦Addison-Wesley

Upper Saddle River, NJ • Boston • Indianapolis • San Francisco
New York • Toronto • Montreal • London • Munich • Paris • Madrid
Capetown • Sydney • Tokyo • Singapore • Mexico City

Illustrations by Andrea Chartier Bain

The publisher offers excellent discounts on this book when ordered in quantity for bulk purchases or special sales, which may include electronic versions and/or custom covers and content particular to your business, training goals, marketing focus, and branding interests. For more information, please contact:

U.S. Corporate and Government Sales
(800) 382-3419
corpsales@pearsontechgroup.com

For sales outside the United States please contact:

International Sales
international@pearsoned.com

Visit us on the Web: informit.com/netobjectives

Library of Congress Cataloging-in-Publication Data

Shalloway, Alan.
  Lean-agile software development : achieving enterprise agility / Alan Shalloway, Guy Beaver, James R. Trott.
      p. cm.
  Includes bibliographical references and index.
  ISBN 0-321-53289-9 (pbk. : alk. paper) 1. Agile software development. I. Beaver, Guy. II. Trott, James. III. Title.
  QA76.76.D47S47 2009
  005.1—dc22

                                                                                              2009032621

ISBN-13: 978-0-321-53289-3
ISBN-10:   0-321-53289-9

Text printed in the United States on recycled paper at Courier in Stoughton, Massachusetts.
First printing, October 2009

To my loving and lifetime partner, Leigh, who has seen me through yet another book and without whom this book would not have been written.

—Alan Shalloway

To my darling family—Genny, Ruth Ann, Meredith, and Ben—for so graciously tolerating the travel required to amass the stories that helped create this book.

—Guy Beaver

To Dr. Bob and Sharon Foote, Lorien, Dedra, and Heather. Mentors in life, in faith, and in thought. Sola gloria Dei.

—Jim Trott

Contents

text

Chapter 7
Lean-Agile Release Planning _____ 117

Chapter 8
Visual Controls and Information Radiators for
Enterprise Teams _____ 137

Chapter 9
The Role of Quality Assurance in Lean-Agile
Software Development

Chapter 10
Becoming an Agile Enterprise

Series Foreword
The Net Objectives Product Development Series

Alan Shalloway, CEO, Net Objectives

If you are like me, you will just skim this foreword for the series and move on, figuring there is nothing of substance here. That would be a mistake. Unless you have read this foreword in another book in the series, please take a moment with me at the outset of this book (if you've already read a foreword from another book, please skip a couple of pages to This Book's Role in the Series).

I want you to consider with me a tale that most people know but don't often think about. That tale illustrates what is ailing this industry. And it sets the context for why we wrote the Net Objectives Product Development Series and this particular book.

I have been doing software development since 1970. To me, it is just as fresh today as it was four decades ago. It is a never-ending source of fascination to me to contemplate how to do something better, and it is a never-ending source of humility to confront how limited my abilities truly are. I love it.

Throughout my career, I have also been interested in other industries, especially engineering and construction. Now, engineering and construction have suffered some spectacular failures: the Leaning Tower of Pisa, the Tacoma Narrows Bridge, the Hubble telescope. In its infancy, engineers knew little about the forces at work around them. Mostly, engineers tried to improve practices and to learn what they could from failures. It took a long time—centuries—before they acquired a solid understanding about how to do things.

No one would build a bridge today without taking into account long-established bridge-building practices (factoring in stress, compression, and the like) but software developers get away with writing code based on "what they like" every day, with little or no complaint from their peers. Why do we work this way?

But this is only part of the story. Ironically, much of the rest is related to why we call this the "Net Objectives Product Development Series." The Net Objectives part is pretty obvious. All of the books in this series were written either by Net Objectives staff or by those whose views are consistent with ours. Why Product Development? Because when building software, it is always important to remember that software development is really product development.

By itself, software has little inherent value. Its value comes when it enables delivery of products and services. Therefore, it is more useful to think of software development as part of product development—the set of activities we use to discover and create products that meet the needs of customers while advancing the strategic goals of the company.

Mary and Tom Poppendieck, in their excellent book, *Implementing Lean Software Development: From Concept to Cash* (2006), note:

> It is the product, the activity, the process in which software is embedded that is the real product under development. The software development is just a subset of the overall product development process. So in a very real sense, we can call software development a subset of product development. And thus, if we want to understand lean software development, we would do well to discover what constitutes excellent product development.

In other words, software in itself isn't important. It is the value that it contributes—to the business, to the consumer, to the user—that is important. When developing software, we must always remember to look to what value is being added by our work. At some level, we all know this. But so often organizational "silos" work against us, keeping us from working together, from focusing on efforts that create value.

The best—and perhaps only—way to achieve effective product development across an organization is a well-thought-out combination of Lean principles to guide the enterprise, Agile practices to manage teams, and technical skills (test-driven development, design patterns). That is the motivation for the Net Objectives Product Development Series.

Too long, this industry has suffered from a seemingly endless swing of the pendulum from no process to too much process and then back to no process: from heavyweight methods focused on enterprise control to disciplined teams focused on the project at hand. The time has come for management and individuals to work together to maximize the production of business value across the enterprise. We believe Lean principles can guide us in this.

Lean principles tell us to look at the systems in which we work and then relentlessly improve them in order to increase our speed and quality (which will drive down our cost). This requires

1. Business to select the areas of software development that will return the greatest value

2. Teams to own their systems and continuously improve them

3. Management to train and support their teams to do this

4. An appreciation for what constitutes quality work

It may seem that we are very far from achieving this in the software-development industry, but the potential is definitely there. Lean principles help with the first three and the understanding of technical programming and design has matured far enough to help us with the fourth.

As we improve our existing analysis and coding approaches with the discipline, mindset, skills, and focus on value that Lean, Agile, patterns, and test-driven development teach us, we will help elevate software development from being merely a craft into a true profession. We have the knowledge required to do this; what we need is a new attitude.

The Net Objectives Product Development Series aims to develop this attitude. Our goal is to help unite management and individuals in work efforts that "optimize the whole":

- **The whole organization**   Integrating enterprise, team, and individuals to work best together.

- **The whole product**   Not just its development, but also its maintenance and integration.

- **The whole of time**   Not just now, but in the future. We want sustainable ROI from our effort.

This Book's Role in the Series

While Scott Bain's *Emergent Design: The Evolutionary Nature of the Software Profession* dealt with how to raise the bar in technical practices, this book is about how to raise the bar in product and project management. Both books, as I suspect all books in the series will be, are based on the belief that there are laws (rules) that must be followed to be effective and efficient.

As Agile has matured, we're finding it useful to go beyond the mere mandate of building in stages and having teams solve their own problems. While both are sage advice, more is needed as our products become more complex. Management needs to become more intimately involved in solving the problems teams face. And although the development teams are the ones who actually deliver the value, they are not empowered to solve the organizational and cultural problems that get in their way.

We believe that Lean thinking provides a new way for management and teams to work together. We further believe that the next generation of Agile methods will be those that promote this cooperative effort instead of being neutral at best and negative at worst. This book is therefore about raising software development closer to a professional level throughout the organization.

The End of an Era, the Beginning of a New Era

I believe the software industry is at a crisis point. The industry is continually expanding and becoming a more important part of our everyday lives. But software development groups are facing dire problems. Decaying code is becoming more problematic. An overloaded workforce seems to have no end in sight. Although Agile methods have brought great improvements to many teams, more is needed. By creating a true software profession, combined with the guidance of Lean principles and incorporating Agile practices, we believe we can help uncover the answers.

I hope you find this book series to be a worthy guide.

Preface

This book was born from need and from knowledge. The need is to expand the knowledge base of software development in both the management and process worlds so as to create a new base. Integrating Agile has transformed the software-development process in less than a decade. Although its mandate applies to all of software development, its focus typically has been on the teams directly involved in the development of software and on the projects they work on. As Agile has begun to transcend the early-adopter phase and move on to the early-majority phase, there are new challenges to address as Agile is applied to quite different situations.

- Larger organizations are attempting to adopt Agile for the first time.
- Organizations that are already using Agile are expanding the scale of their adoption.
- Organizations that are somewhat dysfunctional are starting to adopt Agile.

Extending Agile to these new situations creates the need for a better understanding of what Agile is and a broader set of tools to apply Agile. These two issues are surprisingly tightly related. Many Agile early adopters have learned from any number of excellent books that present a set of practices, mostly oriented around the team. Unfortunately, few of these books explain why Agile works. Rather, they are filled with excellent practices that embody Agile's fundamental belief systems while providing a set of practices that work at the team level in many situations.

The wider adoption of Agility demands more. There is now a need for a greater scope of knowledge as well as an explanation of why the practices work. While almost all Agile methods sprang up independently of Lean thinking, Lean thinking provides insight into why Agile works. This is why most of Agile's methods are compatible with Lean. True knowledge is realized when one can apply principles and practices together to form solid understanding. We use the term "Lean-Agile" for the approach described in this book because it represents our contention that for Agile to work most effectively, it must be applied within the context of Lean.

This book fills the need both to understand why Agility works as well as to expand its base of principles and practices in order to apply it to the enterprise. It builds on the work of others, most particularly, those of David Anderson, Kent Beck, Jane Cleland-Huang, Alistair Cockburn, Jim Coplien, Ward Cunningham, W. Edwards Deming, Mark Denne, Ron Jeffries, Daniel Jones, Michael Kennedy, Corey Ladas, David Mann, Bob Martin, Rick Mugridge, Taichi Ohno, Mary Poppendieck, Tom Poppendieck, Don Reinertsen, Peter Scholtes, Ken Schwaber, Jeff Sutherland, James Womack, Alan Ward, and so many others. This blend of Lean, Agile, XP, Scrum, and other disciplines creates the synergistic blend essential to providing answers, both deep and broad, that the enterprise requires.

I want to give particular thanks to a few people who have helped us personally in our endeavors.

- Mary and Tom Poppendieck for helping me get my start in Lean training. Both have been invaluable to my personal development with their combination of suggestions for improvement tailored by respect and compassion.

- Don Reinertsen for his kindness and encouragement, not to mention the amazing amount of knowledge that his books have conveyed to the community.

- David Anderson for his outspokenness and out-of-the box thinking. He's been an inspiration to go further in my thinking than I have typically dared.

- Ward Cunningham. I know few people smarter than Ward, balanced with such an unassuming nature. His wisdom and manner have been invaluable.

- Our own Alan Chedalawada, who may not have contributed to the writing in this book, but whose ideas formed the basis for much of what we are presenting here that is new. Many of these ideas he first manifested in the real world.

- Our own Amir Kolsky and Ken Pugh for insights into the role of acceptance test-driven development.

While it may seem odd for one author to acknowledge another, I must acknowledge Jim Trott—both a close associate and one of my dearest friends. Without his encouragement, hard work, and efforts on keeping me focused, this book may not have happened.

Alan Shalloway
CEO, Net Objectives
Achieving Enterprise and Team Agility

Acknowledgments

With every book we write, we become more deeply impressed with how important it is to acknowledge those who have helped with its development. Such an effort is indeed the work of a community. The list of people to whom we are indebted is long.

The following people have been especially significant to us:

- Chris Guzikowski, Raina Chrobak, and Chris Zahn from Addison-Wesley, who never grew tired of encouraging us, kept us moving along, and made us look good.

- Our fellow consultants at Net Objectives: Alan Chedalawada, Scott Bain, Amir Kolsky, Ken Pugh, and Brenden McGlinchey, who sparred with us to develop these ideas.

- Doug May, who reviewed early drafts of this book on his own time and gave us such helpful and timely critique.

- Andrea Bain, our talented graphics designer who took our hen scratches and made them understandable.

- Vicki Rowland, the best editor we've ever worked with and who made countless improvements to our grammar.

- Peter Alfvin, who often encouraged Alan to speak up about our unconventional ideas in public. This helped refine many of our ideas.

- Lorien Trott, who so ably and accurately prepared our manuscripts for the publisher with such a good attitude despite the many changes.

- And especially Leigh, Genny, and Jill, our patient wives who put up with us and encouraged us in our dream of this book. After being asked, "Are we done yet?" for the 3327th time, we are glad we can finally answer, "Yes!"

Finally, we have received many deep insights from our reviewers and students along the way. In particular, we recognize: Robert Bogetti, Domingo Chabalgoity, Michael Cottmeyer, Marc Evers, Paddy Healey, Alina Hsu, Kay Johnson, Mark Needham, Richard Karpinski, Armond Mehrabian, Paul Oldfield, Rob Park, and Tathagat Varma. We could not have done this without you!

About the Authors

Alan Shalloway is the founder and CEO of Net Objectives. With 40 years of experience, Alan is an industry thought leader. He helps companies transition to Lean and Agile methods enterprise-wide as well as teaches courses in Lean, Kanban, Scrum, Design Patterns, and Object-Orientation. Alan has developed training and coaching methods for Lean-Agile that have helped his clients achieve long-term, sustainable productivity gains. He is a popular speaker at prestigious conferences worldwide. He is the primary author of *Design Patterns Explained: A New Perspective on Object-Oriented Design* and *Lean-Agile Pocket Guide for Scrum Teams* and is currently writing *Essential Skills for the Agile Developer*. He has a Master of Science in computer science from M.I.T. as well as a Master of Science in mathematics from Emory University.

Jim Trott is a senior consultant for Net Objectives. He has used object-oriented and pattern-based analysis techniques throughout his 20-year career in knowledge management and knowledge engineering. He is the co-author of *Design Patterns Explained: A New Perspective on Object-Oriented Design* and the *Lean-Agile Pocket Guide for Scrum Teams*. He is a trainer and coach in the areas of reflective practices, knowledge management, and process improvement and is a knowledge-management consultant for international relief and development agencies. He has a Master of Science in applied mathematics and a Master of Business Administration from the University of Oklahoma and a Master of Arts in intercultural studies from Hope International University. An Associate Technical Fellow of a large aerospace company, he has also worked in the energy industry, banking and finance, software development, and artificial intelligence.

Guy Beaver is Vice-President, Enterprise Engagements and a senior consultant for Net Objectives. He is a technology executive with a track record of success in Lean-Agile implementations in large, mid-sized, and start-up organizations. He is a recognized expert in Lean, Agile, and Scrum technical development with a proven ability to lead, manage, and motivate organizations to realize significant improvements in productivity and quality. He has more than 25 years of experience in software engineering and IT across several industries, including financial services, defense, and healthcare. Guy has a Master of Science in physics from Wake Forest University.

Introduction

"We can't solve problems by using the same kind of thinking we used when we created them." —Albert Einstein

One of the goals of this book is to give you a better perspective on Lean and Agile and how to use them in software development. This requires an understanding of the roots of Agility, the software development "pendulum," and the importance of paradigms and practices and of being pragmatic. Lean offers a way forward.

This book takes the reader beyond Agile's standard practices by teaching how to incorporate Lean thinking into software development. Although Agile, as it is usually practiced, is effective at the team level, it gives little guidance on how it fits at the enterprise level. This is somewhat for historical reasons, as you will see. Lean-Agile is an approach to Agile software development using Lean principles and practices for guidance.

You can think of Agile in one of two ways: as a set of values and beliefs that leave it to the practitioners to decide how to apply them or as a set of practices that are suggested to manifest good results. Practitioners typically use a combination of both, believing the mandate of the Agile Manifesto and then using either Scrum[1] or eXtreme Programming[2] (or some of each) as the basis for their methods. The challenge with this approach is two-fold—one resulting from the roots of Agility and the other from the lack of a theoretical foundation for the Agile practices themselves—as we will discuss later.

---

1. Scrum is a popular Agile process created by Jeff Sutherland and Ken Schwaber. It is commonly used at the team level and is characterized by self-organizing, cross-functional teams doing iterative development in what are called sprints.
2. eXtreme Programming is an iterative development process for teams centered around several engineering practices. The most common of these is test-driven development, paired programming, and continuous integration.

How This Book Will Help You

This book aims to change how you look at software development. Doing so will enable you to solve seemingly intransigent problems with much less effort than you might have thought possible. One of our guiding principles is that we need to drive from business value: Deliver the value (software) that will provide the greatest return to the business by providing the greatest value to the business's customers. For an IT development group, this could mean either internal or external customers.

Together, we will explore what software development actually is and how it must be managed. We will investigate ways to help our customers through the process of selecting what work to accomplish through development, deployment, and, ultimately, ongoing support and enhancement.

We will drive from principles throughout the book and provide a good many that you can apply in Lean Software Development. This book will not give you all the answers; instead, it will help direct your thinking so you can create answers that will work for you in your company, in your situation, for your customers, and with your products.

The Roots of Agility

The development of the Agile Manifesto (Beck et al. 2001) was a breakthrough event for the software industry. The manifesto, shown in Figure I.1, and its Twelve Principles, shown in Figure I.2, describe the essential ideology that underpins Agile software development.

The Software Development Pendulum

The Manifesto is a strong statement. It is consistent with the intentions of most people in the software development industry. But it says that we must develop in a way that is different from the ways we have often tried in the past. It stands in opposition to the myth that the way to create quality, sustainable software is to conceive large plans and then use command-and-control management[3] to realize them. When it was written, the Agile Manifesto presented a great opportunity for exploring new, better ways of

---

3. Apologies to military experts who properly use this term to mean vision at the top with implementation at the bottom. We're using this term in the way most people interpret it—top-level people telling lower-level people how to get their job done.

Manifesto for Agile Software Development[4]

We are uncovering better ways of developing software by doing it and helping others do it. Through this work we have come to value:

Individuals and interactions	over	processes and tools
Working software	over	comprehensive documentation
Customer collaboration	over	contract negotiation
Responding to change	over	following a plan

That is, while there is value in the items on the right, we value the items on the left more.

Figure I.1 Manifesto for Agile Software Development

Principles behind the Agile Manifesto

We follow these principles:

- Our highest priority is to satisfy the customer through early and continuous delivery of valuable software.
- Welcome changing requirements, even late in development. Agile processes harness change for the customer's competitive advantage.
- Deliver working software frequently, from a couple of weeks to a couple of months, with a preference to the shorter timescale.
- Business people and developers must work together daily throughout the project.
- Build projects around motivated individuals. Give them the environment and support they need, and trust them to get the job done.
- The most efficient and effective method of conveying information to and within a development team is face-to-face conversation.
- Working software is the primary measure of progress.
- Agile processes promote sustainable development. The sponsors, developers, and users should be able to maintain a constant pace indefinitely.
- Continuous attention to technical excellence and good design enhances Agility.
- Simplicity—the art of maximizing the amount of work not done—is essential. — *Burndown*
- The best architectures, requirements, and designs emerge from self-organizing teams.
- At regular intervals, the team reflects on how to become more effective, then tunes and adjusts its behavior accordingly.

Figure I.2 Twelve Principles behind the Agile Manifesto

---

4. Copyright © 2001 Kent Beck, Mike Beedle, Arie van Bennekum, Alistair Cockburn, Ward Cunningham, Martin Fowler, James Grenning, Jim Highsmith, Andrew Hunt, Ron Jeffries, Jon Kern, Brian Marick, Robert C. Martin, Steve Mellor, Ken Schwaber, Jeff Sutherland, and Dave Thomas; this declaration may be freely copied in any form, but only in its entirety through this notice.

developing software. Unfortunately, it also left a huge hole. It did not attempt to describe how to achieve the promise.

 This lack of instructions is not a shortcoming of the Agile Manifesto. The Manifesto's purpose was to create a vision for a better way to develop software. It is instructive to look at the Manifesto in its historical context. During the decades preceding the Manifesto, the principles of and approaches to software management swung like a pendulum, between free-form and command-and-control, from little process to too much process. Each was responding to the challenges of the other.

In the 1960s, several large system failures demonstrated the need for both better engineering methods and better processes. Certainly, software development during this time was not an ad-hoc affair, but the industry was new and there was little experience with large-scale systems. In the 1970s, the idea of software as "engineering" surfaced. We began to use structured analysis and design, top-down programming, and structured programming (goto statements were considered bad form). Notably, the Waterfall model emerged. The industry was growing up, and standard practices for design, programming, and management arose. By the 1980s, PCs and fourth-generation languages enabled small projects to flourish. Small teams produced much more software than large teams did. Prototyping was popular. Speed was king. If you were the first, you were the best.

But quality often suffered. Speed to entry was so important that a product's sustainability was often ignored. This led to different kinds of failures. Since it was easy for anyone to enter the market, the competitive edge of getting in first was lost if the product lacked quality. Failures in this era triggered an upsurge in rigorous process. The sense was that if we can't do it ad hoc, then we'd better control it.

Tick tock. Tick tock. The pendulum continued to swing. Maybe even faster.

The 1990s brought us the Capability Maturity Model (CMM). Y2K dominated the last few years of the decade, emphasizing the need for planning ahead. But the '90s also brought us the Internet, which again enabled small teams to have great impact. The dot-com boom brought rapid software development. Again, a proliferation of small teams found initial success but subsequently had difficulty maintaining the software that they had developed.

Now, the twenty-first century has given rise to Agility—small teams working with customers to develop software quickly. There have been many successes and there have been many failures.

And the pendulum continues to swing. What can we do to stop it? Or can we at least find a balance?

The Agile Manifesto was an attempt to find such balance. Let's respect our teams. Let's respect our customers. Let's work with the business. Process can be good, but process that doesn't help a team get its job done is not.

Unfortunately, the world is messy and the promise of the Manifesto has not been entirely realized. The Manifesto itself showed the potential, but it did not provide a means to stop the pendulum. In fact, it has been used to justify letting teams rule. We have mostly lost the enterprise view, because that view seems to lead right back down the path of command-and-control management. If the choice is between that and using teams with Agility, then abandoning command-and-control seems reasonable.

It is not either-or. There is a way to balance command-and-control with the need for effective teams. Lean provides the way. To see why, we must first examine the beliefs, principles, and paradigms on which we build our thinking.

Principles and Paradigms

A principle is a comprehensive and fundamental law, doctrine, or assumption. Principles may exist at the level of the individual, may be held by a community, or may even apply universally. For example, individual principles may relate to one's integrity or one's way of living. A communal set of principles might include moral or religious beliefs or a set of beliefs that the community accepts as the true way to be living. Universal principles are those that apply everywhere—beyond the effect of the beliefs of any set of individuals. Perhaps we should actually call these laws of the universe. Principles are often stated in the form of guidance since there is often a corresponding principle (law) that should be followed. For example, one of the best known Lean principles is "eliminate waste." That's not a law as much as it is something you should do, as a rule.

A paradigm is a combination of assumptions, values, beliefs, and practices that define how to view reality, how to look at a situation. It is a worldview that characterizes what is true. Paradigms tend to last a long time (consider how long people believed the earth was the center of the universe). Paradigms are shared by a particular community or group of people. In the software world, Waterfall, Scrum, and Lean-Agile each have their own paradigms, or way of looking at how to best build software.

Since a paradigm defines what is real and true for someone, changing one's paradigm is quite difficult. It requires the individuals and their community to grapple with the underlying assumptions, values, and beliefs and assess whether the paradigm actually squares with what is indeed "real" or whether some shift is required.

The paradigms we hold constrain what we consider possible and shape what we do. Unexamined paradigms can therefore be very limiting.

A Pragmatic Approach

Software development professionals are pragmatists (pragmatism is part of our worldview). We favor what works over what is represented as theoretically "correct." It is not that theory is bad, but theory must be grounded in real work if we are going to embrace it.

With that in mind, we would like to suggest taking a pragmatic approach to evaluating the essential paradigms we, as software developers, hold. That approach is to use the scientific method in whatever we do: Propose a hypothesis and then run an experiment to validate or invalidate it. If the experiment supports the hypothesis, then we have some evidence that the hypothesis is correct. If it doesn't, then the hypothesis is incorrect and must be modified.

We suggest that in the software development world, our processes must be consistent with our hypotheses about the best way to practice software development. If we get good results, we have evidence that our process (that is, our hypothesis) is good. If we get poor results, our process needs updating.

Critique the Process, Work Together

Let's be clear: This is all about critiquing the process, not the people involved. How many teams have run into problems because they are following a poor process and yet management, being overly committed to the process, blames the people? Assuming the process is right, they believe "if only the people had done it right, it wouldn't have been such a disaster."

Or how many projects have failed because teams decide to follow their own approaches regardless of the larger needs of the business? They assume management is just getting in the way—bureaucrats who must be worked around.

It seems that the tendency is for management to over-focus on process while teams underestimate its value. One side sees management as crucial to making the process work; the other wants to be protected from management's command-and-control mentality so that they can just get their work done. And so they go back and forth, not working in concert.

What we need is a new attitude about process and how to manage process. Processes must be designed to assist the team in achieving management's goals. Processes help the team get its job done: They represent accountability among team members about how they will work. The team is the steward of its processes—creating, sustaining, and improving them so that the team can improve constantly. Processes are dynamic: They are the team's baseline for change.

Lean Provides the Way Forward

Is this possible? Yes! Lean provides the principles we need to do this. And we will not follow these principles blindly. Blind faith doesn't work. Instead, we will use Lean as a guide and use our own experience to refine our own process.

If you have been building software for a few years, we invite you to use the hypothesis-and-test approach yourself: Run "backward-looking experiments,"[5] that look back over your own past experiences to validate or invalidate the process we are developing. This is a lot more pragmatic and a lot less painful than trying new processes on future projects. You will be able to verify relatively quickly whether the process works.

As we do this, we will be building a pragmatic "theory" about why and how software development works. We recognize the truth in Jan L.A. van de Snepscheut's or Yogi Berra's comment "in theory, theory and practice are the same, but in practice, they are different." We also believe Kurt Lewin's notion that sometimes "there is nothing more practical than a good theory." In other words, do not follow theory when it does not match practice. But when you are not sure what to do, an understanding of why your practices work may give you guidance in unfamiliar situations.

---

5. A backward-looking experiment is a term Alan Shalloway coined to mean looking into your past to validate or invalidate an hypothesis made in the present. For example, if someone says "coding conventions help" he is actually postulating that coding conventions result in better code. You can actually look into your past to see when that was true (adding evidence to the hypothesis) or when it was false (disproving the hypothesis). If you disprove the hypothesis, you can modify it with a condition to see if there is a set of circumstances that would make it true. This enables us to learn about and test our understanding by taking advantage of our past experience.

This pragmatic approach embraces the principles (or laws) that we have discovered work in all situations. For example, the principle that overloading an individual with work, that is, giving her many tasks to do at the same time, degrades her performance.

Principles lead to many practices. However, practices must change depending upon the context, or situation, in which they are used. Relying totally on principles may not work unless the principles are proven. Relying totally on practices will work only if you are in situations you've been in before. Effectiveness requires a proper blend of proven principles with practices appropriate for the situation in which they are being used.

Evaluating Paradigms

As we begin this approach, let's look at some of the core beliefs upon which the Waterfall model and the Agile framework are based. These are described in Figures I.3 and I.4. Are these universal principles? Or are they unexamined paradigms—rules that just must be followed?

We believe that the core beliefs of Agile are more helpful than the core beliefs of Waterfall. Agile's beliefs are helpful, but they are not enough. To follow them effectively, more is required. That is where Lean comes in.

The Core Beliefs of Waterfall

- You can know everything required to build a software product properly at the start of the project.
- Customers can accurately tell you what they want at the start of the project.
- You don't need to get feedback from the customer until the end of the project.
- Managers, developers, and customers can gauge the status of a project by looking at completed milestones as reflected in documentation. That is, given proper documentation, it is not necessary to deliver complete, tested software until the very end of the project.
- You can effectively have separate groups do analysis, design, code, and test. That is, there is little loss of information in the handoff between these groups.
- Handoffs between people in different roles can be done efficiently by writing down what was done in each step.
- You can test at the end of a project and achieve the required quality.
- Management can demand that certain work be done at a certain time and should expect it to happen.
- Giving people many projects to work on simultaneously is a good approach to achieving 100% productivity because then everyone is always busy.

Figure I.3   Core beliefs of Waterfall

The Core Beliefs of Agile

- You cannot know everything required to build a software product at the start of the project.

- Customers cannot accurately tell you what they want at the start of the project; instead, they will gain clarity as the project proceeds.

- You want feedback from the customer as often as possible and you want to give developers feedback on how they are doing as soon as possible.

- Working code is the most accurate way of seeing the progress of the development effort.

- Groups working together minimizes delays as well as the loss of information between people.

- Moving test to the front of the development cycle improves the conversation between developers and customers and testers and, thus, improves the quality of the code.

- While management can set expectations for what work is done, management must not demand how that work is done.

- Working on one project at a time improves the productivity of a team.

Figure I.4   Core beliefs of Agile

We Do Not Know It All

Although software development is not exactly like other types of product development, we can still learn a lot from how other industries approach product development. In particular, Lean gives us a lot of information, based on decades of experience, that can be particularly useful to Agile teams. In fact, Scrum, one of the more popular Agile methods, is based on Lean principles. Unfortunately, an understanding of Lean is not widespread in the software community. It is unfortunate because teams lose out on the potential guidance that Lean offers. Moreover, without a grounding in Lean, software developers often lack the basis for explaining to management why certain practices would be useful. Lean provides a new set of beliefs, shown in Figure I.5. The question still remains: Even if these beliefs are true, how do we manifest good practices that are consistent with them?

Of course, merely believing something doesn't make it so. It is worth looking at the beliefs presented here and then deciding which ones represent actual principles. We suggest using backward-looking experiments for this.

The Core Beliefs of Lean

- Most errors are due to the system within which people work rather than to the individuals themselves.
- People doing the work are the best ones to understand how to improve the system.
- Ad hoc is not an acceptable process.
- Looking at when things are done in a process is a more useful guide than trying to make sure every step of the way is as efficient as possible.
- Our measure for success must be related to the amount of time between when ideas come in and when they are manifested as value to our customers.
- Management must work with the team to improve the way it works to improve its own efficiency.
- Teams are most efficient when the amount of work is limited to their capacity.
- Team eficiency improves by minimizing the amount of work in progress at any one time.
- When evaluating actions, we must optimize the whole, not merely improve individual steps in the process.
- There are principles in software development that must be followed in order to reduce waste.

Figure I.5   Core beliefs of Lean

Lean Provides More than Beliefs

Fortunately, Lean provides more than a paradigm and a belief system. It provides a set of principles in its own right as well as many practices based on them. While these practices cannot usually be taken straight from Lean (since practices must change depending upon the context in which they are used), Lean principles and practices can be readily adapted to software development. By learning these principles and practices, one can manifest the intention of the Agile Manifesto—developing software effectively. And we can do it at both levels—enterprise and team.

We will see that Lean provides a paradigm of management in which managers are not encouraged to command and control teams and developers are not required to insist they are craftsmen who cannot and should not be managed. Rather, Lean provides a paradigm under which managers and developers can work together toward a common goal—providing the best return on software development efforts. Lean provides such a paradigm through its focus on the process by which the team works—but a process that must be the best one for the team to get its job done.

Process is no longer something imposed on the team, but rather something owned by the team to make its work more productive as well as more enjoyable.

Lean combines this management paradigm with concepts, tools, and practices that give both sides a way to work together and improve visibility to management, direction from management, and team productivity.

Going beyond Lean

Of course, Lean is not all there is from which to pull. But our experience is that it is consistent with other useful paradigms, beliefs, and principles that come from other disciplines. For example, we learn from the building-architecture discipline and the software-design-patterns community that we should develop products by starting with the big picture. That is, don't try to create a product by building it from small pieces. Keep the big picture in mind. This, unfortunately, is a lesson many Agile practitioners and consultants have long ignored (probably due to Agile's heritage, which sprang up on smaller projects).

In this book, we incorporate what may be non-Lean practices but they are otherwise consistent with a central principle of Lean: "Optimize the whole." In particular, we'll see this in these areas:

- An enterprise focus instead of a team focus both for product-portfolio management and for team coordination, thereby providing a working alternative to Scrum-of-Scrums.

- A product focus instead of a project focus (where projects are enhancements to products).

- Managing requirement elicitation from the big picture instead of starting with stories and combining them into epics and themes.

- Driving release planning from business value instead of trying to manage the effective release of a collection of stories.

Summary

This introduction explored the roots of Agility, starting with the Agile Manifesto, its principles, and its historical context in the swing between management command-and-control and development teams wanting to apply their local knowledge to get work done. What is needed is a proper understanding of process as both/and: both as a tool for management and a responsibility of the team to steward what it knows.

Getting to this better understanding involves examining core paradigms, principles, and practices that everyone in software development holds. Lean-Agile offers a thinking practice to help form a better way of understanding. It is based on the solid foundation of Lean thinking and is entirely consistent with Agile practices.

Try This

These exercises are best done as a conversation with someone in your organization. After each exercise, ask each other if there are any actions either of you can take to improve your situation.

- Look at the beliefs of Waterfall listed in Figure I.3. Which of these are true?

- Look at the beliefs of Agile listed in Figure I.4. Which of these are true?

- Look at the beliefs of Lean thinking listed in Figure I.5. Which of these are true?

PART I

Extending Our View
beyond Projects

"Computer science is no more about computers than astronomy is about telescopes."
—E. W. Dijkstra

What Is Software Development?

Some have compared software development to engineering or to building construction. Developers take requirements and build products that customers can use. The problem with this comparison is that, unlike those other disciplines, software development almost never starts with clearly defined requirements and rarely specifies clear approaches for construction. What is needed and how to get there often is often more a process of discovery than a clearly defined, up-front plan.

We often think of software as the end goal. But it is not. Software is a means to an end—a way of getting value to a customer. In software products, the software enables the customer to do things (for example, accounting software enables a company to keep its books in order). In IT organizations, the software supports the services and products of the company. Seen this way, software development can be thought of as the process of discovering what is needed, determining how to build that, and then building it. The advantage of Agile over the Waterfall model is that it enables these three to be done in an evolutionary fashion, incorporating what is learned along the way. *iteration /retrospect*

Among other things, this process of discovery helps to mitigate the risks that plague software projects: market risk, the risk that the product specification does not meet the market requirement; and technical risk, the risk that the implementation does not meet the product specification.

1

Don Reinertsen says, "In general, most product failures are caused by market risk. This is not because marketing people are less competent than designers, but rather because market risk is a much tougher problem than technical risk." (Reinertsen 1997)

The Software Development Team and Flow

When introducing Agile to an enterprise, it is common to start by introducing Agile to individual teams. Early on, this makes sense; however, a broader view is soon needed. For Agile to become useful to the entire organization, you must consider the entire value stream:[1] from customers to management to product enhancement to development teams to customer deployment.

As shown in Figure PI.1, the flow starts with customers. In commercial product development, these are external customers; in IT shops, these are

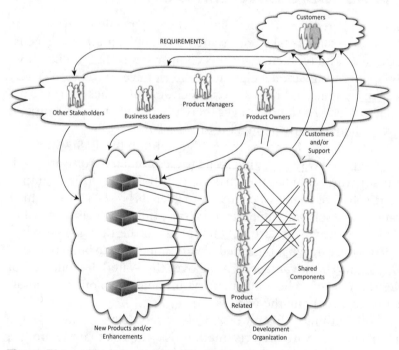

Figure PI.1.   The value stream of software development

---

1. For now, think of a value stream as the chain of actions that flows from customer input/ requirements to product deployment and use.

internal customers who will use the product for business purposes. Ideas originate with recognition of customer needs. They are discussed by management, product managers, product owners, and other stakeholders, such as marketing. These people are represented in the long, horizontal cloud just under the Customers cloud. Together, they determine what products will be built, enhanced, or otherwise supported. They launch projects (shown in the lower-left cloud) that provide a budget for this development work. Development teams (on the lower-right side) work directly on the products to be built or enhanced or as support (component) services that these teams use. When development is completed, product deployment is coordinated by support and management (who initiated the product work in the first place).

IN THIS PART

The chapters in this part describe the piece of the software-development value stream that occurs before the development team gets its hands on it. This is important because many projects seem to take longer in their initiation phase than they do in their construction phase. Shortening this start-up time is one key to reducing the time to market.

This part also offers a brief overview of Lean Software Development. It describes some of the things involved in creating an Agile enterprise:

- Picking the right products and product enhancements in order to maximize return on investment and to enable teams to work efficiently

- Keeping the big picture in mind while working on the small pieces of a project

- Allocating teams to the products approved for creation or enhancement

CHAPTER 1

An Agile Developer's Guide to Lean Software Development

"Time is the most valuable thing a man can spend."   —Theophrastus (372 BC–287 BC)

IN THIS CHAPTER

This chapter describes the basic principles for Lean Software Development, the notion of fast-flexible-flow in the development pipeline, the benefit of value stream mapping, and the way Lean guides Agile teams.

Takeaways

Key insights to take away from this chapter include

- Most errors come from our systems and not from people.

- Lean extends Agile to create a system that helps minimize work-in-process and maximize the speed at which business value is created.

- Lean principles suggest focusing on business value, speed, and quality.

Lean

Lean is the name given to Toyota's method of both producing and developing cars. As software developers, we are doing neither, so why is it of interest to us? The reason is simple: The principles that underlie Toyota's methods are principles that in reality work everywhere. These are not panaceas, though. The principles are universal, although the specific practices may vary.

> Principles are underlying truths that don't change over time or space, while practices are the application of principles to a particular situation. Practices can and should differ as you move from one environment to the next, and they also change as a situation evolves. (Poppendieck and Poppendieck 2006)

The principles that drive Lean can be applied to software. Doing so provides guidance for those who want to develop software more effectively. In this chapter, instead of describing Lean on its own, we describe Lean in terms of the Agile practices it suggests. This illustrates how Agile practices are manifestations of Lean principles. There is power to this understanding—when an Agile practitioner finds him- or herself in a situation where a standard Agile practice cannot be followed, the Lean principles can guide him or her to a better way. Lean principles also often highlight different issues than standard Agile practices do. By making certain things explicit, Agile practitioners will have more power at their disposal to improve their methods.

Lean Applies to Many Levels of the Organization

This book is written for anyone who leads or plays a role in an organization to define, create, and deliver technology solutions. When we refer to the "enterprise," we mean

> All parts of the organization that are involved in the value stream of the product and/or service that is created, enhanced, or maintained. In an IT organization this includes the business and the IT sides. In a product company, it also includes marketing, sales, delivery, support, and development.

The Lean enterprise involves coordinating business, management, and delivery teams so that a sustainable stream of products can be delivered based on prioritized business need. Each area is important. Each area

Table 1.1   A Holistic View: Each Area Has a Part to Play

This area	Must attend to this work
Business	Continuously prioritize and decompose incremental needs across the organization Manage a portfolio of business needs Do release planning
Management	Organize cross-functional teams that can deliver incremental, end-to-end features Manage the value stream Bring visibility to impediments
Delivery Team	Work together, every day, and deliver fully tested and integrated code Learn how to deliver business needs incrementally Become proficient at acceptance test-driven development and refactoring

must be attended to, focusing on certain activities guided by Lean principles, as shown in Table 1.1, above. Like a three-legged stool, if any one area is neglected, the result is shaky.

This book offers guidance on these focus areas to *anyone* in the enterprise who wants to learn how to transition to the Lean enterprise. This includes business people who want to understand Agile and technologists using Agile and trying to make it work. Whether or not you have experience with Agile, this book is a starting point for identifying how to apply the body of knowledge from Lean to the principles of Agile to make your enterprise better.

A Quick Review of Some Lean Principles

The foundation of Lean is based on several fundamental principles; these include

- Most errors are of a systemic nature and therefore your development system must be improved.

- You must respect your people in order to improve your system.

- Doing things too early causes waste. Do things just before you need to do them: This is called "Just-In-Time," or JIT.

- Lean principles suggest focusing on shortening time-to-market by removing delays in the development process; using JIT methods to do this is more important than keeping everyone busy.

These are foundational in the sense that everything else comes from them. The first two form the cornerstone of W. Edwards Deming's work. Deming is the man generally credited by the Japanese with teaching them how to produce high-quality goods. Given that the Japanese did not always do this, it may be worth asking ourselves what the Japanese learned from this man—and what can we learn? Toyota added the JIT concept, which constitutes an essential component of Lean thinking.

Look to Your Systems for the Source of Your Errors

When something goes wrong, our normal tendency is to look for someone to blame. When a plane crashes we immediately ask ourselves, "Whose fault was it?" Was it the pilot's fault? (Blame *her.*) Was it the airline's fault? (Blame *them.*) Was it the manufacturer's fault? (Blame *them.*) Was some part on the plane faulty? (Blame *its* manufacturer.) But is that fair or at least is it sufficient? When we look for some*one* to blame, are we looking correctly? Perhaps it is the *situation* that the people found themselves in that caused—or at least contributed to—the problem.

Here is a typical example from software development. Say you are responsible for writing a feature of an existing system. You are given a document created by an analyst on the team that describes the functionality to be written. You are never afforded the opportunity to talk to someone who will actually be using the software, but rather must rely solely on this document. You write the code and, after testing, the new feature is shown to the customer, whereupon they declare, "This isn't what I asked for!"

Who would you blame? The *customer* for being unclear? The *analyst* for writing it up poorly? *You*, for not being able to follow the spec? The *tester* for not testing it properly? With a little reflection, you may see that no *person* is to blame; instead (or more often), the problem has to do with the way they work together. In other words, in the current system, each person works separately in specialized roles. Feedback loops are nonexistent or inefficient and errors propagate. An Agile system would have the people work as a team. The customer, analyst, developer, and tester would talk among themselves to determine the customer's needs and how to best fulfill them. This is a better system. As errors occur, we look for ways to improve the communication process, continually driving down the number of errors that occur.

Improving communication is a major goal of Agile. Unfortunately, Agile practices tend to emphasize communication at the local level: among the team, between related teams, and with the customer. Agile offers only weak support for improving communication between teams that are only slightly related and practically none for communication up and down the value stream and across the enterprise. On the other hand, Lean practices promote communication in these larger contexts by focusing on the creation of end-to-end value, which provides a common context for everyone involved. This forces the different layers of the organization to communicate more frequently, with an emphasis on continuous process improvement, optimizing the whole, and delivering early and often. Lean thinking helps eliminate the delays that cause waste.

Respect People

Who should be involved in improving systems? Is this primarily a job for management or for the people doing the work? For Henry Ford, the answer was management. To him, management was much more intelligent than the workers and only they could be trusted to decide how to improve the manufacture of his cars. He had very little respect for the knowledge of workers.

The difficulty here is threefold. First, while Ford's policy allowed for setting up a very good static process for building one kind of car, it offered no flexibility. Recall Ford's famous statement that people could have "any color they wanted as long as it was black." Second, most processes are not static; they are always changing. Workers on the line will always understand the local conditions of a changing environment better than management because they have first-hand, local knowledge of what is going on—and that is what's needed to change processes on the line. Finally, Ford could get away with demeaning people in an age when a job's number-one value was providing a way to sustain one's family. Today, monetary compensation is no longer the overriding factor in selecting a job. That lack of respect would now translate into inability to keep quality employees.[1]

---

1. Actually, Ford Motor Company was plagued by difficulties in keeping personnel and had to resort to high wages to do so. In their case, the time to train personnel was short because of how little knowledge one needed to work on the assembly line. This short training (often less than 15 minutes) would not be possible in the software-development world.

Respecting people—management and worker—allows flexibility in the process, continuous improvement of the process, and the ability to attract and retain the people qualified for the work.

In software development, respecting people includes the notion that the team doing the work is responsible for the process they follow. The process becomes their understanding of how to best develop software. When that changes, the process is changed. Hence, the process is the baseline by which the team builds software in the best way they know how within the constraints they are given.

Minimizing Complexity and Rework

A clear mantra for all developers is to minimize complexity and rework. Be clear: we are saying *minimize*, not eliminate. Although complexity and rework cannot be avoided entirely, the Lean principles can help reduce them from what has often been the norm.

Eliminating Waste and Deferring Commitment

Eliminating waste is the primary guideline for the Lean practitioner. Waste is code that is more complex than it needs to be. Waste occurs when defects are created. Waste is non-value-added effort required to create a product. Wherever there is waste, the Lean practitioner looks to the system to see how to eliminate it because it is likely that an error will continue to repeat itself, in one form or another, until we fix the system that contributed to it.

Deferring commitment means to make decisions at the right time, at the "last responsible moment": Don't make decisions too early, when you do not have all the information you need, and don't make them too late, when you risk incurring higher costs. Deferring commitment is a pro-active way to plan the process so that we either don't work on something until we need to or we set it up so that we can make decisions that can be reversed later when we get more information. This principle can be used to guide requirements, analysis, and system design and programming.

Deferring Commitment in Requirements and Analysis   We often think of commitment as an action or decision we make. But it can also be refer to time spent. Once we've spent time on doing something, it can't be undone—that is, we can't get the time back. In establishing requirements, we should ask, Where should I spend my time? Do I need to discuss all of the requirements with the customer? Clearly not. Some requirements are more important than others. Start with those requirements that involve functionality that is most important to the business as well as those that will create technical risk if they are not dealt with early.

The requirements that will be most important to the business are typically those that represent the greatest value to the customer. Agile methods handle this by directing us to delve into the requirements that customers feel are most important. This is one of the basic justifications for iterative development. But just looking at what features are important to customers is not a sufficient guide for selecting what to work on. We must also pay attention to architectural risk. Which requirements may cause problems if ignored? These are the ones that must be attended to.

Deferring Commitment in Design and Programming   Developers tend to take one of two approaches when forced to handle some design issue on which they are unclear. One approach is to do the simplest thing possible without doing anything to handle future requirements.[2] The other is to anticipate what may happen and build hooks into the system for those possibilities. Both of these approaches have different challenges. The first results in code that is hard to change. This happens because one does not consider the changeability of the code while writing it. The second results in code that is more complex than necessary. This occurs because, like most of us, developers have a hard time predicting the future. Thus, when they anticipate how to handle future needs, they often put in hooks (classes, methods, etc.) that actually aren't needed but that add complexity.

An alternative approach to both of these is called "Emergent Design." Emergent Design in software incorporates three disciplines:

- Using the thought process of design patterns to create application architectures that are resilient and flexible

- Limiting the implementation of design patterns to only those features that are current

- Writing automated acceptance- and unit-tests before writing code, both to improve the thought process and to create a test harness

---

2. We are *not* referring to the eXtreme Programming mandate to do the simplest thing possible. That mandate is stated within the context of other actions. Unfortunately, that mandate is often misinterpreted as doing the simplest thing without attending to the need to handle future requirements.

Using design patterns makes the code easy to change. Limiting writing to what you currently need keeps code less complex. Automated testing both improves the design and makes it safe to change. These features of emergent design, taken together, allow you to defer the commitment of a particular implementation until you understand what you actually need to do.

Using Iterative Development to Minimize Complexity and Rework

The biggest causes of complexity are

- Writing code that isn't needed

- Writing code that is tightly coupled together

By doing iterative development, we avoid writing code that is not needed. That is, iterative development helps us discover what the customer really needs and helps us avoid building what isn't of value. Emergent design assists in the decoupling of "using code" to "used code" without adding unneeded complexity in the process.

Create Knowledge

Creating knowledge is an integral part of the Agile process. We build in stages so as to discover what the customer needs and then build it. By doing it this way we deliver value quickly and avoid building things of lesser (or no) value. We believe that software development is more a discovery process than a building process. By itself, software has little inherent value. Its value comes when it enables delivery of products and services. Therefore, it is more useful to think of software development as part of product development—the set of activities we use to discover and create products that meet the needs of customers while advancing the strategic goals of the company.

When viewed this way, it's clear that the role of software in IT organizations is to support the company's products and services. In software product companies, the software exists to support the work and needs of the customers using it. Software is a means to an end—the end is adding value for a customer—either directly, with a product, or indirectly, by enabling a service the software supports. Software development should therefore be considered a part of product development.

You can look at product development as having three steps:[3]

1. Discover what the customer needs

2. Figure out how to build that

3. Build it

In software development, we seem to spend the most time talking about Step 3; however, the first two steps take the most time. Imagine having completed a software development project, only at the end to lose all of the source code. If you wanted to re-create the system as you had it, how long would it take? By re-create, we mean build it essentially the same way without trying to improve it; the only caveat is that you can leave out anything that is unnecessary. Most developers would say that this would take only 20 to 50 percent of the time it took to write it the first time. So, what were you doing the other 50 to 80 percent of the time? You were "discovering what the customer needs" and "figuring out how to build that."

Creating knowledge also means understanding the process that you use to build software to meet this discovered customer need. By understanding your methods, you can improve them more readily.

Deliver Early and Often

Another reason for doing iterative development is to deliver value to the customer quickly. This affords better market penetration, greater credibility of the business with the customer, strong loyalty, and other intangibles. However, it also provides for earlier revenue, allowing initial releases to pay for subsequent development.

This principle has often been called "deliver fast" but we feel it is better to think of it as "remove delays." Delays represent waste—if you remove them you will deliver faster. But the focus is on adding value to the customer without delay. Eliminating the delays results in going faster (from beginning to end). While the benefits of delivering fast are clear, it is essential that this is done in a sustainable manner.

---

3.   This is a gross over-simplification, of course.

Build Quality In

In order to sustain development speed, teams must build quality into both their process and their code. Building quality into their process allows a team to improve it by removing the waste it creates or requires. One way to do this is to define acceptance tests before writing code by bringing the customer, developer, and tester together. This improves the conversations that take place around the requirements and it helps the developers understand what functionality they need to write.

Building quality into code can also be achieved by using the methods described earlier to eliminate waste. Many developers spend much of their time discovering how to fix errors that have been reported. Without automated testing, errors creep in. Poor code quality and code that is hard to understand also contributes to wasted time.

Optimize the Whole

One of the big shifts to Lean thinking from a mass production mentality is discarding the belief that you need to optimize each step. Instead, to increase efficiency of the production process, look at optimizing the flow of value from the beginning of the production cycle to the end. In other words, getting each machine to work as efficiently as possible does not work as well as maximizing efficiency of the production flow in its entirety. Focus on the whole process – from the beginning (concept) to the end (consumption).

The problem with optimizing each step is that it creates large inventories between the steps. In the software world, these "inventories" represent partially done work (for example, requirements completed, but not designed, coded, or tested). Lean proved that one-piece flow (that is, focusing on building an item in its entirety) is a much more efficient process than concentrating on building all of its parts faster. Inventories hide errors in the process. In the physical world, they may represent construction errors. In the software world, they may hide misunderstandings with the customer (requirements), or poor design (design documents), or bugs (coded but not tested code), or integration errors (coded, tested, but not integrated code) or any number of other things. The larger the inventory, the more likely there will be undetected errors.

Fast-Flexible-Flow

A primary goal of Lean is to optimize the whole with speed and sustainability. This can be summarized as "fast-flexible-flow," which is the fundamental phrase used in Womack & Jones (2003). That is, get an idea into the development pipeline and out to the customer as fast as possible. Removing impediments to this flow is critical to improving the process.

This is very much the basis for the Agile practice of building one story at a time: getting it specified, designed, coded, and tested (done-done-done) by the end of the iteration. Scrum's Daily Stand-Up—stating, "Here's what I did, here's what I will do, here are my impediments"—is a direct reflection of this need to improve the process and remove anything that slows it down.

Focus on Time

Mass production looks at machine utilization. Lean focuses on time. In other words, instead of focusing on how well we are utilizing our resources, Lean says to reduce the time it takes to go from the idea to the value. Lean proposes that if we focus on going faster by improving our process, our costs will go down because we will have higher quality with fewer errors and less waste. Unfortunately, focusing directly on lowering costs does not necessarily have the benefit of improving quality or speed. In fact, it typically works the other way.

In the Lean world, we want to eliminate the waste of delays. Some common delays in software include

- The time from when a requirement is stated until it is verified as correct

- The time from when code is written until it is tested

- The time from when a developer asks a question of a customer or analyst until she gets an answer (the delay occurs here especially when e-mail must substitute for face-to-face contact)

Notice how these delays represent both risk and waste. This is because the waste that occurs if something goes wrong multiplies as the delays increase. Looking at these delays also illustrates why resource utilization is the wrong approach. Many individuals work on multiple projects simultaneously because they are often waiting for information or for other resources. For example, when a developer e-mails an analyst and then must wait for a response, she'll have another project to work on. Of course, this has everyone working on multiple projects, which further increases the delays in communication and other events. This doesn't even account for the added inefficiencies of context switching.

In manufacturing, Lean solves this problem by creating work cells that manage their own process and manage their work by pulling off a queue of prioritized tasks. In the software world, this is mirrored by creating self-directed teams that have all of the resources they need (for example, analysts, developers, and testers) and pulling from a product backlog.

Reflections on Just-In-Time (JIT)

There is a parallel between standard manufacturing and JIT in the same way there is a parallel between the Waterfall software model and iterative development. In Waterfall, we take all of our "raw materials" (requirements) and start processing them in big batches. Resources required by the team (DBAs, analysts, testers) are available at different intervals, so we batch-process our work (analysis, design, code, test) to fully utilize them. Since we are building so many things at once, we make a great effort to figure out what needs to be done before starting the manufacturing process (akin to the heavy analysis of Waterfall). In JIT we work only on those parts that we need to, and then, only just before they are needed. This is akin to taking a story in almost any Agile method and doing the analysis on it just before it is built and validated.

By performing work in small, complete steps, JIT in the software arena gives us the ability to change direction at the end of each small completion—without any wasted effort. One of the mantras of Lean manufacturing is to minimize work-in-process (WIP). Agile methods strive for that as well.

Of course, accomplishing JIT is not easy. It requires a smooth, low error-rate process. This requirement, however, makes deficiencies in the process more evident: It makes them easier to see and therefore easier to fix. This parallels the cornerstone of Scrum's efforts to remove impediments to the one-piece flow of stories.

JIT has other advantages. It not only uncovers problems in the process, it also exposes problems in production before they have too much of an impact. In mass production, errors are often discovered only in the later stages of production. If there is a large inventory between steps, a lot of bad inventory may be produced before the error is detected. In software, a delay in discovering the error in a requirement, for example, will result in wasted effort to build and test that piece. It also adds complexity to the system even though it doesn't provide value to the customer (because unneeded features are typically never removed). Essentially, if we can deploy (or at least demonstrate) finished code to customers quickly and in small pieces, we can get their feedback and know if we are producing something of value.

Thus, JIT provides guidance for software development. We can look at Agile methods as an implementation of JIT principles. We don't do full analysis of a story until just before building it. We analyze, design, code, and test just before each stage is needed, which should reveal impediments to our process. JIT encourages us to build things in smaller batches, and it provides the basis for quick feedback from the customer.

Figure 1.1 represents the Waterfall model as a series of steps that take input from the prior step and hand it to the next step.

Table 1.2 compares the hidden costs in manufacturing as compared with the equivalent costs in software. Note, however, that in software,

Figure 1.1   Waterfall as mass production

Table 1.2   Comparing the Costs and Risks in Mass Manufacturing and Waterfall Software Development

	Manufacturing Mass Production	Waterfall Model
Hidden Costs	Transportation	Handoffs
	Managing inventory and storage	Lots of open items; can lead to overwhelming the workforce
	Capital costs of inventory	Cost of training people to build software
Risks	Building things you don't need because production goes on after needs go away	Building things you don't need because requirements aren't clear or customers change their minds
	Inventory becoming obsolete	Knowledge degrading quickly If a line is discontinued, all WIP wasted
	Huge latency if an error occurs	Errors in requirements discovered late in the process Errors in completed code discovered late in testing

the costs are usually greater because "inventory" in software degrades much faster than most inventory in manufacturing.

Value Stream Mapping

The value stream is the set of actions that takes place to add value for a customer from the initial request to the delivery of the value. The value stream begins with the initial concept, moves through various stages to one or more development teams (where Agile methods begin), and on through to final delivery.

The value stream map is a Lean tool that practitioners use to analyze the value stream. Value stream mapping involves drawing pictures of the process streams and then using them to look for waste. The focus is on improving the total time from beginning to end of the entire stream while maintaining this speed in the future (that is, you cannot take shortcuts now at the expense of future development).

One of the great benefits of value stream mapping is that it shows the entire picture. Many Agile practitioners focus on improving the team's performance. Unfortunately, in many cases, the team is not the cause of the development problems—even when it looks that way. Value stream mapping shows how to "optimize the whole" by identifying waste: delays, multi-tasking, overloaded people, rework, late detection of problems, and so on, which affects quality and slows down delivery.

Using Value Stream Mapping to Get to True Root Cause

At one of our Lean Software Development courses, we had two students from a medium-sized company's development team. It was clear to the company that they had problems resulting from poor code quality which, therefore, was an issue for the development team. In a nutshell, when the company's products were installed at their customers' sites, they often had issues that needed to be fixed, which slowed down new development. They came to us for help because they could no longer just hire more developers to fix the problems.

Near the start of the course, students create an "as-is" value stream map. The map that they drew for their organization is shown in Figure 1.2.

The loopback shown in the figure occurs when a customer has a problem that requires work to go back through development. The queues (shown with triangles) indicate that work was often in a wait state, both for development and for deployment. The loopback was particularly disruptive because development teams would start work on the next project only to be pulled off to work on the previous system that had gone awry.

In some sense, the value stream map presented little new information. It illustrated what was known: Developers had a quality problem and were having to do a lot of rework. But the value stream map presented a new perspective. First, it showed the entire development process (including the marketing aspect). Second, a value stream map suggested geting to the root cause of the problem, which was system failure at the customer site. That is, we use value stream maps to identify problems and we use other Lean thinking to get to root cause.

For root cause analysis, it is common in Lean to use the "Five Whys." This technique, credited to Sakichi Toyoda, the founder of Toyota Industries, involves asking why something happened and then why that happened and then why that happened, continuously exploring the cause-and-effect relationships underlying a particular problem until it drills down to the root cause.

In our students' case, the technique started with the question "Why are we having to rework the system?"

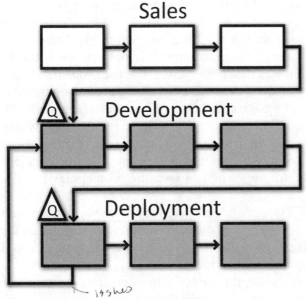

Figure 1.2   As-Is value stream map

A: Because the programs do not function properly on our customers' servers.

Q: Why do the programs not function properly on our customers' servers?

A: Because the code was designed one way, but the servers are configured for another way.

Q: Why are our customers' servers being configured differently from how it was expected?

A: Because our customers are not following our guidelines for server configuration.

Q: Why are our customers not following our guidelines for server configuration?

A: Because they aren't aware of the guidelines.

Q: Why aren't these customers aware of them?

A: Because sales, who is supposed to make sure they know of this configuration requirement, isn't telling them.

Q: Why isn't sales telling our customers they need to do this?

A: Because when a customer is ready to buy, sales tends to shut up and just get the contract signed. Closing the deal seems to be the most important thing to sales.

This series of questions illustrates many points. First, it's not really always *five* whys. Five is often enough, but sometimes you have to keep questioning until you get to the root cause. In this case, sales was not informing the customers that the machines needed to be configured a particular way. Second, the problem may not be what you think it is. In this case, the assumption was that code quality was the problem; in fact, the problem was that the code was not flexible enough to run on misconfigured servers. Either the code could be fixed or the servers could be configured properly. Third, the origin of the problem is not always where you think it is. In this case, the company was fairly sure that this was a development team problem (which is why two people from the development organization were there), when in fact, the problem lay in sales department.

This highlights a critical failure in many Agile approaches that focus on the team: *The problem may not be with the team even though many Agilists say to start there.* A value stream map enables us to see the whole picture and to question our assumptions.

Toward the end of the course, these two participants then created their "to-be" value stream map. That is, a map of their value stream as it should be done. This new value stream map required that their customers were aware of running configuration checks.

The conversation about this change grew quite animated. There was fear that sales would not like this new requirement. After all, here is a customer ready to pay money, but before they can pay, they have to do some additional upfront work. This would seem contrary to sales' desire to close the deal as quickly as possible. Probably, they would not like any perceived impediment to the deal.

But the value stream analysts looked at the bigger picture. They focused on how the customer would react. They felt that most customers would see that the company was acting responsibly and putting the customer's interests first. And if they lost a few customers who did not want to make that upfront commitment, then that was OK. By having all customers either follow the new process or cease to be customers, the organization would remove the bottleneck and be able to deliver more value more quickly. They saw that their problem lay not in having enough customers; it was the waste in their process. The fact was they had more customers than they could support.

It also illustrates how metrics and performance awards can be counterproductive. Sales people were being rewarded on systems *sold*. The rewards should have been based on systems *installed.* Metrics and rewards that focus on only part of the value stream are often counterproductive.

Perhaps most interesting is that this company experienced a significant team performance improvement without changing what the team was doing at all.

The Results

Implementing this "to-be" value stream map resulted in significant conversations across the organization. Everyone, including sales, learned and started to see benefits. Development was pleased not to have to make unnecessary changes to their approach.

A few months later, the company did a second round of value stream mapping. They started with the previous "to-be" map. Armed with a better understanding of their process, they applied the Lean principle to defer commitment as long as practical and to move significant server analysis downstream, doing it just in time for development. They could see exactly where to do this to maximize the needs of development without unnecessarily hampering sales. This reduced delay in their work stream even more! It is also interesting to note that they didn't lose any customers. They cleverly presented the "requirement" of pre-configuring the systems as a service the company offered the customer as the step just before installation.

Lean Goes beyond Agile

By providing time-tested principles, Lean provides guidance for our Agile practices when we are in new situations. Lean tells us to focus on time of development, not resources utilized. Lean reminds us to optimize the whole instead of trying to get each step done as efficiently as possible.

Lean takes us beyond Agile's often myopic focus on project/team/software. To attend to the entire enterprise, we need to look at how products are selected for enhancement and how teams work within the structure of the organization. Agile does not help here but is often severely and adversely affected by the lack of good structures within which the teams must work.

Summary

Lean tells us to focus on improving the system we use to produce software by focusing on processes that support the team. Since the team knows more about how they develop software than anyone else, they need to create and improve these processes.

Lean provides seven principles for software development:

- Respect people
- Eliminate waste
- Defer commitment   *JIT*
- Create knowledge
- Deliver fast
- Build quality in
- Optimize the whole

A fundamental goal for Lean is fast-flexible-flow. That is, it is useful to think of the development process as a pipeline where production takes place. Anything that slows down the pipeline causes waste. In software, waste includes delays, errors, misunderstandings, and waiting for resources. By removing impediments to this flow, we improve our process.

Value stream mapping is a vital tool for analyzing process in order to reduce delay and waste.

Thus, Lean provides guidance for Agile teams. In fact, Scrum can be seen as a manifestation of Lean principles. Understanding Lean can assist in implementing Scrum. Lean also can be applied throughout the enterprise, thereby assisting to implement Scrum throughout the enterprise.

Try This

These exercises are best done as a conversation with someone in your organization. After each exercise, ask each other if there are any actions either of you can take to improve your situation.

- In your organization, how long does it take for an idea to get from business charter (the document used to build the business case and a vision for justifying the project) to delivered capability (months, years)? This is considered the cycle time, which any new system should minimize.

- Does batching ideas into projects increase or decrease this cycle time? *increase*

- What are impediments to smaller, more frequent deliveries in your organization?

- How can you influence your organization to make visible the costs due to delays? *value stream mapping, root cause analysis*

Recommended Reading

The following works offer helpful insights into the topics of this chapter.

Bain. 2008. *Emergent Design: The Evolutionary Nature of Professional Software Development*. Boston: Addison-Wesley.

Kennedy. 2003. *Product Development for the Lean Enterprise: Why Toyota's System Is Four Times More Productive and How You Can Implement It*. Richmond, VA: Oaklea Press.

Poppendieck and Poppendieck. 2006. *Implementing Lean Software Development: From Concept to Cash*. Boston: Addison-Wesley.

Reinertsen. 1997. *Managing the Design Factory*. New York: Free Press.

Womack and Jones. 2003. *Lean Thinking: Banish Waste and Create Wealth in Your Corporation*. 2d ed. New York: Simon & Schuster.

CHAPTER 2

The Business Case for Agility

"The battle is not always to the strongest, nor the race to the swiftest, but that's the way to bet 'em!" —C. Morgan Cofer

IN THIS CHAPTER

This chapter discusses the business case for Agility, presenting six benefits for teams and the enterprise. It also describes a financial model that shows why incremental development works.

Takeaways

Agility is not just about the team. There are product-management, project-management, and technical issues beyond the team's control. Lean-Agile provides benefits for all, such as:

- Getting customers to tell you everything they are ever going to need from you with any sort of accuracy; they tend toward speculation, much of which is inevitably wrong.

- Emerging designs that are change-tolerant, which addresses the need for software development to get a return on investment as quickly as possible in order to respond to changing market conditions as competitors advance and adjust their own products.

- Delivering value incrementally provides much more business value to your customers.

- Lean-Agile methods provide management greater visibility into software-development projects than Waterfall methods do.

> Lean-Agile addresses all of these points. However, it requires the team to pay attention to a few things that *are* in its control:
>
> - Delays and thrashing, which are impediments
> - Resource- and product planning
> - Code quality, coding standards, and planning for future modifications

The Benefits of Agile

Despite the buzz about Agility, it is important to keep in mind that the primary driver is, and must always be, the benefit to the enterprise via adding value to its customers. Helping teams become more Agile is good. It is a necessary part of the journey toward helping the enterprise become more Agile. Enterprise Agility enables an organization to react to market needs and to competitive changes and helps it realize the most value from the resources at hand. In the end, using Agile methods must improve the enterprise's bottom line. If it does not, then we need to question why we are using Agile or if we are using it correctly.

Agile can benefit an enterprise and its teams in the following ways:

- Add value to the business quickly
- Help clarify customers' needs
- Promote knowledge-based product development and better project management
- Motivate teams and allow failing (that is, learning) early
- Focus on product-centered development
- Improve team efficiency

Each of these is important and is discussed below individually. However, there is a synergistic effect as well. Growth in one area spurs growth in other areas, resulting in greater capacity to create value.

Add Value to the Business Quickly

Whether you are in an IT shop that produces software for internal customers or in a company that produces software products for external customers, there is tremendous value when products can be released to the customer quickly[1]. The benefits to the business include the following:

- **Revenue/Return on Investment** The sooner customers can begin using a product, the sooner the business begins to receive a return on its investment—either in direct revenue or as a way to satisfy business needs.

- **Increased Customer Satisfaction** All things being equal, customers prefer to get new or improved features sooner rather than later so that they can begin to use them.

- **Market Position** The best way to maintain or increase market position relative to the competition is to deliver valuable features sooner than they can. Products that look fresher and more capable satisfy customers more deeply, which creates credibility for the business and builds customer loyalty. In today's world, competition often comes from smaller, more nimble (as in Agile) companies, and so releasing quickly is more important than ever.

- **Lower Risk** Releasing quickly shortens the feedback loop with the customer, enabling you to discover mistakes in your project earlier. It gives you an opportunity to fix the product—or abandon it—in order to minimize your losses.

- **Greater Profit Margins** Investment costs are recouped sooner on products that are released more quickly and are further mitigated by the incremental delivery of smaller releases. Additionally, it is often possible to charge more for your products if you are considered a market leader.

A Financial Model for Software

Suppose you are responding to a Request for Proposal (RFP) which spells out the following:

- Scope
- Due date

---

1. Merely releasing a product or software supporting a service adds no value if the customers of the organization can't actually use the product or service of the company.

- Quality

- Cost

The RFP says that none of these four can be modified. That is, you cannot charge less for the product or give better quality without being disqualified. Where can you compete? Credibility may come to mind, but that might be difficult to establish. What else could there be?

Mark Denne and Jane Cleland-Huang offer valuable guidance here in their brilliant book, *Software by Numbers* (Denne & Cleland-Huang 2003). The following is based on their analysis.

Figure 2.1 shows the cost and return for a typical, successful software project. In this graph, the "Investment Period" represents the time spent creating the software. This is when work is being done before money can be made. The Payback Period begins when the customers begin to realize value from—and start paying for—the product.

What would this curve look like if you could release the same product in two phases? Each phase of the system would contain half the features required. Suppose the team can build and release the first phase in half the time period and the second phase during the remainder of the time period. Each of these releases would have a financial curve similar to the one shown in Figure 2.1, except that they would occur at different times. For example, on a 10-month project with 100 features, you might release

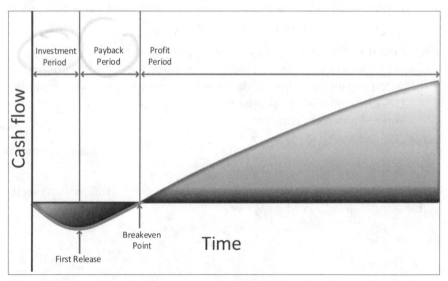

Figure 2.1   A successful application development project

features 1–50 after five months and features 51–100 after another 5 months. Figure 2.2 shows these two curves overlaid on each other.

Each half contributes some value and some revenue. If you are a product company, you are getting revenue for half the system; if you are an IT organization, you are providing new value to your internal customer. It is often the case that the first half of the system provides more than half the value (remember the Pareto rule, "80 percent of the value comes from 20 percent of the work"). However, it is also possible that no value will be returned until all of the system is in place (for example, you cannot release an airplane guidance-control system that only partially works). Let's suppose we have the former case, in which half the system provides half the value. Figure 2.3 shows the total profit generated from these two phases.

Figure 2.4 compares two release strategies: a single-release strategy, in which all of the features are delivered in one release package, and a strategy of staged (iterative) releases, in which features are delivered as they are ready. With the single-release strategy, the business must wait significantly longer to realize revenue than with the staged-release strategy. The amount of money that the business must fund on its own, before money begins to come in, is significantly more, the breakeven point is significantly extended, and the ultimate profit is significantly less. The business realizes less overall value and so does the customer. Too much delay may actually prevent the business from entering or extending the market altogether.

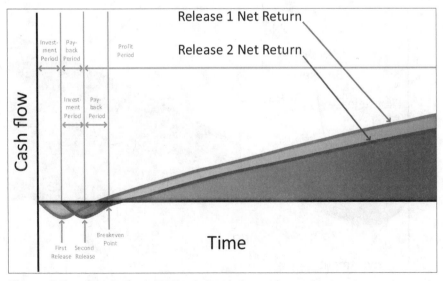

Figure 2.2   Developing a system in two halves

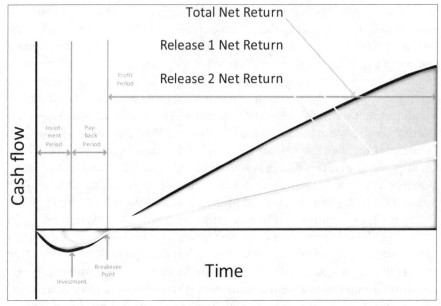

Figure 2.3   The net return on a successful software project built in stages

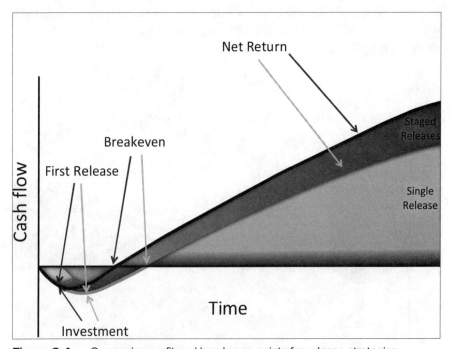

Figure 2.4   Comparing profit and breakeven points for release strategies

Releasing features sooner means that everyone gets value sooner: profit, market penetration, and utility. Additionally, it helps clarify what the ultimate product feature set *should* be: As customers understand more about the product, they can speculate less about what they think they need.

Of course, there are other considerations such as delivery and installation costs; but even so, we have understated the case. For example, in many large projects half of the requested features often represent 80 percent of the entire project's value. In that case, the first curve would be sloped higher than we have shown.

Although not all software can be delivered in stages, very often it can be—particularly in IT organizations. How do we determine which aspects of a product can be delivered quickly? Denne and Cleland-Huang (2003) suggest identifying "minimum marketable features" (MMFs). A minimum marketable feature is the smallest amount of functionality that makes sense to market.

This can be taken further: Plan which features to deliver first so that the business and the customer get the most value as soon as possible. A relentless focus on adding value is at the very core of Lean thinking.

Help Clarify Customers' Needs

Frequently, developers complain that customers do not really know what they want. They change their minds; they cannot specify what the software should do; their requirements are imprecise and incomplete.

It is easy to think that if this is true, it must be a customer issue. But dig deeper. The developer team is also involved. Consider the following case study.

Case Study: Building Components

Alan was working on a system that involved four components: scheduling, accounting, resource management, and content delivery. The intended development approach, as shown in Figure 2.5, was to build and release each component in turn until the product was completed. From the perspective of contributing value, delivering with four iterations would be good because customers would get the components sooner.

Unfortunately, it was clear that the customers did not really understand the fairly complex scheduling aspect of the product. At first, Alan thought that if each component could be delivered in stages, perhaps the customers would be required to know less up front and would be able to build on what they did know. So he asked the team, "If we build *half* of the scheduling component, would that provide value?" This would require the customer to know only

Initial Development Sequence

Figure 2.5   Time frame for initial development sequence

Iterative Development Sequence

Build and deliver the first half of all features. Then go back and build the rest of system.

Figure 2.6   Building the components in stages

Suggested Development Sequence

Figure 2.7   Building components 25 percent at a time and cycling through them until the whole project is done

half as much. We would deliver half of each component, release it, go to the next one, and release that until the first half of each component was done. We would then repeat the process to add the features we hadn't built yet. The thinking was that after the customers had used each component for a while they would know how to describe the rest of the features. This is shown in Figure 2.6.

The team's response was disappointing. "Yes, we could deliver half and find value, but our customers don't even know *half* of what is needed."[2]

This was when he asked a simple question that resulted in an epiphany for him. "How much do customers *really* know?" How often do we developers have the attitude that customers really aren't sure about *anything*? The truth is that they do have certainty about *some* things, even if it isn't everything. It seems reasonable that they usually understand about 20 to 25 percent of their problem domain.

This leads to an even more useful question, "What *part* of the system do they know?" Do they know the core stuff or do they know the fancy, extra stuff? In fact, customers typically know more about the core stuff, the things that led to the project and product enhancements in the first place. In other words, the customers know what we can start with.

The key insight is this: Start with what customers know.

Alan asked the team if building and delivering the components in pieces representing only 25 percent of the system would be valuable. They responded, "Yes." This evolved into the plan shown in Figure 2.7.

---

2. We are not suggesting that you can always deliver in stages; that is why we had to ask the team. But you should always look for the opportunity to deliver value in stages when you can.

This has become a fundamental approach for us:

> Start building the system based on what the customer is clear about, even if it is only 20 percent of what is required. Build a little, show them, gain more clarity, and repeat. That is the best way to address constantly changing requirements.

When customers are changing their minds frequently, it is probably because developers are asking them to speculate and try to be clear about things that they do not yet know. What happens? Anything built under those circumstances will, of course, be inadequate. Note that the word "speculate" is never used—but the pressure for more information causes the customers to do just that.

The reality is that customers usually do know some of what they want, at least the features that are most important to them right at the moment. What many cannot do well is speculate about what is unknown. ("This is a six-month project, so tell me what you will need six months from now"). Speculation is risky.

To mitigate the risk of uncertainty, Agile prescribes short iterations with lots of feedback. As customers learn more about what the system looks like and what it can do, they get clearer ideas about what they really need and can ask for it more precisely. The design emerges with experience over time.

Lean product development takes this further with its focus on delivering value. It guides teams to concentrate on what their customers have the greatest clarity on: the core functionality of the product. Core functionality is closely tied to the business process, to what they are already doing, even if it is not automated or is poorly done. Customers can be very specific about these features. What they are not clear about—and so what they have to speculate about—involves user interface, esoteric features, and other cool bells and whistles. Often, these offer the least real value to the customer but are the most seductive—both to the customer and to the developer—and thus are the most likely to get them off track.

The Lean principle here is to create knowledge all the time. Focus on delivering value! Start with what the customer is clear on, on core processes. Let them gain experience and knowledge and then specify the next bit.

This is a better approach to product planning than trying to specify every requirement at the beginning. Even if it is not possible to release in stages, it can still be useful to build in stages because doing so concentrates first on that part of the system that the customer is clear about; it develops customer clarity. We do customers a favor by not requiring them to speculate, by focusing on what they are comfortable with. And it does developers a favor by reducing risk, making it less likely that they will build unnecessary features. And not building unneeded features means less wasted time and, even more importantly, a less complex system.

The point is to involve the business and the customer in planning for quicker delivery in multiple iterations, adding value in stages. This is Lean thinking.

Promote Knowledge-Based Product Development and Better Project Management

The most obvious benefit of Lean-Agile product development is that you discover how you are doing very early in the project. In non-Agile projects, you don't really know about the quality of your code until you enter the test phase of the project, which is usually late in the schedule if not at the end itself. You also don't know how customers will react to your product until the first beta testers see it. This is a bit late in the cycle. In many ways, the feedback you get on a project at this point, which is illustrated in Figure 2.8, is really only useful for setting up the next release.

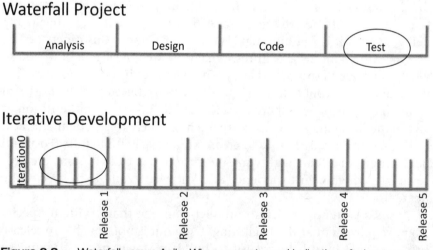

Figure 2.8   Waterfall versus Agile: When you get a real indication of where you are

This feedback covers both the pace at which you are working and whether or not you are building what the customer wants. In a Waterfall project, although customers may see the system while it is being built, it is often difficult to incorporate their feedback into the system. Agile processes are geared toward enabling the developer to utilize the feedback rapidly, as soon as it is given.

Most of us have been on projects that were doing fine after six months but then were two months behind after seven months without being given any new requirements. Unless you are not using source control, this actually isn't possible (you could back up to where you were one month ago and be just one month behind schedule). The reality is that you were not on schedule at the six-month mark but did not know it. Now you do, but it's a bit late in the project to do anything about it.

Imagine a ten-month Agile project in which you discover after a couple of months that you are behind schedule. You have many choices at this early point—add more resources, remove scope, reset the end date, even cancel the project. When we learn late in the game that a project is in trouble, it affords little opportunity for management to adjust. We talk about "death marches" at the end of many projects. At that point, management is often angry and upset. And where there is anger, there is usually fear. Fear runs rampant in many non-Agile projects when management senses that the team has lost control of the job. That can happen when a team relies on too many predictions and assumptions that do not bear themselves out.

What is different about Lean-Agile projects is the way they are planned, the role of testing, and the sense of urgency about them. These present new challenges for the project manager, who must facilitate communication between teams and customers, manage sustainability and a constant sense of urgency, maintain visibility, and communicate the true pace of progress to all concerned. But these are relatively positive challenges to have.

Short Planning Horizons

One of the myths of Agile is that you do not plan. In fact, you are constantly planning—just in smaller increments and with more people than you are probably used to. You plan for releases. You plan before each iteration. You plan in the daily standup meetings. Maybe 15 percent of the team's time involves some sort of planning. The difference is that, at the project-level, you plan for what is known: two to four weeks out, the next iteration, and the work we will do today. Planning for what is nearly certain is a whole lot easier than planning for what you don't know. This is what makes Lean-Agile projects easier to plan.

Testing to Improve the Process as Well as the Quality

A key Lean principle is to aim for perfection, to improve constantly. In Lean-Agile projects, this strongly drives the way testing is done. Testing occurs very early in the development process in order to shorten the cycle-time between finding a defect and fixing it. This makes it likely that fairly well perfected code is delivered at the end of an iteration. It also makes it more likely that any defects that are found will not have serious consequences.

Perfection means that testing is not just for finding bugs. Even more, the testing activity should discover the *causes* of errors and eliminate them. Root-cause analysis is part of testing's portfolio of work. This approach to testing is different from the usual approach, in which bug elimination is done by developing rigorous specifications and then testing in a separate phase, usually after development is completed. Removing the delay between development and testing is what makes risk management easier in Lean-Agile projects. Many errors stem simply from misunderstanding customer requirements. Creating acceptance tests up front (at least defining them, if not implementing them) changes the conversations between customers, developers, and testers. Discussing things at the implementation level as well as the requirements level improves the conversation, which assists developers in understanding what customers really mean and need.

Planning without Fear

Lean-Agile projects always have a sense of urgency about them. Short deadlines and close contact with the customer tend to ensure this. However, there is rarely a sense of panic or fear. Even if there is a setback, the project never feels out of control, and that helps prevent management from getting angry and afraid about the project. They get a sense early on whether the project is on track or at risk and they can adjust to it; they don't get surprised by a lack of progress at the end of a long project (and surprising management is always a bad thing). The stress level among Agile development teams seems moderate and healthy. Contrast this with more traditional approaches, where the workload at the front end is relatively low and then ramps up to crises and all-consuming 80+-hour weeks at the end; and then when there are setbacks, the consequences feel dire and the pressure builds. Such a pace and environment cannot be sustained or be healthy for long. Lean-Agile projects tend to feel more in control and to be more sustainable over time.

Motivate Teams and Allow Failing (Learning) Early

The feedback that customers get with Lean-Agile helps them clarify their needs and instills confidence that their needs will be met. This feedback helps developers, too.

By and large, developers enjoy working with the business and with customers when there is a sense of common purpose and teamwork. They like doing work that positively impacts users of their product; they have a passion to help. Developing short iterations and working closely with customers results in lots of good feedback and lots of quick wins. This is a great motivator for development teams.

In this process, both customers and developers discover very quickly what is not working[3], what assumptions are invalid, and what they do not know. That information, too, is a good motivator. It may not make them happy but at least it presents them with challenges to overcome while they are still in a position to react positively. Nothing feels worse than discovering a major flaw late in the cycle.

By getting early feedback on how the team's methods are working, developers can make changes quickly and avoid waste. Sometimes this feedback has more to do with the progress of the project than with its process. If it is slower than desired, management can chose to add more resources, de-scope the project, push out the end date, or even cancel the project early in the cycle. With wise project management and Lean think-ing, this should be a motivator: Stopping early on the wrong project or on a project that is more costly than feasible is in everyone's interest. It prevents the agony of working on a project for six months or a year only to find out that there is no business support for it and that it is going to be cancelled. That feels just terrible, especially if the team was doing what it was asked to do and was doing it well. Ultimately, it is better to work on projects that have a solid business tie-in.

---

3. In the Agile community, they say that they want to "fail fast" but we prefer to say that we want to "learn fast." That may involve failing, but it may not. It is better not to fail if you don't have to! But if you are failing, learn fast . . . and correct quickly.

Focus on Product-Centered Development

Suppose you are working on a project for which the following are true:

- There is no benefit from a partial release of the product; the entire product must be finished before it can be released. (This is not uncommon.)

- The customer has perfect clarity about what is needed. (This almost never happens; even with rewrites, the customer usually has better ideas the second time around.)

- Management trusts the team to produce the result that is needed; therefore, the project does not have to be controlled through iterations. (This happens on occasion.)

- The team perfectly understands Agile. There is no learning curve.

Would you still want to use Agile and an iterative approach? Yes!

Why? Because building software in stages enables you to take advantage of what you have learned as you build it. All developers know much more at the end of a project than they do at the beginning. When you design everything up front, there is a tendency to overdo the architecture, to include more than you need. This adds complexity that the team has to deal with for the life of the project.

Lean gives insight into how to manage unfolding requirements and design, as described in detail in *Emergent Design: The Evolutionary Nature of Professional Software Development* (Bain 2008).

Improve Team Efficiency

A problem many teams face is that key people are busy with several projects. This degrades their efficiency not only because they are pulled in multiple directions and must continually switch tasks, but because it creates delays for everyone else who needs their assistance. Large projects tend to have more people working on several projects at one time, which lowers the teams' efficiencies.

Lean helps us minimize the time it takes to complete prioritized business and customer solutions. For most legacy organizations, this means they should organize around sequencing and completing smaller, high-value requests before starting new ones. In these organizations, the drive to keep people busy (to maximize efficiency) seems to motivate professionals to start more and more projects without concern for the consequences. The Lean approach is to finish work and deliver it to the end user before starting something new. In simple terms: Stop allowing queues of unfinished work to build up. This tends to reduce contention for critical resources because projects go through the development pipeline faster; this alone can generate huge efficiency improvements.

Summary

This chapter describes six benefits of using Agile for software development:

- It adds value to the business quickly.
- It helps clarify customers' needs.
- It focuses on knowledge-based product development, which leads to better project management.
- It motivates teams and allows "failing early."
- It promotes product-centered development.
- It improves team efficiency.

It also offers a financial model that describes the benefits of realizing the value of products incrementally rather than in final releases. In addition to financial benefits, everyone on the team—customers and developers—can learn more quickly and incorporate that learning back into the product and process while there is still time to do it.

Try This

These exercises are best done as a conversation with someone in your organization. After each exercise, ask each other if there are any actions either of you can take to improve your situation.

- How involved are customers and stakeholders in day-to-day product development?
- What are impediments to frequent feedback from users of products in development?

- How would smaller, more frequent deliveries of verifiable components help improve the ability of customers and stakeholders to provide feedback?

Recommended Reading

The following works offer helpful insights into the topics of this chapter.

Bain. 2008. *Emergent Design: The Evolutionary Nature of Professional Software Development*. Boston: Addison-Wesley.

Denne and Cleland-Huang. 2003. *Software by Numbers: Low-Risk, High-Return Development*. Upper Saddle River, NJ: Prentice Hall.

CHAPTER 3

The Big Picture

"It is only possible to make a place which is alive by a process in which each part is modified by its position in the whole."   —Christopher Alexander

IN THIS CHAPTER

This chapter discusses the larger goal of going for Agility at the enterprise level. What is involved? What is required to create real value for the organization? Everything must drive toward delivering value for the overall organization.

Takeaways

Enterprise Agility requires looking at an organization's entire value stream—from idea to implementation, from concept to consumption. In order to achieve Agility, several enterprise areas must be addressed:

- Identify the products whose creation or enhancement will make the greatest impact on the company's bottom line.

- Match these product enhancements (projects) to the organization's resources.

- Manage these projects so the product enhancements are achieved with the greatest quality and speed possible.

- Organize the software-development teams so they can work with each other in the most effective manner.

- Use proper software-engineering methods both to support the project management and to ensure long term viability and low-cost sustainability of the products created.

- Create a learning environment so that the process is continuously improved.

Aiming for Enterprise Agility

Many people have focused on introducing Agility at the team level. This can be the easiest place to start but often it is not the principal challenge that a development organization faces. And it definitely isn't where to end.

The real goal should be to create *enterprise* Agility. That is, the enterprise needs to be Agile. It needs to be able to respond to external competitive forces, better understandings of the marketplace, its own errors, changing technologies, and anything else that can have an adverse or positive influence on the enterprise. Team Agility is necessary but not sufficient. Enterprise Agility requires team Agility; but team Agility is only a means to an end: Enterprise Agility. Enterprise Agility enables a company to deliver higher quality products and services to their customers at a faster rate than their competition. This is a strong competitive advantage in any industry.

Getting to Enterprise Agility

Enterprise Agility requires looking at the entire value stream of an organization. By "value stream," we mean the stream of delivered software solutions that flows from the delivery organization to the customer or consumer of those solutions, driven by business need. By focusing on the value stream, enterprise Agility clearly shows the time required for ideas (triggered by market opportunities, competitive threats, or business need) to flow through the entire life cycle through to deployment and use. As much as possible, we seek to minimize this cycle time and to remove waste and delays in this flow.

Figure 3.1 shows a rough timeline of a project. At some point, the project is envisioned. Management determines what value the project

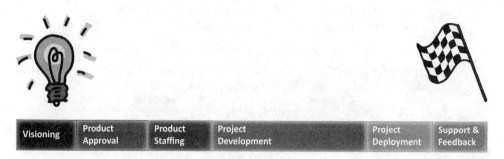

Figure 3.1   A rough timeline for software development from initial concept to consumption

might have, how much it will cost, and whether it should be initiated. Once a project is approved, it gets staffed; shortly after that, software development begins and then it is deployed and supported. Feedback should occur throughout the development process, but once deployed, a new level of feedback is also available—how customers are using the software and what real value it has contributed to the business.

Unfortunately, many companies attend to only a part of the entire timeline. For example, one client hired us to help make their teams Agile. They said their projects were typically six months long. When we casually asked how long it took to go from idea generation to project initiation, they said, "Two years." That means that, start to finish, a project runs for two and a half years and development is only 20 percent of that time!

This was surprising. Surely, they did not hire us to help them with only 20 percent of their problem. Yet, they asked us to focus on development because that is where they were spending most of their software-development dollars. True, they spent 80 percent of their budget during these six months. But Lean tells us we need to focus on the time spent, not the money. Focusing on removing delays by improving quality results in quicker time to market and lower costs. Focusing on lowering costs typically degrades quality and takes longer. Time and again, focusing on lowering costs instead of removing delays and improving quality slows development and lowers quality. Even focusing on the development time may not improve the value stream since it represents only one part of it. It is crucial to look at all of the work done from envisioning the product until it is actually deployed. Had we helped them with only their project management, we could have helped them with only that small 20 percent included in the Agile/Scrum ellipse (shown in Figure 3.2). We would have missed the greater opportunities for improving the steps prior to project initiation.

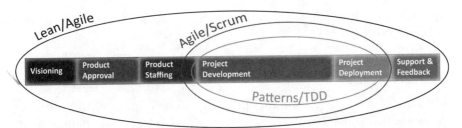

Figure 3.2   Where Lean, Agile/Scrum, and technical methods apply to the software-development timeline

Time after time, this is the case. In theory, Agile could apply broadly. In practice, most Agilists focus on the local team or teams and, as a result, concentrate mostly on the project level and the challenges of the team. Too often, they view issues of staffing, project and process, and impediments through the lens of their impact on the local team. They consider technical disciplines, such as design patterns and test-driven development (TDD), because these help teams get their work done. And make no mistake: Scrum and other Agile methods do make teams much more effective than they were before. But more guidance is needed to address the challenges of multiple teams working together across an entire organization. Lean thinking inherently offers the approach and guidance required to address the entire value stream.

How to Create Real Value for an Organization

To improve software development, several essential areas must be addressed, including:

- Identify the products whose creation or enhancement will make the greatest impact on the company's bottom line.

- Match these product enhancements (projects) to the organization's resources.

- Manage these projects so the product enhancements are achieved with the greatest quality and speed possible.

- Organize the software-development teams so they can work with each other in the most effective manner.

- Use proper software-engineering methods both to support the project management and to ensure long-term viability and low-cost sustainability of the products created.

- Create a learning environment so that the process is continuously improved.

Identify Value

In many organizations, the identification step is done by the software department itself (IT in IT organizations and product development in software product companies). This is the wrong driver—the tail is wagging the dog. Software creation or enhancement should be driven by business needs—so it should be driven by the business-management end of the organization.

The question is not, "What can we technologists build" (a software-development perspective) but rather, "What products will return the greatest value to the business?" and "When can the business or customers start using them?" (business-driven perspectives).

That last question is important. Just because software has been released does not mean the business realizes value from it; there is often a lag between release and use. People must be trained, product must be shipped, support processes must be set up, and marketing and communication must be implemented. The value does not begin until all of that is in place. The relevant value stream must extend from when the idea is formulated until value is realized.

Manage the Organization's Resources

The difficulty of assigning resources to projects varies from company to company. Mary and Tom Poppendieck (Poppendieck and Poppendieck 2003) say that we should adopt a *product* focus, rather than a project focus, in our development efforts (and therefore in our staffing practices). Project thinking assumes a well-defined beginning and end to the work. And it staffs for the project rather than for the life of the product: Resources are put together and disbanded. Ideally, the same people could work on a product throughout its lifetime. However, resources often become scarce and it becomes increasingly difficult to keep teams together in the most effective way.

When many projects are in process, the contention for resources becomes so great that projects get scheduled based on resource availability or political clout rather than what would contribute the most value to the business. We've seen extreme cases where it seems that teams don't even exist; rather, there are several people working on a project together while they also work on other projects with other people. In organizations like this, creating a business focus is often the impetus for creating effective teams. Project thinking virtually guarantees inefficient use of personnel.

Suppose we have a company that is organized as shown in Figure 3.3. This is a typical organization. Resources are assigned to projects one at a time according to project need. For example, Figure 3.4 shows how staff will be assigned to Project 1: a business systems analyst, an architect, three UI people, and so on.

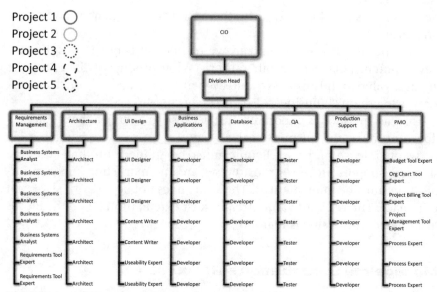

Figure 3.3 Matching project needs to available staff

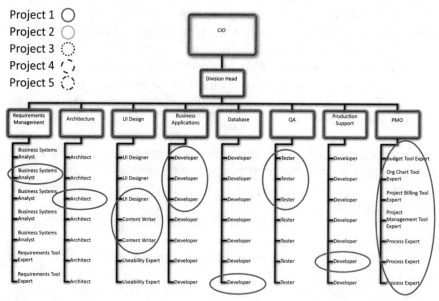

Figure 3.4 Matching resources for one project

The next project also needs resources: a requirements tool expert, an architect, some UI designers, and so on. Note the new circles in Figure 3.5.

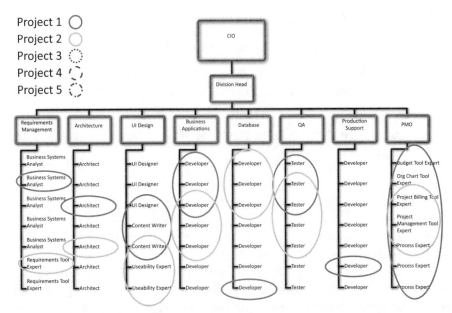

Figure 3.5   Matching resources for another project

Continue staffing the projects in this way and you get something like Figure 3.6.

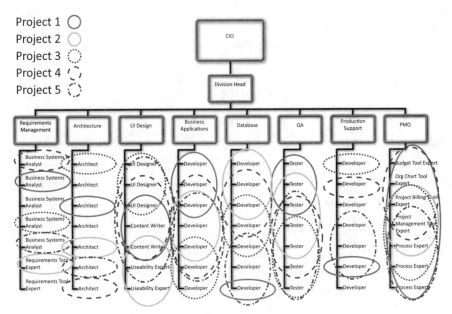

Figure 3.6   Resource map for all projects

Unfortunately, this causes many problems, including:

- People are assigned to multiple projects.

- We now require projects to start and stop on time so that resources are available as needed; that is, we are assuming a predictable future.

- Resource constraints make it impossible to accelerate the truly critical projects.

The first problem, having people work on multiple projects, is particularly bad. Studies[1] have shown that when people are working on even two projects at a time, their efficiency decreases by 20 percent. If they work on as many as three projects at a time—and this is not uncommon in IT organizations—their efficiency drops 40 percent! They are operating at only 20 percent of their capacity on each project. This has a staggering impact and it is often ignored. The continual stopping, restarting, and waiting for information causes a tremendous productivity loss.

It is even worse for key staff. They are certainly being pulled in many more than three directions at once. As keepers of some crucial information, as many as five or six projects are vying for their attention at any given time. This drives their productivity to very low levels—people who, given their essential knowledge, should be the most productive. Just as damaging, most of the others in the development organization waste time waiting for these people—further degrading the productivity of the entire organization.

The second and third problems mentioned above make this even more challenging. Lean thinking provides a better way.

Manage Projects

Once the product creation or enhancement has been committed to, and resources allocated for it, we must be able to efficiently and effectively manage the projects themselves. This is where Agile and Scrum come in. As we have already seen, these projects are not being done in isolation. If we attempt to manage the projects individually and merely coordinate them while doing so, we are likely to miss a variety of opportunities as well as cause great inefficiencies.

---

1. For one example, see (Aral, Brynjolfsson, and Van Alstyne 2008).

Agile project management done in isolation violates the Lean principle of optimizing the whole. Chapter 5, Going beyond Scrum, describes how Scrum can be readily extended to include Lean principles and be much more effective than Scrum by itself. *Kanban*

There are other alternatives to Scrum, including Crystal, feature-driven development, and Kanan software development. They are good and they address specific challenges for teams; however, they, like Scrum, do not entirely address the bigger picture.[2] By themselves, they do not address the entire value stream, which is what is needed.

Proper Software Engineering

Although software development itself may not be the limiting factor in organizations, ignoring the best practices of software development eventually results in a major impediment: poor code quality. Software must be well written and properly tested to be sustainable over the long haul. Our experience dictates that emphasis on quality design through the use of design patterns and up-front automated testing are essential protocols that need to be understood and applied by the development team.

Case Study: Financial Services

One of our consultants was working with the IT department of a large financial-services company. The team was working on a software product that supported the company's consumer financial-service offerings (for example, IRAs or money-market funds). The team was getting ready to roll out some product enhancements that would greatly simplify the experience for the consumer. In fact, they based their business case on the hope that these enhancements would reduce support-desk headcount.

One of the enhancements was "basic" functionality—the usual experience the consumer would have when things were working fine. Another enhancement supported consumers when things were not so simple. As you can imagine, the second enhancement was much more complex. They developed three estimates for completing the work:

- Time to do both enhancements: nine months

- Time to do the basic enhancement: six months

- Time to do the second enhancement (handling complex situations): four months

The extra month was required because they would need to re-factor the database schema and transition the data from the first release to the new one.

---

2. This is not necessarily true of Kanban, which can be used to include the beginning part of the value stream. We are referring here to when Kanban methods are used to manage only the development team.

What would you say? What would you expect the business to say?

The development team felt that splitting up the project was a bad idea because it would take them an extra month and would require extra work. Looking chiefly at costs to themselves and the project, this might seem reasonable. However, the business saw it differently. Releasing the first enhancement three months early would result in cost savings that greatly outweighed the extra month of development. In fact, they gained so much with that first release that they decided not even to do the second enhancement. They could realize more value by having the developers do something else and retaining the support-desk people to handle those complex situations.

The point is that simply focusing on speeding up development teams is insufficient. Instead, you have to see the product in the context of the bigger picture—the entire value stream. Doing so lets the enterprise see all the alternatives for achieving its objectives, realizing more value (and more cash), and satisfying its customers. Agile approaches help teams do well; adding Lean thinking and technical best practices extends the enterprise's capacity to optimize the entire value stream.

Summary

Transitioning to Agile software product development is not done in isolation. It operates in the larger context of integrating Agility at the enterprise level. Enterprise Agility entails looking at the entire value stream of an organization, from initial concept to when the customer can utilize the product.

Try This

These exercises are best done as a conversation with someone in your organization. After each exercise, ask each other if there are any actions either of you can take to improve your situation.

- How is your product-development staff organized? By product? By skill set? By process activity?

- Sample your organization for the average number of projects assigned to each person or group. Can you justify the productivity losses due to task switching?

- How can you reduce the amount of work-in-process with your current organizational structure?

- How can you restructure in order to bring control to the number of projects in flight?

Recommended Reading

The following works offer helpful insights into the topics of this chapter.

Aral, Brynjolfsson, and Van Alstyne. December 2008. *What Makes Information Workers Productive*. http://sloanreview.mit.edu/smr/issue/2008/winter/12/ (accessed October 2008).

Bain. 2008. *Emergent Design: The Evolutionary Nature of Professional Software Development*. Boston: Addison-Wesley.

Collison and Parcell. 2004. *Learning to Fly: Practical Lessons from One of the World's Leading Knowledge Companies*. Milford, CT: Capstone.

Poppendieck and Poppendieck. 2003. *Lean Software Development: An Agile Toolkit*. Boston: Addison-Wesley.

Townsend and Gebhardt. 2007. *How Organizations Learn: Investigate, Identify, Institutionalize*. Milwaukee, WI: ASQ Quality Press.

CHAPTER 4

Lean Portfolio Management

"There is nothing so useless as doing efficiently that which should not be done at all." —Peter F. Drucker

IN THIS CHAPTER

This chapter describes the approaches for selecting products and how to size them for creation and enhancement. The challenge is to select projects well so that the organization realizes the greatest return on investment (ROI) possible and provides high-quality, sustainable products. To achieve this, organizations use some form of product-portfolio management. We explore some of that approach's shortcomings (delays, staleness) and offer a better one—one that uses Lean thinking.

Takeaways

Key insights to take away from this chapter include the following.

- The Lean product portfolio should consist of minimum marketable features (MMF) to enable quick delivery of small product enhancements.

- Teams should be organized so that they can work efficiently on these product enhancements.

- Minimizing work-in-process improves efficiency while reducing risk.

- Increasing customer value must encompass all product lines.

The Challenge of Selecting Projects

Improving the product-development process is only half the challenge for software development. The other half, even more fundamental, is selecting the most important products to create and enhance. This approach is called "portfolio management."

Portfolio management applies to both product-development organizations and IT organizations. Each type of organization has its particular set of challenges, but the general approach, which we describe here, works for both. You must adapt it to your own situation, of course.

Introducing Terms

At the outset, it always helps to define terms. This section introduces terms we use throughout the rest of the book.

Enterprise

As defined in chapter 1, An Agile Developer's Guide to Lean Software Development, when we refer to the "enterprise," we mean all parts of the organization that are involved in the value stream of the product or service being created, enhanced, or maintained. In an IT organization this includes the business and IT sides. In a product company, it also includes marketing, sales, delivery, support, and development.

Product Organization and Customer Organization

"Product organizations" create software products for companies that derive revenue directly from the software. Customers are primarily external to the organization and developers are managed along product lines. In contrast, "IT organizations" create products for companies whose principal products are not software but that depend on software and applications to deliver or manage their products or services. Examples include financial institutions, healthcare providers, and insurance companies. Customers are primarily internal to the organization and developers are managed by roles. Table 4.1 illustrates the differences. Of course, these are just two endpoints on a spectrum; companies might have a mix of both.

Table 4.1   The Issues Facing Product Organizations and IT Organizations

	Product Organization	IT Organization
Who are the customers?	External	Internal
How are developers assigned to projects?	Along product lines	By roles
What is being developed?	Products to be sold externally	Software to be used by internal and/or external clients
How is planning done?	Yearly, based on marketing	Yearly, based on requests from business side
Who decides which products/projects to do?	Program managers	Typically a team of managers with representatives from the business side and IT

Customers

Customers are the end users of the software products, the people who consume the product for some purpose. The goal of a software organization is to add value for its customers.

In IT organizations, customers usually come from the business side of the company. Software exists to support the business as it provides products or services to external customers. If external customers use the products and services directly (for example, a banking Web application), the business side represents those customers to IT.

Product Champion

We use the term "product champion" to describe someone who makes the decisions about which products to create or enhance. Product companies may use the term "program manager" or "product manager." IT organizations may call this role the "sponsor."

Project

We use the term "project" to represent a fixed body of work selected to be implemented. It is the work required to create or enhance a product. For "project," you can substitute the phrase "product creation," "product enhancement," or "product fix" if that helps orient you toward product thinking.

Process

"Process" means different things to different people. In software development, we think of a process as an agreement by a team about how they will work together.

The team is responsible for its process. Teams employ their local knowledge about what is required to do their work, complementing required enterprise standards. The team agrees to use and improve its own processes.

Processes exist to serve the people, to help them get their work done. No process is perfect; when problems arise, the team is responsible to stop, change the process, and start again, all without affixing blame to any one person.

Project Portfolios

Virtually all large organizations have a portfolio of projects that they must manage. The mix of these projects is designed to maximize the return on their software-development investment. Ideally, the most important projects would be selected and then given to the development teams; but the larger the portfolio, the harder it is to administer.

Project Portfolios Are Idea Inventories

Administering the project portfolio involves a planning life cycle. The organization uses the life cycle to identify the sources of greatest ROI and then defines a plan to achieve it. It is common to use a yearly project planning cycle. An unintended outcome of the annual cycle is an ever-widening gap between what delivery organizations are working on and what the business needs. The wider the gap, the staler and the less relevant the projects become. The annual cycle becomes a sinkhole into which ideas descend.

Think of project ideas as a type of "work-in-process" (WIP). As long as an idea is in process, the business does not realize value from it. The quicker you can turn it into a real product, the sooner it has value.

What causes excess WIP? Planning teams start out with great intentions. They develop tight business cases and project visions during the project vision "season." Program managers lead value-driven discussions about the capabilities and features they need to respond to market opportunities or competitor threats.

Then they enter the technical analysis season. All of that high-bandwidth communication between business and development degrades while technical organizations take time to analyze the requirements. Work drops into various technical silos (QA, mid-tier, UI, and the like). Technical integration is pushed off farther and farther.[1] It becomes a downward spiral—people need to be kept busy while they wait for answers to planning questions; the busier they are, the longer it takes them to answer other questions.

Business is savvy about these delays. If they anticipate long delivery cycles, they may end up piling on poorly prioritized requirements (the kitchen-sink effect) in the hope of getting some work that is useful. The more work they give, the larger the portfolio grows. And the larger the portfolio, the harder it is to administer. And the harder it is to administer, the more delays there are. And so on. It is a vicious cycle.

Should We Avoid Delays by Batching Project Analysis?

To address these delays in analysis, technical organizations often batch together various business requirements that seem to involve similar technical issues. Then, the technical analysts, who are always in short supply, can focus on those common issues at one time (see Figure 4.1). That seems to be more efficient for the technical resources, but it significantly delays overall delivery and decreases the efficiency of the organization as a whole.

When you batch requirements together, you hold up the release of the most important one(s) in the batch until the least important one is ready. If there is a delay in one part of the bundle, the whole package is delayed. What is the true objective?

---

1. Analysis in silos is a type of Lean "anti-pattern"—a known violation of Lean principles that should not be done (see Shalloway 2008).

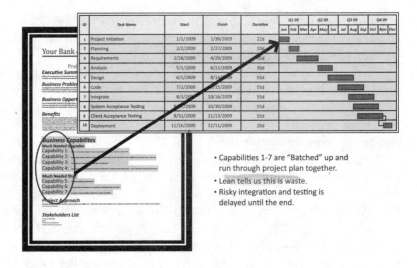

Figure 4.1   Batching business needs into projects

The obstacle comes from letting projects drive planning. The focus is on minimizing cost and maximizing resource utilization rather on speed and realizing ROI quickly.

Should We Avoid Delays by Increasing Releases?

One approach to narrowing the gap between idea and delivery—between concept and consumption—is to increase the frequency of a product's releases. This is good in that it gives the business a predictable schedule of changes. And it gives the appearance of rapid delivery. But if there is still a 12- to 18-month gap between idea and delivery, there is still significant delay. The ideas are still stale.

Lean Portfolio Management

Lean thinking offers a way out of the vicious cycle that can come with managing a large product portfolio. We start by thinking about the relationship between the portfolio's needs and development team's needs. As shown in Figure 4.2, there is a pipeline and a feedback mechanism between the two. The goal is to promote a fast-flexible-flow of work while selecting projects that return the greatest value to the organization. Lean thinking says to focus on sustainable speed by delivering the most impor-

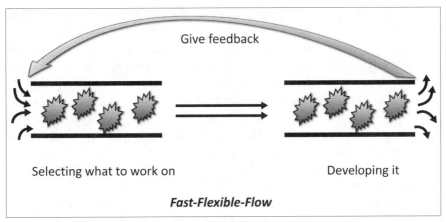

Figure 4.2   Selecting what work feeds the development team

tant aspects of a system first, by minimizing work-in-process, and by limiting the amount of work to the organization's capacity. Lean addresses the risk in software development by creating feedback and focusing on value rather than by the classic method of planning everything up front.

Lean directs us to select smaller projects to work on whenever possible. This does not mean picking small projects from the batch that has already been identified; rather, it means that, early in the planning, projects are defined as small as they can possibly be. This ensures that essential projects are being worked on all the time. Projects that are too large run the risk of bundling together features that are less important to the organization overall.

This approach delivers value to customers more quickly by prioritizing which business features to work on based on business value and then managing the project in a visible portfolio. We call this Lean portfolio management.

Why It Works

The Lean portfolio-management approach allows stakeholders and clients to identify and prioritize features that create the highest ROI for the business. The Lean organization is structured so that cross-functional teams can review and break down both business features and system dependencies in order to build minimal marketable software solutions. As opposed to the traditional approach, which is task-based and resource-driven, the Lean portfolio approach is a results-based, validation approach. Status reviews are not based on tasks completed but instead on validation of technical results.

This solves the dilemma that to deliver sooner seems to require more bodies or lowered quality. Lean thinking says that concentrating on delivering the most important features of a product maximizes both team efficiency (by eliminating task switching and waiting times) and team effectiveness (by working on the most important parts of the product). By focusing on small, marketable features, with the goal of getting completed software all the way through the system, an Agile team immediately improves efficiency by avoiding the costs of multi-tasking and its subsequent thrashing. Furthermore, critical projects are not slowed down by working on less important projects in parallel. Additional benefits are achieved because Agile methods quickly expose impediments to rapid delivery that are normally hidden in large Waterfall projects, where processes to transform handoffs create the illusion of control.

It Is OK to Plan Releases

On the other end of the spectrum, some Scrum practitioners believe teams should stay focused on the current work iteration and never look ahead (or not much). This attitude has led to many failed Agile teams. In fact, Lean thinking agrees with Scrum's view not to look too far ahead (trying to achieve JIT); but decisions that need to be made early still need to be made early.

The Lean product portfolio enables priorities to be set, and elaboration of details to occur, at the right, responsible moment. Value is realized incrementally. As more is learned about requirements, that knowledge is fed back into the planning for future increments.

Thus, Agile methods allow a learning organization to emerge, which results in predictable estimation of features described at the capability level. These features can be deconstructed in advance of the iteration in which they are actually implemented by establishing Lean flow that is conceptualized as the planned release of features.

With Existing Systems, Plan to Use Incremental Delivery

Building and delivering incrementally works when converting existing systems, too. Customers may say that they "want everything we had in the old system." But that means they haven't done an analysis of which features have been valuable. It is extremely unlikely that every feature in the existing system is truly valuable. By building in steps, business value drives and it allows the development team to focus only on high-value, required features, and not to waste time converting the system's unneeded features (or worse, bugs). It also allows the business to embrace market changes and opportunities that arise during the conversion project. [2]

The Benefits of Lean Portfolio Management

This section describes four of the benefits that Lean portfolio management provides to a business.

Speed and Quality

A development organization that is truly in synch with its business customers positions itself to help identify minimal marketable features and is structured to be able to release them quickly. Organizations successfully making the transition to Lean-Agile discover that attempts to deliver quickly expose delays that are impediments to both effective and efficient product development. This enables the organization to adjust and to remove these delays and so deliver value more quickly. When the entire enterprise is focused on speed, market opportunities can be leveraged and threats bypassed; the result is rapid savings and realized profits. In order to accommodate this, the development team must begin to see delivery and quality as sustainable activities that are constantly improved by short-cycle feedback loops. Once time-to-market becomes the focus, actions taken to reduce delays cause quality to go up since these delays are the cause of quality problems. The shorter cycles also reduce the development cost by eliminating wasteful steps.

Another benefit of focusing on speed is that the team's understanding of what they are building increases and they can therefore avoid building what they don't need. This creates less complex systems because they are smaller—again, resulting in higher quality. Creating smaller, high-quality modules creates an upward spiral of competitive strength by enabling future changes to be more easily manifested.

---

2. This does require that the technology organization understand Agile design patterns and Test-Driven Development. These practices allow teams to create change-tolerant architectures that give confidence to make aggressive design changes, since the architecture supports them, and suites of automated regression tests allow verification that nothing existing is broken as changes are implemented.

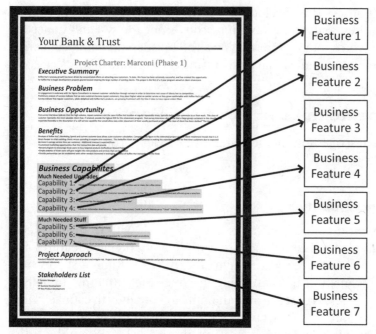

Figure 4.3   Business features of the project vision

Line of Sight to Business Needs

Think of the Lean portfolio as a set or container of capabilities, defined at a high level, that the business requires to implement its market or response strategies. These capabilities map loosely to capability statements called out as business solutions in the project vision statement or a typical project charter. Call these capabilities "business features" (see Figure 4.3). The Lean portfolio gives the entire business and development organization a focal point, in which line of sight to the business needs is established for all work undertaken, with the goal of minimizing work-in-process and completing each capability as quickly as possible.

The Lean portfolio can be tracked for reporting, but the real value to the business organization is that it creates a visible representation where business features are listed to establish both priority and technical effort required (which continually must be traded off).

Minimizing Work-in-Process

Building in smaller chunks has the side effect of minimizing work-in-process and enabling the formation of well-defined, Agile teams that work on one feature after another. When they complete one, they pull the next one from the prioritized list of features. This enables teams to work on—and complete—one product or enhancement at a time, which ensures that they are always working on the highest-priority product enhancements.

Smaller chunks make it easier to manage key resources that have to be shared across teams. If the work is smaller, there is less contention for these precious resources, so thrashing is minimized.

Minimizing Interruptions

Interruptions are also more easily handled when working with small chunks. When team members are involved in many projects at once, it is tempting to interrupt the team when a manager has an urgent task come up—just to get the task done—when there is no clear break in work activity or the breaks are too far in the future.

When teams are working on smaller chunks of functionality, it is more likely that the manager's urgent task can wait until a team is done with its current work. This avoids forcing the team to multi-task, which increases thrashing and lowers efficiency.

The Approach

The basic approach for Lean portfolio management starts with a breakdown of business features, as shown in Figure 4.3. We will use these business features to transition from a collection of project visions to Lean portfolio management. Instead of batching up capabilities into a large project, Lean organizations can deliver minimal marketable feature sets. This requires cross-functional, continuously integrated Agile teams pulling prioritized work based on capacity.

Taking all of the business features for all of the projects, we can get a plan for our product development, as shown in Figure 4.4.

Select those business features that will return the greatest value, as shown in Figure 4.5.

Note: In the following figures, "BF" means "Business Feature."

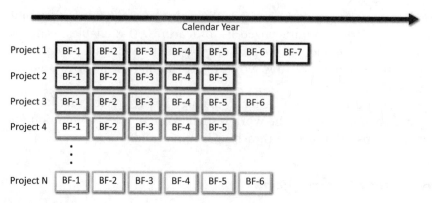

Figure 4.4   Development schedule for business features

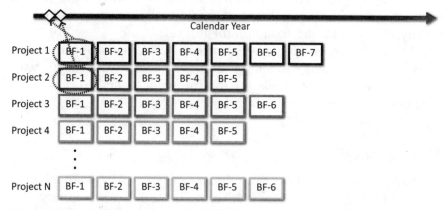

Figure 4.5   Initial business features developed

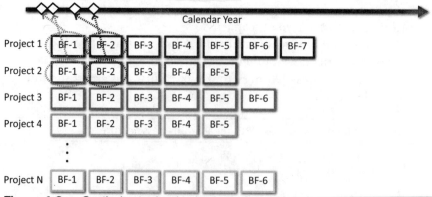

Figure 4.6   Continuing to develop business features as planned

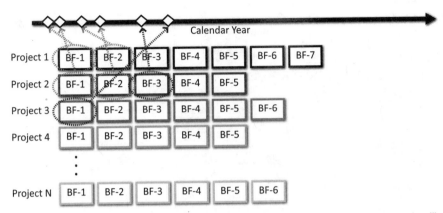

Figure 4.7   Developing a business feature from another product line when it will return more value to do so

As long as our understanding of the world and our projects does not change, the team keeps to the schedule and develops the next most important business features as originally planned, as shown in Figure 4.6.

At some point, a business feature of another product may become more important than some feature in the current plan. Business conditions change all the time; something is learned that gives it more urgency. Because we are using short release cycles, it is easy to modify the plan and give that new business feature a higher priority so that it will be worked on next, as shown in Figure 4.7.

This even works for new features that were not part of the original plan. Just insert the new feature and give it higher priority, as shown in Figure 4.8.

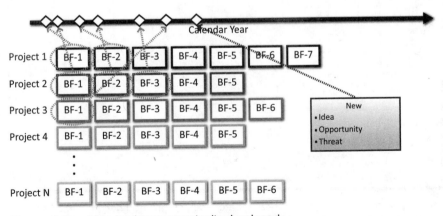

Figure 4.8   New business opportunity developed

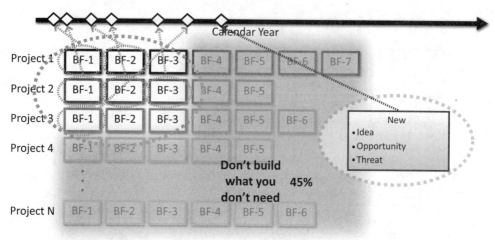

Figure 4.9   Build what you need; avoid building what you don't need

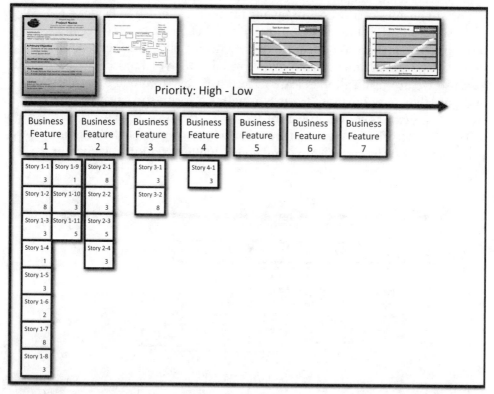

Figure 4.10   The product backlog: prioritized feature set, staged and decomposed into user and system stories (under the features); higher priorities to the left, lower ones to the right

The point is to focus on building those functions that are most needed and most important, and to avoid building features that are less useful. The iterative approach of focusing on the most valuable business capabilities enables us to take advantage of the Pareto rule: Find the 20 percent of the work that provides 80 percent of the value. This is illustrated in Figure 4.9.

With this approach, it is straightforward to create a prioritized product backlog for each team. As shown in Figure 4.10, each team has a product backlog that lists its features across the top and the story breakdown under each feature. The priority of each feature on the team's backlog must align with the priorities of the overall portfolio. The priorities are shown graphically: Higher-priority features appear on the left and lower-priority features on the right. Figure 4.10 shows an actual team's product backlog.

Shorter Planning Cycles

Figure 4.10 illustrates the extreme position of planning at the business-feature level based on minimal marketable features. You can still realize significant value without going that far by focusing on the time delays that occur in the regular annual planning cycle.

A typical annual planning cycle runs from July 1 to December 31. This means that we spend the last six months of this year collecting ideas and developing plans for work that begins next year. Then, in January, any new ideas that come along go into the hopper to wait until the next planning cycle, next July 1. If you have worked in IT for any length of time, this is not surprising.

But what is the result? It is that the ideas we are working with are likely stale. To compute the average amount of time it takes from when an idea enters the planning cycle until it is completed, add the following:

- The average time it waits for planning

- The time it takes for planning

- The average time it takes for completion

As shown in Figure 4.11, assuming everything gets done in a year, each of these steps takes 6 months, which means that the entire time from idea to delivery averages 18 months.

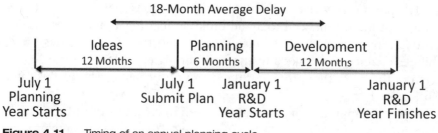

Figure 4.11   Timing of an annual planning cycle

Figure 4.12   Timing and delays of quarterly planning cycle

What happens if we plan on quarterly releases instead? The average age of the items waiting to be planned is only 1.5 months. The planning cycle is 3 months, and with a quarterly development cycle, the average time until implementation is 1.5 months. Quarterly planning, even with the same development methodology, reduces the delay between idea and implementation from 18 months to 6 months (see Figure 4.12).

Estimating and Tracking Progress

Traditional portfolio management often tracks progress against a plan rather than against value created. Progress means finishing various engineering phases. How often have you seen projects that show "green" status through requirements, analysis, design, and build stages—successfully finishing each phase on time—but then become "red" overnight when it comes to release?

In Lean thinking, the most valuable indicator of status is working software. Building smaller, complete pieces of functionality simplifies the principles of continuous integration. Furthermore, working software exposes otherwise unseen problems that will not reveal themselves until too late in the development process. Avoiding long integration cycles and hidden snags is a great way to prevent waste.

By creating a Lean portfolio of business features, businesses can focus on prioritization and can clearly see business value versus cost. This is accomplished because teams learn how to estimate with just enough accuracy for businesses to determine the best value returned from effort. An effective practice for institutionalizing this estimation skill is by using story points (Cohn 2005). The portfolio view simplifies budget decisions because funding centers can be determined by what percentage of features (along with costs) are staged in the portfolio. Once Agile teams establish their velocity, planners can create accurate release schedules that give clear time-to-market for business goals (see Figure 4.13).[3]

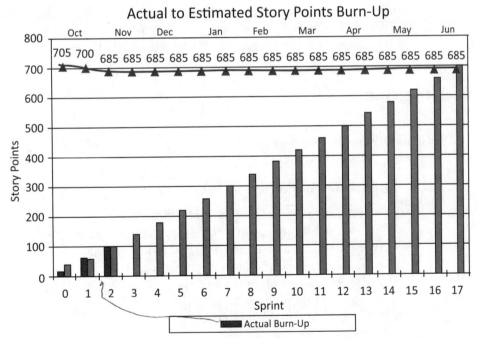

Figure 4.13   Each iteration delivers working software, measured in "story points," and release status can be easily tracked in a burn-up chart.

---

3. Team velocity is defined as the effort or story points the team can complete per iteration

Summary

This chapter presents the Lean approach to portfolio management, which has several advantages over other, traditional project-portfolio approaches. A Lean portfolio of features allows the business and technologists to view ROI versus technical risk. Planners can allocate correct proportions of budgeted work and create right-sized work that can be accurately estimated and pulled into a large Agile organization. The enterprise can issue a predictable release plan that establishes a means to deliver technology solutions guided by business. With focus on correct engineering practices, enterprise Agility will emerge, allowing the organization to be change-enabled, which provides the competitive advantage afforded by quick time-to-market.

The essence of Lean thinking is "fast-flexible-flow." We can get more value through our development pipeline by selecting minimal marketable features to ensure we are building the smallest sensible features we can. This improves effectiveness. And, by working with smaller pieces that can be completed more quickly, we can minimize work-in-process, limit work to capacity, focus on eliminating delays, and avoid thrashing. This increases our efficiency. Lean enables an upward spiral to the speed of delivering value while increasing quality and decreasing costs.

Try This

These exercises are best done as a conversation with someone in your organization. After each exercise, ask each other if there are any actions either of you can take to improve your situation.

- Think about the projects you have worked on in the past.

  - Was there a subset of these projects that could have been released without all of the features of the project that was released?
  - What would have happened had you released the product enhancements in smaller increments?
  - Are there reasons other than the product itself (for example, cost of release) that prevent partial releases?
  - What should you do about these?

- How many projects at a time does the typical person in your organization work on?

- What does this accomplish and what does it cost?

- Do key people work on even more projects than a typical person?

Recommended Reading

The following works offer helpful insights into the topics of this chapter.

Aral, Sinan, Erik Brynjolfsson, and Marshall W. Van Alstyne. 2008. *What Makes Information Workers Productive*. http://sloanreview.mit.edu/smr/issue/2008/winter/12/ (accessed October 2008).

Beaver, Guy. February 11, 2008. *Knocking Down Silos: Transitioning the Enterprise to Agile*. www.agilejournal.com/content/view/753/76/ (accessed February 09, 2009).

Cohn, Mike. 2005. *Agile Estimating and Planning*. Upper Saddle River, NJ: Prentice Hall.

Poppendieck, Mary, and Tom Poppendieck. 2003. *Lean Software Development: An Agile Toolkit*. Boston: Addison-Wesley.

Reinertsen, Donald G. 1997. *Managing the Design Factory*. New York: Free Press.

Shalloway, Alan. 2008. "Lean Anti-Patterns and What to Do About Them." *Agile Journal*. www.agilejournal.com/content/view/553/39/ (accessed February 2009).

Townsend, Patrick L., and Joan E. Gebhardt. 2007. *How Organizations Learn: Investigate, Identify, Institutionalize*. Milwaukee, WI: ASQ Quality Press.

PART II

Lean Project Management

"Management is doing things right; leadership is doing the right things."
—Peter Drucker

"An empowered organization is one in which individuals have the knowledge, skill, desire, and opportunity to personally succeed in a way that leads to collective organizational success." —Stephen Covey

Lean Provides Guidance

Complex problems often require complex solutions. Simple solutions that work in some situations may fail miserably, and at great cost, in others. If we hold on to solutions because they work in one area, we may never quite understand, until it is too late, why they don't work in others.

Software development is clearly a complex problem. It takes place over a wide range of circumstances. Many factors vary widely, such as the following:

- Physical location of team members (together, apart)

- Size of team (2–2000)

- Number of teams (one to hundreds)

- Skills of teams

- Experience of teams

- Organization of skill sets (distributed or in silos)

- Problem domain (IT application, embedded system, product)

- Technology used (Java, .Net, specialized)

- Availability of customer (none, full-time)

- Quality and style of management (command-and-control, leader-ship)

One size does *not* fit all.

Currently, one of the biggest challenges to advancing Lean-Agile meth-ods throughout the software industry is the lack of foundational thinking being presented to new practitioners. Some proponents of popular meth-ods take pride in this, but we think this approach is flawed. In particular, Scrum is represented as a framework within which to hold what you need to know. Although many people in software-development organiza-tions are very capable, there is no reason to reinvent the wheel. Developers should be encouraged to take advantage of what has been discovered in other industries as well as within our own.

Lean provides a new paradigm for management, one that can help managers transition from a command-and-control stance to one in which they are leading teams. From this leadership position, managers can assist teams in adopting the best practices of the Agile industry. These include using the Lean concept of fast-flexible-flow to improve product-portfolio management, Scrum and Kanban for team management, and design pat-terns and Test-Driven Development to enhance teams' technical skills.

In simple situations, we can afford for teams to figure things out on their own. But transitioning to an Agile enterprise presents bigger prob-lems. It requires incorporating all the knowledge and skills we have along with what others have demonstrated. One of Lean's great strengths is its ability to incorporate knowledge into a framework that can be used in a consistent, unified manner.

IN THIS PART

The chapters in this part address Scrum because it is currently the most popular Agile method. To many, "Agile project management" conjures up the title Scrum Master. Unfortunately, Scrum, as it is often applied in the industry, has many limits. Some of these are true limits of the method. More are due to people believing that some process examples are fundamental truisms of Scrum that must be followed. That is, most of Scrum's failings are not in Scrum at all, but in the way it's adopted. This is exacerbated by Scrum's focus on being a framework with a few practices, but having few principles on which to rely—other than inspect and adapt to remove impediments. This part begins by discussing Scrum's actual limits while also pointing out that many of its "truisms" are really just misunderstandings.

This part uses Lean thinking to extend Scrum in three areas:

- How to prepare for your first iteration

- How to manage your product backlog when all planning cannot be accomplished during the planning day

- How to integrate development and testing and use QA to improve your process

These extensions to Scrum all focus on how the team is managed. Other extensions are presented in the next part, which deals with how teams work together.

Lean brings to consciousness many practices that good managers and teams already manifest. We have learned that being explicit about the rules you follow is the best way to ensure that you use them whenever possible.

Chapter 5

Going beyond Scrum

"It isn't what we don't know that gives us trouble; it's what we know that ain't so."
—Will Rogers

IN THIS CHAPTER

This chapter discusses how to approach learning a new methodology and how to extend your knowledge of the methodology. We start with Scrum as a base because it is widely used in Agile projects. Although Scrum is quite effective at the team level, it needs to be expanded to work well throughout an Agile enterprise. We explore several of the mistaken beliefs that Scrum practitioners (new and experienced) hold and the unfortunate consequences of these beliefs as well as some of Scrum's actual limitations. After considering these issues, we offer two approaches to help teams go beyond Scrum: Scrum# (which embeds Scrum within Lean thinking) and Kanban software engineering (which focuses directly on the flow of work). The chapter concludes with a brief case study to illustrate these ideas.

Takeaways

Key insights to take away from this chapter include

- Scrum is a powerful, purposely lightweight framework that naturally limits work-in-process at a team level and empowers teams to work effectively with business partners.

- Scrum, executed correctly, exposes impediments so that an organization can react.

- While Scrum works well at the team level, using it as the primary method to guide Agility at the enterprise level has severe challenges.

- Lean brings proactive guidance to Scrum, and offers clear principles that explain why Scrum works (and why it fails when it does).

- Both teams and management have a common responsibility for good process.

- Always use the best practices and approaches for your particular situation, informed by good principles and the experience of others. And then improve continuously through Plan-Do-Check-Act.

- Scrum# is an enhancement of Scrum that results from embedding Scrum with Lean thinking.

- Kanban software engineering is a Lean approach that manages WIP directly to improve the flow of work through the value stream.

Learning a New Way

There are many models that describe how people learn new skills. It is widely acknowledged that people go through different stages: beginner, basic competency, competent, advanced, expert, virtuoso, master. Transitioning from stage to stage involves starting with a basic set of principles and practices and then expanding on them as the learner becomes more adept. The model evolves by building precept upon precept.

For example, when learning how to drive a car in the United States, a new driver may be told a few principles, such as "first be concerned about safety" and "use your own judgment . . . don't let others hurry you." They will also be given a few practices, such as "drive on the right side of the road," "don't follow anyone too closely," and "put on your blinker before you make a turn." This is the basic set, the "100-level" for a beginner.

Before long, the beginning driver has to transcend these rules and understand the principles upon which they are based. "Driving on the right side of the road" actually is a manifestation of a principle: "Driving in the same direction as the other cars in your lane is safer than driving in the opposite direction." But, even in the US, if you want to make a left turn on a two-lane, one-way road, you should do it from the left lane. So the rule, "drive on the right side of the road," is insufficient.

The point is that to become adept at any new process, we need to keep adding principles and practices to what we already know. For some methods, this can be burdensome. If we have no guiding force, it can be overwhelming. Fortunately, Lean-Agile has a mindset that can give guidance without being burdensome. Lean-Agile presents a way of thinking to solve new problems as they come up as well as a way of organizing practices that have been established to work in particular situations (contexts).

Defining a Method while Not Being Restricted by It

In the introduction, we discussed how our industry seems to cycle between too much process and not enough process. Processes can be used to micromanage teams or can be so loose as to be useless to the organization. Teams react against or are cowed by rigid processes. But they also go astray when process is missing.

Product development requires discovery and feedback so that what is learned can be incorporated; it also requires systems so that what is learned can be incorporated efficiently. It requires both fire and a fireplace: bright people with passion and a structure to help focus them.

Lean-Agile balances the extremes of too much or not enough process by looking for a process that supports the team. Lean thinking assumes that most errors are systemic in nature. To resolve them, it is critical to understand the way we do our work. Team members must understand the process they are following. Lean thinking assumes that the purpose of the process is to support the team. The team understands their work and conditions better than anyone else; therefore, the team is responsible for their process. When the process dictates actions that don't best fit the situation, the team must modify (improve) it.

Defining a Process

How do you define a process that supports teams? By balancing the following:

- Principles apply in all contexts; practices apply in only certain contexts.

- When learning something new, people are in transition and can learn at only a certain rate.

- Process definitions need to be updated as the team learns, and they should help people progress from beginner to expert.

We want a model that can be picked up fairly easily by beginning teams and that can then expand as the team learns and becomes capable of incorporating more knowledge into the model. This balance enables us to provide a definition of a methodology that is not too overburdening to new practitioners yet is rich enough for people once they gain experience.

This concept represents a significant break in thinking between Lean-Agile and many other Agile methods. eXtreme Programming (XP) started with a dozen practices and a few values. As it became more popular and people became more skilled with it, however, little was done to explain the principles on which XP was based.

Several practitioners went beyond the specified practices and used their intuition and experience to take XP beyond situations where the practices as specified would work. This was a good thing. Unfortunately, little effort was made to codify these new practices or the thinking behind them, which meant it was hard for others to transition quickly from beginner to expert. A lot needed to be relearned. This learning was expedited, of course, with coaching from others who had already undergone the transition. But coaches of this nature are often either unavailable (if one looks internally) or expensive (if one has to learn externally).

We see the same thing happening with Scrum. Scrum is propagating through the industry because it is easy for individuals or small groups of teams to adopt it. Scrum's practices readily work inside organizations that have well-defined teams, good communication channels with customers or their representatives, few interruptions to support existing products (where the teams adopting Scrum are the only ones to support them), and there are not many projects in process at any one time (about one at a time per team). This is the context in which the basic Scrum practices work well.

However, most organizations comprising several teams do not work under these conditions. Very often, an organization decides to adopt Scrum and it creates special cases, such as the one just described, for one select team; the result is success with Scrum for that team. Unfortunately, when they try to expand Scrum to other situations in the organization, it does not work nearly as well because they haven't first addressed the necessary core organizational issues.

Scrum, like XP before it, has responded to these challenges by relying almost entirely upon developers learning as they go. Developers are expected to "inspect and adapt." This is good, but it's not nearly enough. Both XP and Scrum have good belief systems and values but speak little of the principles underlying their practices.

Lean thinking uses a richer approach, the "Plan-Do-Check-Act" (PDCA) cycle. PDCA requires the team to do its work according to an explicit plan of execution—a "model" if you will, that is guided by experience, good principles, and lessons that others have learned. This plan becomes their standard process. They do their work according to the plan then stop and check their experience against the plan. Based on their observations, they decide how to adjust the *plan*—what to change and what to keep doing. Then they begin to plan again.

The difference between "inspect and adapt" or "sprint plan, execute, retrospect" and PDCA is that PDCA includes an explicit statement of the workflow that the team is using. We plan what and how we will do our work. We do that work. We check to see the results that this "model" achieved. We then act accordingly—planning again, as necessary. The former approaches leave the team to figure out for itself what to do based on their own intuitions and with little guidance. PDCA, built on a model of Lean principles, provides more specific guidance and enables us to check the validity of our understanding of the work involved.

PDCA also applies more widely; it is not limited to the development cycle but becomes part of the mindset in all aspects of the team's work. A testing team can use PDCA in its work that is founded upon test-driven development (TDD) principles. A UI team adjusts its interview process after each set of user interviews based on what they got versus what they expected.

For software development to become a true profession, we must use work processes that are guided by good principles and by the experience of others while constantly being open to critique and learning.

Principles and Practices Open the Door for Professionalism

There is an analogy here with design patterns. In 1994, Gamma, Helms, Johnson, and Vlissides published their seminal book, *Design Patterns:*

Elements of Reusable Object-Oriented Software. Most people have understood patterns as "solutions to recurring problems in a context." That is good for the beginners' level. But patterns are much more than that. Christopher Alexander, author of *The Timeless Way of Building* (1979) inspired the patterns community when he said that patterns are really about resolving the forces (or issues) that need to be resolved in recurring situations. Learning how to resolve these forces leads to a discovery of much deeper principles rather than mere solutions. This deeper understanding of patterns[1] can become a foundation for establishing a Lean-based thought process to use for designing practices that solve problems teams face.

The Lean-Agile approach to creating a model for undertaking software development is a combination of foundational principles, beginning practices, and a thought process that teams can use to expand on their knowledge and to incorporate lessons learned from others. This creates the basis for a level of professionalism in software process that heretofore has not been achieved.[2]

Knowing Where You Are

Any skill that is really useful in life takes time to master. Sometimes you make great progress when you are first learning a skill. Danger lies in thinking that your surface understanding is deeper than it is. Wise people keep pressing on to learn and improve so that they can handle the inevitable challenges. You need to be prepared when the crisis comes—that's not the time to begin preparing.

As educators in several different areas (Lean, Agile, Kanban, Scrum, product management, design patterns, Test-Driven Development), we have seen the importance of clearing away misunderstandings before proceeding on to new concepts. While we never want to forget what we know, misimpressions about what we are learning can stand in our way.

We have chosen to discuss the misunderstandings of Scrum to illustrate the difference between Lean-Agile and other Agile methods because Scrum is widely used and reasonably well known. It represents much of the current attitude in the industry about Agile and is therefore representative of much of the industry's thinking, particularly with new teams attempting to adopt Agile methods.

---

1. See *Design Patterns Explained: A New Perspective on Object-Oriented Design* (Shalloway and Trott 2004).
2. This is analogous to Scott Bain's exhortations of creating a basis for the technical aspects of software development in *Emergent Design: The Evolutionary Nature of the Software Profession* (2008).

The following sections cover several beliefs we have encountered that impede learning Scrum effectively. The first involves misunderstandings about Scrum itself—things that people believe but that are not true about Scrum. The second takes on concepts that Scrum does seem to advocate but that we feel are not effective. Errors in understanding must be cast aside before the true intentions can be grasped. Whenever we discover limitations in our thinking, or in this case, the thought process we are learning (Scrum), that becomes a place where we can expand our thinking.

Scrum is a really useful approach. It seems simple and yet it, too, requires skill and determination. To be prepared, you have to understand its principles and practices so that you can adapt to and address the challenges you will face.

After we explore some misunderstandings we have witnessed in the industry and how to get beyond them, we will conclude with a few concepts that many Scrum trainers believe but that we do not agree with.[3]

Scrum Is a Framework

Scrum is a framework for creating an effective Agile development process. It is based on the belief that software development must be controlled by responding to feedback received during the course of development. That is, although software development is inherently empirical (you can't predict it) you can *control* it with feedback. The more frequent the feedback, the more effective developers can be. Scrum suggests building software in stages—say, every two to four weeks. Assess where you are, reprioritize, and develop the next step. Doing this helps expose problems and impediments. And problems are not to be avoided, but rather to be solved. For example, a team may find it does not have enough contact with someone who can speak for their customers. This is a problem that needs to be solved (increase the level of contact) or the team's efforts will be hampered.

Following Scrum means bringing problems to the surface, solving them, then moving forward until more problems surface, and then solving them.

---

3. We are not saying that experienced Scrum practitioners cannot succeed at the enterprise with Scrum. After all, Scrum is merely a framework for building software and the team members need to fill in the framework with their own knowledge. What we are saying is that many of the things Lean provides fit nicely into that framework and should be used. Also, experienced Scrum practitioners know when to break the rules, so to speak—that is, use their intuition. We believe many of the things they intuit on their own can be explained consciously with Lean thinking. Our experience is that intuiting solutions is good, but being able to explain why you did what you did is better.

There is not a one-size-fits-all approach to this because each team—and the problem domain they work in—is different. They must learn to learn. They must also throw away any limiting beliefs.

Misunderstandings, Inaccurate Beliefs, and Limitations of Scrum

This section discusses a variety of beliefs about Scrum that we have heard from many Scrum practitioners, both new and experienced. These can be grouped into three categories as follows:

- Misunderstandings commonly held by new Scrum practitioners

  - There is no planning before starting your first Sprint.
  - There is no documentation in Scrum.
  - There is no architecture in Scrum.

- Scrum beliefs we think are incorrect

  - Scrum succeeds largely because the people doing the work define how to do the work.
  - Teams need to be protected from management.
  - The product owner is the "one wring-able neck" for what the product should be.
  - When deciding what to build, start with stories: Release planning is a process of selecting stories to include in your release.
  - Teams should be comprised of generalists.
  - Inspect-and-adapt is sufficient.

- Limitations of Scrum that must be transcended

  - Self-organizing teams, alone, will improve their processes beyond the team.
  - Every sprint needs to deliver value to the customer.
  - Never plan beyond the current sprint.
  - You can use Scrum-of-Scrums[4] to coordinate interrelated teams working on different products.
  - You can use Scrum without automated acceptance testing or up-front unit testing.

---

4. Scrum-of-Scrums is a method to coordinate activities among several teams that are working together. Each team sends a representative to a meeting that occurs as often as necessary—very often weekly or even twice a week.

Misunderstandings Commonly Held by New Scrum Practitioners

These are only a few of the misunderstandings we have run across. We mention them because they are some of the most frequent and some of the most damaging.

There is no planning before starting your first Sprint.   Many people think that Scrum says just to jump in on day one and build the first part of the system. Actually, Scrum acknowledges that some pre-planning is necessary. We will talk about this in great detail in chapter 6, Iteration 0: Preparing for the First Iteration.

There is no documentation in Scrum.   Actually, Scrum doesn't address this directly, but it suggests that there be no documentation unless there is business value for it. This does eliminate many types of documentation. As in all Agile methods, document things only when that documentation will actually be useful. Don't write documentation simply because the process says to do so (and if your process *does* say this, you should change your process).

There is no architecture in Scrum.   Again, Scrum doesn't address this directly. Scrum is more about managing the team than defining the work the team should do. Chapter 13, The Role of Architecture in Lean-Agile Projects, discusses the proper use of architecture.

Scrum Beliefs We Think Are Incorrect

We have found that these beliefs either lower a team's effectiveness or make it less likely that improvements will be made. This is not a complete listing, but these are what we see as the more common and harmful beliefs.

Scrum succeeds largely because the people doing the work define how to do the work.   It is true that Scrum follows Lean's mandate that the people doing the work define how the work is done. However, the biggest improvement that many teams achieve when they initially practice Scrum has little to do with this. Consider "teams" that

- Have to pull people from other parts of the organization to get all of their needed skills

- Work on many projects at a time

- Are not co-located

- Have to follow what amounts to bureaucratic policies that are counter-productive

Now, imagine that you are to pilot a Scrum project and are told:

- You will have a cross-functional team with all of the skills you need.

- You will work on only one project at a time.

- You team will be co-located.

- You will not have to follow bureaucratic polices that are counter-productive.

You probably would expect a great productivity increase. We have seen teams like this be three times more productive than other teams in the same company even when they work on the same types of projects and have the same level of personnel. We believe that Scrum's first times-three improvement level is often because thrashing stops and delays are cut out. There may be cases when we're unable to do iterative development to the extent we would like, but we still see a huge productivity increase by taking advantage of this.

We want to understand this because we can often make productivity improvements by implementing these items even if Scrum can't be started. Misidentifying the cause of improvement can result in missed opportunities for further improvement.

Teams need to be protected from management.   Many Scrum practitioners say that the team should be insulated from management. They misunderstand the Scrum mandate to protect the team from *interruptions*.

This misunderstanding is based on the experience in some organizations that management causes most of the interruptions and therefore the team must be protected from management. This creates an "us (developers) versus them (management)" conflict that has caused so many problems in the software industry. Some generally understood Scrum principles are closer to folklore than actually a part of Scrum. Many of these tend to undermine management.

The famous "chickens and pigs"[5] story used by many Scrum practitioners encourages this attitude. The intent is to illustrate how some people on a project are committed to it while others are merely interested in it. Unfortunately, it is usually used as a way to keep management from being involved. Management is not an impediment to be removed—it's an asset that keeps the entire enterprise moving in the right direction. Chapter 11, Management's Role in Lean-Agile Development, describes attributes of good Lean-Agile management. Again, Lean provides a way for management and workers to work together. Lean's directive that management supports the team while the team creates their process provides guidance here.

It is true that in some organizations teams won't self-organize unless management steps back and allows them to. In this case, the Scrum Master must encourage the team to make decisions in the new vacuum that management's disappearance has created. But this views managers as capable only of managing and not leading. Lean-Agile considers management's role as one of leadership, which is a distinct difference from the way many Scrum practitioners view it.

Leaving this attitude unchecked can result in dysfunctional teams that never quite become effective due to thrashing and poor integration with other groups. At that point, only management's involvement can bring the situation under control.

Beyond this, there are times when management is essential because teams are constrained by their own local concerns. For example, if reorganization is needed, management must be involved; if impediments are introduced by factors outside the team's control, then management can help resolve them.

Management is a partner in improvement.

The product owner is the "one wring-able neck" for what the product should be.   Actually, no one's neck should be "wring-able"! The product owner is the keeper of priorities but the entire team is responsible for building a quality product. Lean provides a way for developers and managers to work together. It starts with the name of this role: To indicate that it is leadership—not ownership—that we need, Lean uses "product champion" instead of product owner.

---

5. "Chickens and Pigs" is based on an old joke. A chicken and a pig are in a bar having a drink when the chicken says to the pig, "We should open up a restaurant." The pig says, "Oh? And what will we serve?" The chicken responds with "ham and eggs." The pig considers for a moment and then answers, "I don't think so. While you would be interested, I would have to be committed!"

The product champion leads the developer team in discovering what the customer truly needs, and she or he assists and guides the rest of the team in this discovery. The product champion and the team are responsible for the quality of the product. The product champion may be responsible for prioritizing stories, but the development team is no less responsible for the product as a whole.

Practical experience from the field suggests that the product champion role comprises a team of product managers, business stakeholders, business analysts, and client-facing personnel who are committed to providing the required service levels of feedback and validation so that the development organization can move quickly. Chapter 10, Becoming an Agile Enterprise, covers this in detail.

When deciding what to build, start with stories: Release planning is a process of selecting stories to include in your release.   It is almost always better to start with the big picture. In particular, Agile analysis should be a progression from business capability to sets of features to stories to tasks. The concept of minimum marketable features, described in chapter 4, Lean Portfolio Management, is essential. If you are losing the big picture while working on little pieces, this misunderstanding may be why—you shouldn't be starting with the little pieces. Lean's principle to "optimize the whole" helps provide guidance here. Chapter 7, Lean-Agile Release Planning, describes this in greater detail.

Teams should be comprised of generalists.   This is an overly simplistic view. If everyone on the Scrum team can do every task then it is definitely easy to manage how stories are built. In reality, many applications have complexities that require specialists, such as database analysts and developers of stress-test algorithms in aviation.[6] What is really needed is a team that is organized so that it has all the skills it needs to complete the work in a short time. The more knowledge is shared, the better. But the guiding rule is that the team have the necessary blend of skills.

Inspect-and-adapt is sufficient.   We discussed this earlier, but it bears repeating. Inspect-and-adapt is good and necessary but it is not sufficient unless it includes explicitly improving the process with which the team works. It is also necessary to incorporate learning and guidance from

---

6. Some of these skills require a Ph.D. and years of experience—not an easy thing to replicate.

others and from past experience. The better model is Plan-Do-Check-Act. Having to relearn should be considered a type of lost knowledge.

Limitations of Scrum That Must Be Transcended

Scrum works extremely well for teams within functional organizations. Unfortunately, many people are trying to adopt Scrum in less than fully functional organizations. Although Scrum may help teams isolate themselves from dysfunction in the organization (which can lead to limited improvement), it is better for them to help the organization become more functional. While this is not necessary for an individual team to accomplish its work, it is necessary for multiple teams to work together effectively. Lean-Agile's broader perspective can help here and it is essential if we are to achieve enterprise Agility.

Self-organizing teams, alone, will improve their processes beyond the team.   This clearly relates to the prior misconceptions concerning management. Purely self-directed teams have a history of not succeeding well. Scrum teams should be self-organizing, not self-directing. Continuous process improvement can be accelerated by a partnership between teams and management. Although the Scrum Master can provide some of the leadership necessary to prod teams into self-assessment, it is not enough. In fact, the Lean Enterprise Institute (Womack and Shook 2006) described the crucial role that middle management plays, such as asking intelligent questions and establishing an environment in which there is both leadership and collaboration while avoiding being either an autocrat or a hands-off manager. Lean's paradigm of management providing leadership to teams that continuously improve their process provides guidance here.

Every sprint needs to deliver value to the customer.   Until the software is released, there is no value delivered, no matter what you do. While each iteration (which Scrum calls a "sprint") should include something that can provide feedback, it is not necessarily true that the iteration is always for the customer's benefit. There are cases when you need to learn something about the system. These situations don't occur as often as some developers think—usually the biggest risk is in building what the customer doesn't need. But there are times when not discovering something about the system now will cause you great problems later (such as redesign or higher integration costs). In these cases, building what can most mitigate your risk may be more appropriate. Lean's principles of "optimize the whole" and "eliminate waste" provide guidance here. We don't want to overbuild, thus adding waste, but at the same time, we must keep the big picture in mind.

That said, you risk losing interest and feedback from key business stakeholders if iterations fail to show verifiable progress against a roadmap. Being able to deliver end-to-end slices of capabilities is a higher-level technical skill that cannot be achieved in a hand-off, legacy organization. It requires cross-functional teams working together. In making the tradeoff between delivery of infrastructure and verifiable business value, always lean toward the latter to ensure that business and stakeholders stay attentive and engaged. They should serve as a natural constraint to "building what is not needed" or looking too far ahead.

Never plan beyond the current sprint.   Oh, if only this were possible! On small teams and small projects, it might be; however, as the effort gets larger, it becomes increasingly difficult. An iteration backlog (visual control) sophisticated enough to handle multi-iteration and multi-team stories can manage this, and it isn't really that complicated. We talk about this in chapter 8, Visual Controls and Information Radiators for Enterprise Teams. Lean's larger view together with its mandate on eliminating waste helps here again—look as far as you need, but no farther. Dependencies among teams that work at different rates require looking ahead to make sure their efforts are well coordinated.

You can use Scrum-of-Scrums to coordinate interrelated teams working on different products.   Scrum-of-Scrums is a great practice for coordination. However, when the different teams involved in the Scrum-of-Scrums have different purposes, motivations, or driving metrics, Scrum-of-Scrums simply does not work well. When the pressure is on and when teams have different motivations, they tend to home in on solving their problems. It is human nature to focus on those closest to us—so when we try to coordinate teams, naturally we will do what is in our own team's best interest.

Lean can provide a bigger view. We all know the challenge of creating teams from individuals—we must provide a common goal. Creating an organization from individual teams has the same problem. Having a product coordination team that reaches across teams can solve this. Chapter 12, The Product Coordination Team, provides a better alternative.

Another characteristic of Scrum-of-Scrums is that often they become reactive in nature, and are simply a place to discuss impediments. Lean guidance would suggest that if impediments exist, then the process must be improved. The product-coordination team is proactive and creates a structure for cross-team planning and visibility, which is critical for scaling and sustainability.

You can use Scrum without automated acceptance testing or up-front unit testing. Most people are not aware that Scrum, as Jeff Sutherland orig- inally created it, included automated testing practices and other quality engineering practices. Unfortunately, these were removed so that Scrum would catch on more readily. We say unfortunately because without them the quality of your code will degrade and you will find it hard to change and dangerous to change as well. In addition, the process of getting good acceptance tests helps clarify the customer's needs and therefore lowers the risks of both building the wrong and thing building things wrong.

It is interesting to note that the Lean principles "optimize the whole" and "build quality in" are almost always violated when automated testing is not included. Optimize the whole, in this situation, means that when you are building a product you need to consider the entire time span of both the coding and testing as well as its whole lifespan, not merely the coding phase. Getting out a quick release that will cost a lot to maintain is not a good practice. As Scrum teams mature, most are starting to realize that automated testing should be a part of Scrum.

Here are three essential references if you want to learn more about this:

- *Emergent Design: The Evolutionary Nature of the Software Profession* (Bain 2008)

- *eXtreme Programming Explained, Second Edition* (Beck and Andres 2004)

- *Working Effectively with Legacy Code* (Feathers 2004)

Unfortunate Consequences of These Beliefs

These beliefs compound to form additional challenges.

Management should not prod teams for information if the teams decide they don't need to give it. This sometimes arises from a combination of the fallacy that self-organized teams don't need management's help (they do!) and that teams need to be protected from management. The visual controls used by most teams should provide information to both the team and to management. Management has a need and a right to understand what is happening in the team. If it is difficult for a team to show this, there is something wrong with how the team is tracking their work. Lean's use of visual controls provides guidance here.

No part of a team's process can be dictated from the outside.   It is unfortunate that many people still have the attitude that a central process group can find the right process for all teams. This is a holdover from a legacy mentality that does not work. Teams need to be responsible for their own process. However, Lean's principle of optimizing the whole does mean that certain standards need to be established for how teams work together. Typically this is better accomplished with a "here is what needs to be achieved" mandate and not a "here is how to do it" one. Requiring teams to use consistent methods when they work together is a good practice—as long as each team can determine how best to meet this requirement.

Lean Thinking Provides the Necessary Foundation

Leaving teams to figure out for themselves their practices, workflows, and approaches almost guarantees misunderstandings, errors, and limitations; at best it is inefficient. Teams that guess well will succeed because Scrum is a useful approach. Teams that do not guess well may fail. Certainly, that is inefficient and results in a lot of unlearning, relearning, and adjusting.

The most effective method is to approach Scrum within the system of Lean thinking. Lean offers a well-established model to guide a team in its practices and in its workflow. Table 5.1 illustrates what help Lean thinking provides.

Introducing Scrum#—Scrum Embedded in Lean Thinking

From Table 5.1, it is reasonable to expect that a team operating from the perspective on the left would get significantly different results—even with the same practices—than one using the explicitly stated Lean perspective on the right. Since both are following Scrum, we have chosen to label this second type—practicing Scrum within Lean's context and belief system—as Scrum#. Scrum# is Scrum infused with Lean thinking.

It is useful to take this a little deeper than simply the beliefs. Using Lean thinking, what approaches should Scrum# practitioners follow?

Table 5.1.   Scrum and Lean Perspectives

Belief	Scrum Perspective	Lean Perspective
Iteration structure	Use time-boxed iterations; discover and build in relatively small iterations.	Use the type of iteration structure that best addresses your needs (e.g., time-boxed as in Scrum or flow-based as in Kanban).
Product direction	The product owner is the "one wring-able neck."	The team is responsible for the product. The product champion sets priorities and leads the team to discover and build what is needed.
Management	Scrum tends to insulate teams from management.	Managers lead and coach teams. Management and teams work together.
How to organize	Get teams working and then scale them by coordinating teams with Scrum of Scrums.	Create a context for all work, such as the value stream. Teams learn how to work in this context.
How to learn	Inspect the results of your work and then adapt to improve your situation. Focus on the team's practices and try to improve them.	Work from known, good practices. Understand the fundamentals of flow and WIP and do everything with the big picture in mind. As such, plan your work, do it, check it against your understanding, and then act accordingly. Don't just "inspect and adapt"; create a model of how things work and refine it.
Story prioritization	Focus on value to the customer.	Focus on value to the customer and to the business but also pay attention to the cost of delays, not necessarily what the most valuable feature is.
Where to start	Let teams figure things out for themselves.	Begin with a solid understanding of Lean thinking. While teams may be able to solve problems on their own, it is essential that we know as much as possible about what we are doing. Pay particular attention to batch sizes, queues, WIP, and flow.

At the beginning of any Agile transition, it's best to avoid making too many changes at once; but starting with the four in Table 5.2 virtually guarantees better results. The quality of the team's work will improve and cycle time will decrease.

Table 5.2   Four Essential Practices for Scrum#

Practice	Description
Make timely builds and use swarming.	Many new teams are plagued by difficulties creating builds in a timely manner. Everything may compile and link but still the code fails because of unknown dependencies—such as some other team using an old API, not realizing it has changed. This happens when teams are working on the same stories but are not in sync. A cure is to use team swarming on stories. Difficulties in getting quality builds often result from not enough swarming. Swarming is the practice of bringing together all of the people required to work on a story at the time when it will do the most to decrease the overall time required to complete the story. This is the Lean approach of focusing on cycle time instead of individual productivity.
Define acceptance tests prior to writing code.	This practice enhances conversations among customers, analysts, testers, and developers. It also helps testers stay in sync with developers. If developers cannot write code before the testers specify the tests, then the developers need to help prevent testers from getting behind.
By the end of the iteration, complete all stories that have been started.	Avoid opening new stories just because someone is slightly impeded. Many new Agile teams do not realize that having a lot of WIP is an impediment itself. It is better to have fewer completed stories than to have many that are 90 percent done—you cannot demonstrate a 90-percent story to the customer at the end of the iteration.
Ask good, reliable questions.	This provokes the team to think about what they are doing and helps them learn to recognize the gaps between what they are doing and what is expected.

Anti-Patterns: Practices to Avoid

Teams just starting out with Scrum seem to make the same mistakes again and again. They try an approach that seems good only to discover that it causes problems. While some coaches contend that teams must learn for themselves, we believe it's better to learn from others' mistakes. There are already plenty of other, new things to learn. We have seen these common missteps so often that we can describe them as "anti-patterns"—approaches that are known to work against you. Some common anti-patterns for Scrum teams are

- Stories are not completed in an iteration.

- Stories are too big.

- Stories are not really prioritized.

- Teams work on too many things at once.

- Acceptance tests are not written before coding starts.

- Quality Assurance/Testing is far behind the developers.

Here are questions we always try to use.

- Does the team's workload exceed its capacity?

- When was the last time you checked your actual work process against the standard process?

- When was the last time you changed the standard process?

- Where are the delays in your process?

- Is all of that WIP necessary?

- How are you managing your WIP?

- Are developers and testers in sync?

- Does the storyboard really help the team keep to its workflow?

- Are resources properly associated with the open stories?

- How much will limited resources affect the team's work?

- What resource constraints are you experiencing?

continues

- Can these constraints be resolved with cross-training or are they something to live with?

- Does the storyboard reflect constraints and help the team manage them?

- What needs to be more visible to management?

- How will you manage your dependencies?

Introducing Kanban Software Engineering

This section introduces Kanban software engineering,[7] a relatively new approach to developing software rooted in Lean thinking. Based on long experience and good principles, many development teams see it as a healthier, Leaner alternative.

As Table 5.1 shows, most Agile methods use time-boxing, that is, managing software development by discovering and building in relatively small iterations. This indirectly improves workflow because the team works on small things and gets quick feedback to ensure it is working on the right things. Kanban software engineering focuses more directly on workflow.

Kanban software engineering (referred to as Kanban from now on) is based on the following beliefs: [8]

- Software development is about creating and managing knowledge.

- Software development processes can be described in terms of queues and control loops, and managed accordingly.[9]

- As information flows through the system, we must have some representation of it.[10]

---

7. "Kanban software engineering" is perhaps an unfortunate name because it conjures images of the *kanban* cards that Toyota uses to manage their pull-manufacturing systems. Kanban software engineering is much more than merely using cards to manage WIP.

8. Most of the ideas regarding Kanban in this chapter come from Ladas 2009 and Anderson 2009.

9. Ladas 2009, page 10.

10. Ibid., page 26.

The Kanban model, illustrated in Figure 5.1, is based on the notion that the team works on the appropriate number of features through completion. When the team is ready to begin on the next feature, they pull a feature from a small queue of potential work. This allows for proper management of both selecting what to work on and how to do the work.

- It focuses the team on building features that are as small as possible and that add value to the customer.

- The development pipeline has small queues and batches and so is more efficient.

- The team still gets quick feedback to keep them on track.

The differences between Kanban and common Agile approaches include

- The queues in front of software development teams stay small.

- The software development teams focus on completing features as quickly as possible but are not constrained by a time-boxed system.

- Kanban is explicit about including the entire value stream, from concept to consumption. Ideas from the customer start the value stream, and the product managers are directly tied to the teams because of the work-in-process limits that Kanban puts on this flow.

- No estimation is required in Kanban.

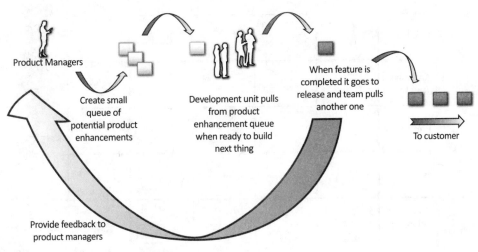

Figure 5.1   Flow of Kanban software engineering

Managing the Work in the Kanban Team

Kanban does not specify a technique for managing how work is done: It can be done individually or by a team swarm. Instead, Kanban seeks to control the amount of WIP that is allowed. Kanban accomplishes this by specifying slots for each available type of activity. Simply by limiting the number of slots available, we can limit the amount of WIP the team has at any step. By defining WIP limits for each activity, we can minimize the average cycle time for any activity.

The Kanban board (illustrated in Figure 5.2) helps the team manage its work. As team members complete a task, they move the card representing that work to the next step in the workflow. At any point in time, the board represents the current state of work. It also shows the process that the team is using and its WIP limits. The Kanban board could be considered a perfect "visual control" (discussed in chapter 8, Visual Controls for Enterprise Teams) because it accurately shows both process and status with minimal effort.

Kanban's approach—based on Lean thinking—is inclusive of management. This means that management is included in the conversations about how the work is being performed and tracked. This is important

Kanban

Status	Support	Project X	Project Y	Project Z	WIP Limit
Backlog	▭▭	▭▭		▭	5
Analysis (right size)	▭▭	▭	▭		4
Implement			▭▭	▭	3
Test	▭▭			▭	3
Done/ Released	▭▭	▭▭▭	▭▭▭	▭▭▭	

Smooth Flow

Figure 5.2   A Kanban board limiting WIP

because it also means that management cannot just say "do more!" Instead, they agree to abide by the methods the team has selected to do their work. Chapter 11, Management's Role in Lean-Agile discusses how managers lead and coach teams. By creating visibility into the team's process (transparency), management can work with the team on improving that process.

Another diagram used by Kanban is the cumulative flow diagram (CFD), which describes the overall flow through the Kanban system; it provides a measurement for every significant step in the workflow. Figure 5.3 shows an idealized case with four steps: backlog (to be done), analysis, implement, and done. For each step, it shows the count of features at the given time interval. Wide lines indicate an impediment or blockage of flow while thin lines indicate that WIP is too small (sometimes called an "air bubble").

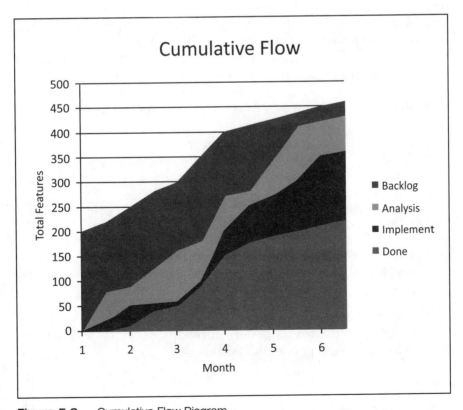

Figure 5.3   Cumulative Flow Diagram

Advantages of Kanban

Many Agile teams spend ten to twenty percent of their time breaking down features into stories and estimating them. Sometimes this can be valuable for improving their understanding of the stories; however, when the story breakdown is required simply to make stories fit into an artificial deadline set by a time-boxed iteration scheme, it is wasted work. Compound this with the cost of estimating these smaller stories and it is a whole lot of expense and work for no extra value. Kanban eliminates this type of waste by managing for flow rather than for time boxes.

Kanban doesn't assume all estimation is unnecessary, but it suggests looking at value received for time invested. Kanban pulls well from the features identified by the portfolio team. If you are fairly certain of your feature estimates, you may discover that detailed story estimates are not necessary.

The true value of Kanban lies in its requirement that the team create a workflow with explicitly defined rules and limits. This enables team members to discuss objectively what is working and what is not. That is, it helps the team focus on the *process* rather than on blaming a *person*. Yes, a person might have made a mistake, but what is it about the process that allowed the mistake to happen or to go undetected? Fix the process.

Think of Kanban this way; it combines

- Defining a workflow based on queues and control loops.

    and

- Managing this workflow by limiting the amount of WIP at any step in the workflow.

Evidence suggests that teams learn continuous process improvement faster with Kanban. Some of the reasons are as follows: [11]

- Kanban reduces the fear of committing to a per-story estimate, which is a significant risk for some teams. Fear always impedes learning.

- Kanban is explicitly a team process rather than one for individuals. It highlights the team's performance rather than individuals' and can reduce the fear of embarrassment.

---

11. Thanks to John Heintz for several of these insights.

- Kanban focuses on how the workflow process can be improved rather than blaming an individual.

- Kanban allows reflection about concrete measures such as, "Should WIP be 4 or 5?" Reflection about concrete issues is often easier in the beginning than reflecting about more abstract or personal issues.

- A transparent process allows management to be involved in improving it.

Case Study: Contrasting Scrum and Kanban

This example contrasts how Scrum and Kanban play out in the real world. Imagine two Agile teams at two different companies. One company uses Scrum, the other, Kanban.

At the first company, the Scrum team and management agree that the product owner prioritizes the features on the backlog and, once the team selects features, the team is free to do whatever it wants in whatever sequence so as to meet its commitment. There is not much collaborative work between the team and the product owner. Management prioritizes (through the PO) and the team implements. If management tries to get heavy-handed and demand something, the team can decline to work (that is, they can abort the sprint). If something urgent comes up, managers must wait until the end of the sprint in order to add it to the list. The team thinks this isn't so bad; on average, management will have to wait only a week or, at most, two. Management is none too pleased; they can no longer get the team to work on something immediately as they used to do.

At the second company, the Kanban team spells out to management its workflow and its rationale for the WIP limits. They use language that managers understand: Here is where we figure out what the customer wants (analysis), here is where we decide how to verify that we have done what they want (test specification), here is where we design it, here is where we build it, here is where we validate that we built it right (acceptance test), and so forth. They make it clear that they are managing their work and limiting that work to the team's capacity. This keeps their efficiency high, yet enables them to respond quickly to requests.

The team reaches an agreement with management that they will always pick the top item in each work queue and do it as quickly as possible, using the best development methods they know, to meet quality objectives. If management must expedite something that is more important than existing WIP, they agree to a "silver card" convention, which always moves the item to the top of each queue. If necessary, the team can also establish different service level agreements (SLAs) with management so that certain tasks are generally put into the queue before others (e.g., critical bugs).

At the Scrum Team

Imagine the following conversation at the company that is using Scrum. A vice president is putting some pressure on the development manager.

PRODUCT MANAGER (PM): Joe (one of their VPs) just told me we need to get Feature X done immediately.

SCRUM MASTER (SM): Great. We'll move that to the top of the backlog and do it next sprint.

PM: What part of "immediately" do you not understand? He wants it done now.

SM: Yes, I understand what he wants, but that'll be disruptive and have an overall negative effect. When we started Scrum we agreed that we could work without interruption during the sprint.

PM: Well, that's true, but that was intended for when things are going normally. Now I'm getting heat to get this done. I'm sorry, but just have the team work a little harder this next week to get it in. I don't ask very often.

SM: Well, I think if we put this thing in, we have to take something out.

PM: You know we can't do that. If you don't keep your sprint commitment then that'll impact the other teams that are depending upon you.

SM: Can't you just go back to Joe and tell him it'll be disruptive?

PM: Would you want to do that?

SM: Well, no.

PM: Good. Then we're agreed. You'll all just buckle down a little and get this small thing done. I really appreciate it.

SM (TO HIMSELF): Great. I guess I could have told him about our agreement to abort the sprint but I know that'll be a CLM [career limiting move]. Well, having the team work an extra weekend is still better than the way it used to be.

At the Kanban Team

Pressure from VPs is nothing new. Here is the conversation that might take place at the company using Kanban when the VP goes to the development manager with something urgent.

PRODUCT MANAGER 1 (PM1): Joe (one of their VPs) just told me we need to get feature X done immediately.

KANBAN TEAM LEADER (KTL): Great. Just move it to the top of the queue and we'll pull it next.

PM1: What part of "immediately" do you not understand? He wants it done now.

KTL: So you want us to drop everything we are doing and get to this?

PM1: Yes, that's what immediately means.

KTL: Do you think it'd be OK for us to let people finish the current task they are working on so they can at least get closure on that? Most everyone would only need a day or so to complete that. Then we'd get on this by using the "silver card" and everyone appropriate would give it their full attention.

PM1: Yes, that's OK. Joe'll be pleased to know that he's going to get his work done without being too disruptive.

KTL: Oh, it'll disrupt us, but if that's the right business decision, no problem.

KTL puts silver card with Joe's request on the board and notifies the other product managers and VPs of its presence.

PRODUCT MANAGER 2 (PM2) CALLING PM1: I see you've silver-carded feature X. Are you aware that this will slow down the three features we're currently working on? I need those features to be able to hit our release schedule.

PM1: Well, Joe said we needed to get this done. We just got a big account that needs feature X. If we get that done quickly we can make thousands of dollars.

PM2: OK, but we've made a lot of other promises as well. I don't think we can knee-jerk react here.

Now, we could take this conversation either way. Perhaps the PMs resolve it, perhaps they go to Joe. Maybe Joe realizes his mistake or decides the impact is too great or stays stubborn and can outrank everyone else. The point is the conversation is elevated to where it should be—at the product-management level.

Compare this with the typical situation in Scrum, which deals with conflict primarily at the level of a single product manager and the team. The problem is not between the product manager and the team, it is that the product managers aren't prioritizing among themselves.

By creating transparency into the process, the demand's impact is seen across the organization. The Kanban team doesn't have to take a strong and uncomfortable stand, they merely let the business side see the impact their decisions will have on the productivity of the organization. Because the software team is not a black box to management, management can work with the team more effectively.

Selecting an Approach

Many choices, which one to use? Use the one that that fits the needs of your own particular context. There is not necessarily a right or wrong answer. Learn as much as you can and then consider the various tradeoffs. Table 5.3 compares how XP, Scrum, Kanban, and general Lean thinking address different factors. [12] Use this to help you select an approach for your team.

---

12. We believe Waterfall is virtually never appropriate if you have Kanban and Lean alternatives. Whereas XP and Scrum may not work in certain situations, with Lean and Kanban you can always use the underlying principles to figure out what to do.

Table 5.3   Selecting an Approach

Factor	XP	Scrum	Scrum#	Kanban	Lean Thinking
Keep teams intact	Prescribed	Prescribed	-	-	-
Use time-boxed intervals	Yes	Yes	Yes	No	-
Prioritize stories across a team	Yes	Yes	Yes	No	-
When to release completed work	At end of selected iteration	At end of selected iteration	At end of selected iteration	Whenever, at discretion of team	-
Works in a support environment	No	No	No	Yes	Yes
Co-located teams*	No guidance	No guidance	Use fast-flexible-flow to create optimal workflow	Manage with appropriate WIP limits	Use fast-flexible-flow to create optimal workflow
Support for the product- management organization	No	No	Yes	Partial	Yes
Code quality	Yes	Not discussed	Use a workflow that increases quality	Use a workflow that increases quality	Use a workflow that increases quality

* This is incredibly valuable for all methods. The issue is how each method might help you overcome the challenge of having teams that are not co-located.

A Case Study: Process Control

Recently, we worked with a medium-sized group in a process-control company that was just starting its transition to Agile. This group was comprised of 70 product managers, leads, developers, and integration/build support organized across eight teams. There were three product champions for all eight teams.

As is common in development teams building on specialized hardware, the teams were organized around the hardware, each team working on a different component. This is less than ideal: It is like having teams organized around the tiers in an n-tier architecture: one team for the UI, one team for the mid-tier, and one team for the database. It is the exact opposite of swarming and can cause a lot of problems (for example, it is hard to integrate code).

Our first inclination was to reorganize the teams so that each team had expertise on all types of the hardware component. Upon reflection, the pain of reorganization seemed greater than the benefit, especially given they were just learning Agile. Instead, remembering that principles—not prescribed practices—should drive any approach, we looked for the principle that should guide us. To find this, we asked what problems they currently were having. Their main problem was integrating the work of several teams when a feature cut across several components. It was clear we needed to swarm to avoid the problems (waste) they were having integrating features that cut across the hardware components on which the software resided.

It turned out that 80 percent of the features they were working on were isolated to one hardware component. For the majority of cases, their structure was fine. What they needed was a way to handle the features that required more than one hardware component.

Another question was how could we know that we were building features as efficiently as possible or, alternatively, how could we know when we were not building efficiently? This question arose because the team was facing such long build times: Doing a build took less than an hour; fixing the build's problems often took a whole day. This occurred because features across components were being built over a long time span. Each developer (on a different component) would have a branch and then check it in after many changes. This practice was essentially creating errors and then delaying when they would be discovered.

How to create efficient builds? The answer turned out to be fairly simple, if unusual. We decided to create special teams to work on a cross-component feature. This way, 80 percent of the time they could work with the component-oriented structure in place, but when the team needed to swarm, it could. Our approach was to let the cross-component stories drive the work: When the appropriate members of the cross-component team were available, they would pull the cross-component story from the backlog; otherwise, people would continue working on the single-component stories.

This approach required an unusual form of iteration planning. The three product champions agreed to meet on iteration planning day with the team leads to determine the amount of work to be done for the iteration. This worked because the team leads were the most knowledgeable about the effort required to build the features. For each team, they created a backlog of work for that team's hardware component. Then, they created a special backlog made up of cross-component work.

During the iteration, when it was time to pull work, they would look first to the special backlog to see if a "teamlet" was available to work on it; otherwise, they would pull from the team's own backlog.

Summary

While Scrum is an effective Agile project-management framework, its history, and the common misinterpretations of it, tend to limit its effectiveness when you want to extend it beyond a few teams. It never pays to be dogmatic in following Scrum. Scrum is meant to be a framework for creating an effective process for Agile development. One of its great mandates is to find impediments and remove them. While Scrum tells you not to follow an ineffective practice, it often doesn't tell you what to do when its practices don't seem to apply.

It is much more effective for teams to begin with approaches that are known to be good than to have to start from scratch. There is always more to learn; but you start out ahead when you can learn from the mistakes and successes of others. One effective approach is to let Lean thinking guide the practices of Scrum, to "embed Scrum in Lean thinking." We call this approach Scrum#, and offer some specific practices that this approach prescribes.

Kanban software engineering is an emerging approach to software development that is also based on Lean thinking. Kanban seeks to improve the flow of products through the value stream by managing WIP directly. This is often a better approach than trying to manage flow through short iterations.

Wise development teams will use the approach—Scrum# or Kanban—that best fits their context.

Try This

These exercises are best done as a conversation with someone in your organization. After each exercise, ask each other if there are any actions either of you can take to improve your situation.

- If you have examples of failed Scrum projects in your organization:
  - What was the reason(s) for failure?
  - How did the organization react?
  - Did anyone observe any of the misunderstandings presented in this chapter?

- If you are planning to use Scrum for the first time, are any of the misunderstandings we've talked about cited as justification for resistance?

- Review Table 5.3. What approach is best for your situation?
- How much WIP do you currently tolerate?
- How should you organize your storyboard so that it helps
  - Control your WIP
  - Management quickly grasp what they need to know
  - Make visible and address resource constraints
  - Manage dependencies in a visible way

Recommended Reading

The following works offer helpful insights into the topics of this chapter.

Alexander. 1979. *The Timeless Way of Building.* New York: Oxford University Press.

Anderson. June 8, 2009. *Agile Management Blog: Thoughts on Software, Management, Constraints and Agility.* www.agilemanagement.net/Articles/Weblog/KanbanBlogosphereRoundupJ.html.

Bain. 2008. *Emergent Design: The Evolutionary Nature of Professional Software Development.* Boston: Addison-Wesley.

Beck and Andres. 2004. *Extreme Programming Explained: Embrace Change* 2d ed. Boston: Addison-Wesley.

Denne and Cleland-Huang. 2003. *Software by Numbers: Low-Risk, High-Return Development.* Upper Saddle River, NJ: Prentice Hall.

Feathers. 2004. *Working Effectively with Legacy Code.* Upper Saddle River, NJ: Prentice Hall.

Gamma et al. 1994. *Design Patterns: Elements of Reusable Object-Oriented Software.* Boston: Addison-Wesley.

Kennedy. 2003. *Product Development for the Lean Enterprise: Why Toyota's System Is Four Times More Productive and How You Can Implement It.* Richmond, VA: Oaklea Press.

Ladas. 2009. *Scrumban: Essays on Kanban Systems for Lean Software Development.* Seattle, WA: Modus Cooperandi Press.

Poppendieck and Poppendieck. 2006. *Implementing Lean Software Development: From Concept to Cash.* Boston: Addison-Wesley.

Reinertsen. 1997. *Managing the Design Factory*. New York: Free Press.

Shalloway and Trott. 2004. *Design Patterns Explained: A New Perspective on Object-Oriented Design*. Boston: Addison-Wesley.

Shalloway and Trott. 2009. The Lean-Agile Pocket Guide for Scrum Teams. Seattle: Net Objectives Press.

Womack and Jones. 2003. *Lean Thinking: Banish Waste and Create Wealth in Your Corporation*. 2d ed. New York: Simon & Schuster.

Womack and Shook. 2006. "Lean Management and the Role of Lean Leadership Webinar." *Lean Enterprise Institute*. www.lean.org/Events/ LeanManagementWebinar.cfm (accessed October 23, 2007).

CHAPTER 6

Iteration 0: Preparing for the First Iteration

"People only see what they are prepared to see." —Ralph Waldo Emerson

"There are no secrets to success. It is the result of preparation, hard work, and learning from failure." —Colin Powell

IN THIS CHAPTER

This chapter discusses what needs to be accomplished prior to actually building working code in your first iteration. It offers a checklist for a minimum set of "critical mass" prerequisites that can help ensure the success of a new Lean-Agile project. If any of these logistics are not in place and visible, the chance for success is compromised and the project risks pitfalls that might have been avoided.

Takeaways

The simple message to take away from this chapter is this: Before you write a line of code, set up the following:

- The product
- The team
- The environment
- The architecture

> **Note**
>
> In chapter 3, The Big Picture, we talked about the importance of *product thinking*. In this chapter, we use the word "project" to mean "a defined enhancement to a product that is focused on adding value for customers via the product being enhanced."

Getting Ready for Iteration 1

A common cause of project failure is beginning without properly setting up for success. While Waterfall projects tended to spend too much effort on setting up, in Agile and Scrum projects many failures have occurred from not doing enough. Better is a middle ground—just enough to start up the project effectively so that it will develop and deliver incrementally, but not so much that we get overburdened before we even begin.

Start with the question, "What do the team and the organization each need to do to prepare for the first iteration?" That is, what is required so that we can begin building value in the *first* iteration?

This question is the basis for the rest of this chapter. To answer it, we need to consider four general areas, as shown in Table 6.1.

The time required to complete Iteration 0 (also known as Sprint 0) will vary; it depends on the needs of the team and the product. Typically it

Table 6.1   Focus Areas for Iteration 0

Focus on . . .	Think about how you will . . .
Product	Establish and make visible the vision and the pipeline of work that the team will do
Team	Ready the team with knowledge, skills, tools, and processes
Environments	Install, configure, and test tools; set up workrooms and collaboration spaces; create visibility
Architecture	Define the high-level architecture and design goals that will guide emergent and incremental delivery of business value

takes one week for each three months of scheduled project-time. The team should time-box each week of Iteration 0 to ensure they don't spend more time than necessary.

Set Up the Product

In order to drive software delivery from business value, the team needs a product champion who can clearly describe the vision of the undertaking and make it visible to the team. The product champion needs to be able to speak for the customer and the stakeholders. She answers the question, "Why are we here?" and establishes line of sight between the team and the business requirements.

For the team, line of sight ensures they understand the highest priority—for the day, the iteration, the release, and the product vision. Transparency and visual controls need to be established that create visibility of all work underway. Visual controls provide a powerful mechanism for keeping the development team tightly coupled to, and aware of, the product backlog—which the team should review regularly.

The Lean portfolio (described in chapter 4) can provide insight into what feature or features can be delivered for the most return on investment (guided by what business the organization is in). This portfolio and the release plan must be established, estimated, and made visible before any attempt is made to execute an iteration. This preliminary work is necessary because the time it would require to decompose and estimate a high-level plan and to establish enough stories ready to be broken down into tasks would overload the first iteration undertaken. In other words, we need to "prime the pump" of high-value work so that the team can focus on delivering business value and have the right amount of visibility into future work. The structure should support "responsible looks ahead," but not so much that the team focuses too far into the future and risks doing unneeded analysis or building unneeded features.

Set Up the Team

Lean guidance dictates that limiting work to the team's capacity is fundamental to efficient workflow. This environment is created by forming dedicated teams that pull work from a prioritized backlog and focus on completing it before starting new work. Iteration 0 is the time to form and locate the team(s) and assign roles well-established in Lean-Agile methods, including product champion and Scrum Master. Decide on the following:

- The logistics for both daily stand-up meetings and visual controls (product portfolio, road map, release plan, and iteration backlog)
- How to manage impediments
- How to ensure transparency (WIP, impediments, status)

Lean mandates that the team focus on quality and preventing waste, particularly delays. Additionally, the development process should help prevent the creation of technical debt.[1] It is recommended that the team transition to a test-first approach. If this transition is not underway, Iteration 0 should include a plan for the team to establish testing approaches at the unit, functional, system-acceptance, and user-acceptance levels. The agreed-upon strategies for driving all work under the context of testing should be documented, and incremental creation of a fully automated test suite, with visual controls in place to monitor progress, should be a clearly stated goal.

At the story level, the team needs standards of work that specify the agreed-upon definition of "done." This can be a simple document that describes the visible quality steps that the team must achieve prior to closing and demonstrating a story, including all updated compliance documentation, an updated design deliverable, code inspections, architecture review, and finally, product champion acceptance.

Set Up the Environment

In order to maximize the delivery of business value, the team needs to put in place as much of the technical setup as possible in Iteration 0. Install, configure, and validate all components of the development environment, including IDEs, version control, testing tools, and bug-tracking applications.

A common approach is to have the team test-drive these components by pulling in at least one build story in order to verify from end to end that business value can be delivered within the environment.

---

1. There are two types of technical debt. One is merely writing poor-quality code that makes future changes more difficult. The other results from not taking advantage of what you've recently learned about your system to improve its design.

TIP During Iteration 0, have the team perform any support work (bug fixes) that they may be responsible for. This also helps to test the environment.

Set Up the Architecture

Other items that require attention and buy-in from the team in order to set standards of work include high-level identification of dependencies and risks, architecture goals, and documentation. These may require enterprise review and sign-off, and should be addressed during Iteration 0. How to do this is discussed in greater detail in chapter 13, The Role of Architecture in Lean-Agile Projects.

Iteration 0 Checklist

Use the checklist shown in Table 6.2 at the beginning of a project to ensure that all of the issues for Iteration 0 have been covered.

Table 6.2   Iteration 0 Checklist

✓	Activity	Description
☐	Vision	Product champion has prepared vision statements for the project and release.
		The team understands and agrees to the vision, drivers, and expected outcomes for the release.
☐	Product Backlog	Features have been prioritized and estimated.
		High-level architectural milestones have been specified.
☐	Story Estimation	Stories have been decomposed and right-sized.
		Validation criteria for stories are understood.
		Stories have been estimated for first few iterations' work.

continues

Table 6.2   Iteration 0 Checklist, *continued*

✓	Activity	Description
☐	Iteration Backlog	Iteration length is set.
		Iteration backlog is established and visible.
		The team has committed to Iteration 1 plan.
		Stories are assigned for the first few iterations.
☐	Team	The team is staffed with all of the needed roles, dedicated to the release, and co-located as much as possible.
		The team has received required training: Lean-Agile software development, Test-Driven Development, engineering practices.
		Artifacts and deliverables are determined (and visible).
☐	Testing Agreements	Definition of done has been established and documented (unit, integration, acceptance).
☐	Team Environment	Lessons learned from previous releases have been intentionally incorporated.
		Tools for testing, coding, integrating, and building have been selected and installed.
		Logistics have been established for daily stand-up (time, location, conference-call information, portal, and so on).
		The ground rules for team life have been agreed to.
		The team workspace is organized (and cleaned up): physical, communication, and collaboration issues have been addressed.
		The team's project board is set up.
		The build environment has been established and tested.
☐	Architecture	Architectural goals/approach have been identified and made visible.
		Dependencies and risks have been identified and made visible.
		Conceptual design has been completed.

Summary

This chapter describes Iteration 0 (also known as Sprint 0), the work required to set the stage for the team to start work on Iteration 1 and beyond. The length of Iteration 0 can vary depending on the needs of the team and the project. There are four primary focus areas: the product, the team, the environment, and the architecture. Time spent here sets up the team for early success.

After discussing each of these, the chapter concludes with a checklist for Iteration 0 activities.

Try This

These exercises are best done as a conversation with someone in your organization. After each exercise, ask each other if there are any actions either of you can take to improve your situation.

- Discuss a time when you did too much up-front preparation.
  - How could you have avoided the excess preparation?
  - What did this cost you besides your time?
- Discuss a time when you did not do enough up-front preparation.
  - Can you tell the difference between doing too much and not enough preparation?
- What do you think is the minimal preparation required for virtually all projects?

CHAPTER 7

Lean-Agile Release Planning

"If anything is certain, it is that change is certain. The world we are planning for today will not exist in this form tomorrow." —Philip Crosby

"In preparing for battle I have always found that plans are useless, but planning is indispensable." —Dwight D. Eisenhower

IN THIS CHAPTER

A major reason enterprises transition to Lean-Agile software development is the need to plan releases predictably and accurately. Release planning is the process of transforming a product vision into a product backlog. The release plan is the visible and estimated product backlog itself, overlaid with the measured velocity of the delivery organization. It provides visual controls and a road map with predictable release points.

Lean-Agile says the release plan must be driven by the needs of the business. We prioritize to maximize value to the business. We sometimes call this approach "business-driven software development."

To understand how to do this, we must understand some fundamental concepts about process. Therefore, the chapter begins with a conversation about the issues that underlie process—predictability, level of definition, and requirements for feedback.

Takeaways

Key insights to take away from this chapter include

- Release planning is a continual activity of the Lean-Agile enterprise. It is the transformation of the product vision or business case into a prioritized and estimated list of features.

- Once a feature list is created, its completion plan is determined by the velocity of the teams involved. Effective release planning requires a delivery organization that is skilled in predictable estimation, a skill readily gained by leveraging short-cycle iterations in order to get rapid feedback.

- Effective release planning emphasizes rapid return by focusing on discovering and manifesting minimum marketable features.

Issues that Affect Planning

One of the most frequent questions we get is, "How can you predict what is going to happen if you are working with an Agile process?" We believe that this question comes from a misunderstanding of some key issues that underlie process.[1]

Evaluating Processes

We think of processes as having the following:

- A degree of process definition; that is, to what extent the process has been defined

- A degree of predictability, or the randomness of its output

- A degree of feedback, or the amount of feedback that the process uses

Degree of Process Definition

Let's first clean up the terminology: We can view the output of a process as deterministic or nondeterministic (stochastic). In a deterministic process, the outputs are 100 percent determined by the inputs; in a stochastic one, the output is a random variable—it has different values that occur with different probabilities.

---

1. Special thanks to Don Reinertsen for an e-mail laying out many of these ideas. Used with permission; any inaccuracies should be considered ours.

Fully determined systems do not exist, except in academia and thought experiments. Virtually all real-world manufacturing and development systems have stochastic outputs. That is, they are partially determined.

It is useful to distinguish between a process that is fully determined versus one in which its *output* is fully determined. Although many people tend to assume that a defined process produces a deterministic output, this is not always true—a precisely defined process can still produce a random output. For example, the process for obtaining and summing the results of fair coin flips may be precisely defined; its output is a random variable.

Well-defined systems can produce outputs that range on a continuum from deterministic to purely stochastic. Just as we can structure a financial portfolio to change the variance in its future value—by ranging from all cash to all equity—we can make design choices that affect the amount of variance in a system's output.

Degree of Predictability

Thinking of system output as a random variable may be more useful than labeling it as either unpredictable or predictable. We could think of it as completely unpredictable, macroscopically predictable, or microscopically predictable. It is unclear if anything falls into the first category—even a random number generator will produce uniformly distributed random numbers. It is the zones of what we would call "macroscopic" and "microscopic" predictability that is most interesting.

We can make this distinction using the coin-tossing analogy. When we toss a fair coin 1,000 times, we cannot predict whether the outcome of the next coin toss will be a head or tail—we would call these individual outcomes "microscopically unpredictable." There may be other microscopic outcomes that are fully determined since we have a fully defined process. For example, we could define this process such that there is a zero percent chance that the coin will land on its edge and remain upright. (If the coin lands on its edge, then re-toss the coin.)

Even when the outcome of an individual trial is "microscopically unpredictable," it is still a random variable. As such, it may have "macroscopic" or bulk properties that are highly predictable. For example, we can forecast the mean number of heads and its variance with great precision. Thus, just because the output of a process is stochastic, and described by a random variable, does not mean that it is "unpredictable." This is important because the derived random variables describing the "bulk properties" of a system are typically the most practical way to control a stochastic process. That is, even though a process may be unpredictable on its own, it can still be controlled with feedback.

Degree of Feedback

The degree of feedback needed is another variable we should add to our duo of degree of predictability and degree of process-definition. In the software-development world, feedback is probably essential; in other areas it may not be. But for us, feedback is likely the most cost-effective way to achieve our goal—but deciding how and when to use it is really an economic issue.

It is important not to confuse process definition with the level of determinism or the amount of feedback required to keep things on track. The key to this section is to understand that although we may not be able to predict microscopically the result of each story, we should be able to predict macroscopically the timing and the cost of the business capabilities encompassed in our features.

Transparent and Continuous Planning

Lean-Agile release planning is a continuous activity that the entire organization can observe. This makes it possible for anyone to contribute to discussions about the value of items in the plan and the effort required to produce them. Release plans enable delivery in small, end-to-end slices. This enables validation in a regular, predictable rhythm that is defined by the iteration length. As we described in chapter 4, Lean Portfolio Management, we want the product portfolio to serve as the transparent focal point for the business to sequence releases of minimal marketable features.

In all but the simplest cases, a feature requires several iterations before it is ready to be released to the customer. Reasons for this include

- The feature is too big to finish in one iteration.

- Multiple features may need to be released together in one package.

- The customer can only "consume," or put to use, features at a certain pace or at a certain time of year.

- Marketing, training, support, and packaging for an otherwise completed feature will not be ready after a single iteration.

Release planning must account for all of these when developing the release schedule.

We think of release planning as continuously decomposing a product vision while focusing on those features of greater priority (value) to the business. This decomposition uses just-in-time methods to prevent wasted effort on lower-priority or unneeded features. That is, we expand on features just as much as we need to according to our expectations of when we will build them (this order is determined by the value they provide to the customer). This plan enables the team to look ahead responsibly so that large-effort activities can be broken down in small enough segments (right-sized work) and balanced against higher priority items that come up. A good release plan provides a clear visual control and obviates the need to look too far ahead and work too far in advance on future, larger features. The continuous activity model is shown in Figure 7.1.

Release planning starts with a vision provided by the product champion, who can make decisions regarding value priority for both the customer and the business. We typically look to the organization that creates project charters to find ideal candidates for this role. The vision should be reviewed and understood by the delivery team and should be revisited as market conditions change priorities. The vision should be visible (for example, with posters on walls) and re-reviewed as part of every iteration's planning session.

Target dates are determined by looking at the estimates in relation to the team's velocity. For example, if a team can deliver 40 story points in

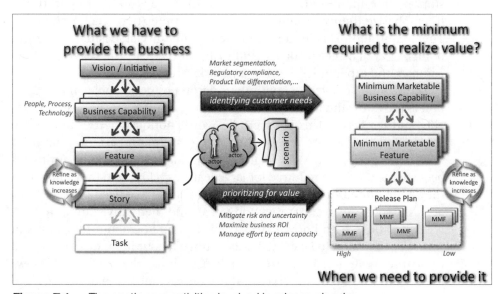

Figure 7.1   The continuous activities involved in release planning

a two-week iteration and we have 200 story points to achieve, we can fairly estimate that it will take five two-week iterations to complete the work at hand. Short cycle times (one to four weeks) enable quick feedback on both the rate of completion and how well we are meeting our customers' needs. During each iteration, teams must focus on coding only the most important feature at any one time. This provides a clear picture of business value (features) juxtaposed against system constraints (technical stories) and enables high-value decisions regarding minimum releasable features.

A project charter should make a business case for new capabilities or capability enhancements. We look to these capabilities to find business features, or "features." It is important to realize that features derive from the vision and capabilities; they do not appear by aggregating lower-level requirements into larger chunks, which is sometimes suggested in the literature as the creation of "epics." Trading business value against effort in search of minimum marketable features leads to decomposing capabilities to form features and stories.

To perform Lean-Agile release planning effectively, the development organization must visually establish (and continuously improve) its ability to determine velocity (story points per iteration), as described in chapter 4, Lean Portfolio Management. The visible velocity is a powerful measure of enterprise capacity (see Figure 4.13 on page 69). This approach requires that the delivery organization be skilled in the art of three-level story point estimation (feature, story, task). Here is another opportunity to emphasize the importance of short cycle time (two-week iterations): The organization is able to recalibrate the quantity associated with story points, as well as get feedback and institutional learning regarding how complex the capabilities, stories, and tasks are.

These multiple levels of continuous decomposition enable an organization to provide estimates required for creating a visible release plan predictably and fearlessly. This is especially worth noting when estimates are required at the feature level, when the least amount of information is known. Experienced Agile teams are confident in providing estimates because the precision required for large features is low, and they know that they are required to commit only when features have been broken down at least two more levels (stories and tasks), and then only commit to two-week iterations with known tasks (which should be about four hours in size). In a transition to Lean-Agile, allow three to four iterations for this skill to mature well enough to produce reliable release plans. Table 7.1 shows the various levels of requirements, their sources, and estimation units.

Table 7.1   Various Levels of Top-Down Requirements Utilized in the Lean-Agile Approach

Requirement Level	Description	Source	Units
Feature	Business solution, capability or enhancement that ultimately provides value to the business and/or its customers	Business/customer value, charter document, business case	Story Points
User Story	Describes interaction of users with the system	Feature	Story Points
Story	Any requirement that is *not* a user story (e.g., technical enabling, analysis, reminder to have conversation)	Development team, analysis work, large story decomposition	Story Points
Task	Fundamental unit of work that must be completed to make progress on a story	Development team (during iteration planning)	Hours

The rate at which teams complete features can be measured in average story points completed per iteration. This provides a velocity of production. After a few iterations this should converge to a somewhat steady rate. If it doesn't, the teams need to investigate why it hasn't yet happened. Once a reasonable velocity is established, it can be used to estimate delivery dates of the releases. Prior to this, release planning will need to rely on comparing current work to the amount of time it took to perform similar work in the past.

In practice, it is never possible to focus on only one feature at a time. Some features may require longer lead times due to dependencies and waiting to complete system-enabling work. WIP should be constrained by an overall focus on the delivery of features (as opposed to the completion of tasks). The constraint is naturally held to because the visual control would quickly expose a feature that is too large. The mature organization continuously challenges the need for large features to find the minimum scope required to deliver maximum return. Metaphorically, this means that sometimes the business value requires only a "bicycle," while the development organization is creating a "motorcycle." In organizations that exhibit enterprise Agility, visible release plans serve as catalysts for communication, where business value and technical constraints are continuously decomposed and visible along with multiple options based on effort and value. The end result is an organization that incrementally demonstrates and evaluates the value of the release, one feature at a time. A business develops true Agility when it can make real-time verification that what it has built meets the minimum scope required for the feature to deliver its intended value. This is achieved by continuously fighting the waste that comes from building too much. The resulting increase in speed of delivery now enables the organization to meet the demands of rapidly changing markets, customer needs, and business opportunities.

Depending on the release structure of the organization, dedicated release iterations may be required to actually deploy the product to the enterprise production environment. It is an acceptable practice to have a so-called "release iteration" for this activity. It is important that this iteration is constrained to the minimum amount of time required by the release organization, and it should be used only to perform activities required for sign-off and compliance of the release acceptance organization (no new scope).

Releases and Elevations

In an ideal world we could release straight to the customers after every iteration. Unfortunately, for many reasons this is often impractical. For example, if you are on a team that builds embedded software, you may need to create an internal release for the integration team (a team that tests your software, and possibly others' as well) on a hardware platform. Or you may build code that another team will use, so you'll need to release it internally to the other team. There are also times you'll need to release code to selected customers to get feedback—possibly as an alpha test, but maybe just to play with.

We have coined the term "elevation" for all of these "releases" that are not quite real. We don't use "internal release," as elevations sometimes go to customers, but they are not the real releases.

Example: Release Planning Session

This section describes a typical release planning session. Such sessions often follow a sequence like this:

1. Identify features.

2. Prioritize features.

3. Split features using the minimum-marketable-feature perspective.

4. Estimate the value of the features.

5. Estimate the cost of the features.

6. Elaborate further by writing stories for features, repeating until you have reasonable clarity on what the features are and their high-level values.

7. Create a specific release plan by date or by scope.

8. Plan elevations.

How long does a release-planning session take? Small projects (three months or less) can often be done in a day. Larger projects will take a few days.

During the session, the team has to remember constantly that it is being driven by two forces:

- **Add value for the customer.** The focus is not on building software; it is to increase the value of the software product we create to those who will use it. The software is a means to an end, but it is not the value itself.

- **Get to market quickly**. Develop plans around minimum marketable features (MMF). View features from the MMF perspective: What is required to develop and release them?

Using Tools in Release Planning

We want tools to support the Lean-Agile process. The early stages of release planning, though, are best supported with lower-tech, higher-touch tools: everyone present in the room, using stickies or index cards on the wall.

This creates the best environment for the nonlinear, multi-dimensional thought processes release planning requires.

Once the release plan has been created, it is good to move the data into an Agile planning tool.

In the following sections, we examine each of the steps in a bit more detail.

1. Identify Features

Begin by writing features on stickies or index cards. Briefly describe each feature (usually just a few words), as shown in Figure 7.2. At this point, the team is just trying to establish a high-level scope of the system.

2. Prioritize Features, Left to Right

Once the features are identified, the team does an initial prioritization: Place the most important features on the left and the least important on the right, as shown in Figure 7.3. This only represents a first cut; the team is not committed to this order. It will certainly change as they work through the steps.

Even this initial prioritization should prompt some interesting conversations. The conversations should focus on sharing knowledge and helping everyone learn more about the features. Don't get hung up on whether the prioritizations are absolutely correct. Focus on learning as much as possible and consider all decisions tentative.

3. Split Features Using the MMF Perspective

Once the initial set of features is described, it is often easy enough to split up some into what could be called minimum marketable features and then further split into one or more enhancements to those MMFs.

For example, suppose Feature F in Figure 7.3 must be supported on five different platforms: Linux, Windows, Solaris, HP, and AIX. Talking with the customer, the team discovers that only Linux and Windows need to be supported at first. Feature F can be broken into two parts: the core MMF for Linux and Windows and an extension MMF for the others. Call these F1 and F2, respectively. Other features can likewise be decomposed, as shown in Figure 7.4.

4. Estimate the Value of Features

Since the product champion is driving from business value, the first thing to do is estimate the relative value of each feature. We can do this using the Team Estimation Game.[2] The value of each story is assigned business-value "points" (shown as "BV" in Figure 7.5). However, do not reorder

---

2. Appendix A, Team Estimation Game, contains a description of the Team Estimation game, which we prefer over "Planning Poker."

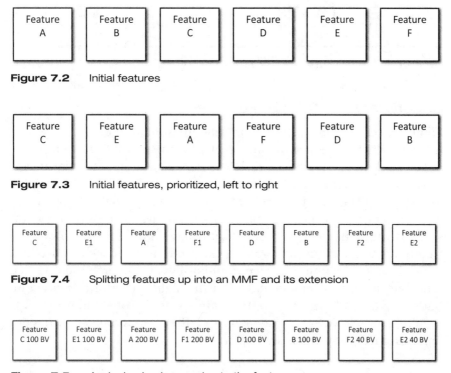

Figure 7.2   Initial features

Figure 7.3   Initial features, prioritized, left to right

Figure 7.4   Splitting features up into an MMF and its extension

Figure 7.5   Assigning business value to the features

the features based just on these points. Features may have to be developed in a particular order or you may need to get a sense of the cost required for each business value.

You may find that you have difficulties quantifying features by points this way. In this case, just identify the general sequence in which the features need to be built. We have found that many organizations cannot initially set values to the core, required features. In some sense, this doesn't matter: They will all need to be built before release anyway. If that is the case, don't worry about it. You should find that, after the release of the core MMFs, you can set relative values for the remaining features.

Remember: Business or customer value is independent of cost. First, determine business or customer value and only then ask the team to estimate the cost. Then, you can calculate ROI.

Figure 7.6   Assigning cost in story points to features

5. Estimate the Cost of Features

You can use the Team Estimation Game to estimate the cost of the features that are represented in "story points" (shown as "SP" in Figure 7.6).

Once you have the cost for each feature, the product team may decide to reprioritize them. In effect, you now have the capability to evaluate Return (business value) on Investment (cost), which enables new insight into selecting what brings the highest return to the business for the effort spent by the delivery team. A significant value of this technique is that it clearly de-couples business value prioritization from technical effort, which is an opportunity to drive from business value first. We find that most business organizations have lost the ability to prioritize based on business value alone because they are so used to batching up large requirement sets with faraway dates that they see no need to sequence features since "they are all important."

6. Elaborate Features

You might be surprised at how well this approach works at a high level. It works by comparing one item against another—something teams are reasonably good at. Going further requires more accuracy. This requires a more detailed understanding of the features.

Start by writing stories for each of the features, beginning with the higher-priority features, the ones you will be working on sooner. This is called "elaboration."

After elaborating a few features and increasing your understanding of what is required to build them, you may need to re-estimate both business value and cost. (Notice that this technique has a built-in feedback loop that continuously calibrates the accuracy of the feature estimates. The elaborated stories for each feature are individually estimated and then summed to compare with the feature.) Continue this process until you have a set of features comprised of the core and extension MMFs, along with a number of elaborated stories, and you are confident in the relative estimates of the features. This is shown in Figure 7.7.

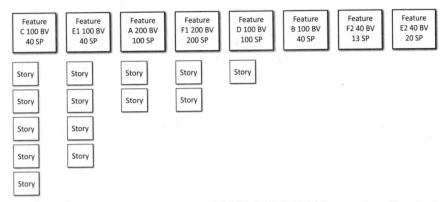

Figure 7.7   Result of feature and story elaboration

7. Create the Release Plan

Now the team is ready to plan releases. There are two approaches to this: planning by date and planning by scope. Which to use depends on your needs, which are often mandated by governmental regulations or market conditions.

Planning by Date

There are times when a project must come in by a certain date: Government regulations require certain features by a certain time, software is required for a conference, or our industry requires major releases at a certain time of year. If this is the case, then the release plan entails setting the date and ensuring the right amount of functionality can be achieved within the allotted time.

For example, suppose you have four months to finish product development and every feature except B, F2, and E2 is required by that date. The release plan is shown in Figure 7.8.

Add up the estimated number of story points for these features. That determines how many points must be completed in each iteration. In this example, there are 480 story points. There are 17 weeks available. Suppose Iteration 0 requires a week at the beginning and there are two weeks at the end for alpha testing. That means 480 points over 14 weeks for development, or 34 story points per two-week iteration.

Total Points/Number of Weeks Available for Development = Required Team Velocity

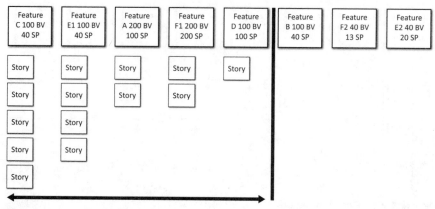

Figure 7.8   Planning by date

If the team can handle that level (velocity), that is great. If not, you have to focus on what is truly minimal for each of the identified features. What can be cut out? What must be left in? At the beginning, you cannot know for sure, which is why the focus must be on starting work on only the features, or aspects of features, that are truly essential. Iterative development will enable you to discover the core functionality need.

Agile Estimation Isn't Exact, but It Is Better

In our classes, we are often asked how we can get precise estimates with Agile methods. This question seems to imply that the asker is somehow getting these desired accurate estimates with his or her non-Agile method. We don't claim that using Agile methods will improve accuracy over non-Agile estimating at the very beginning. It will, however, create clarity at a faster pace. But when it comes to the claim that we must be accurate, we are reminded of the following joke: Two campers are awakened in the middle of the night by the sounds of a bear snuffling at their tent entrance. One calmly starts putting on his shoes. The other exclaims, "Are you crazy? You can't outrun a bear!" The other responds, "I don't have to outrun the bear, I only have to outrun you!"

This type of estimation does not necessarily give you better accuracy than traditional methods. But it does show you where you need to look to make your decisions. Very often it becomes clear that the true MMFs can be built in time, whereas you are uncertain about features you would just *like* to have. Sometimes, it becomes clear you are in trouble. If you are somewhere in the middle, then at least you have an idea about which features you need to investigate further.

Planning by Scope

Another approach is to plan by scope. This works much like planning by date; however, this time you begin with those MMFs that are required. Calculate the number of story points in the MMFs, divide by the team's velocity (the ability to complete stories in an iteration) and the result is the time required to do the work.

Total Points/Team Velocity = Number of Weeks Required for Development

If the result is too long, reassess to see what features or elements can be dropped to make it shorter.

Proper Planning Avoids Risk

Both of these approaches help teams focus and avoid risk. They help teams:

- Work on the most important features
- Avoid starting less-important features until the more important ones are finished
- Minimize WIP

These are crucial. Consider a time when you were working on a project only to discover you were going to have to cut scope. The predicament is that at this point, you have:

- Already completed some less-important features—which you started because at the beginning of the project you were confident it was all going to happen; and
- Started some features you would like to cut but doing so now would cause you to lose work you've already done—you'd have wasted time and added complexity for no value (almost certainly the code that's in there for these features will stay in there).

Planning-by-date and planning-by-scope methods help ensure that the team works on the most important features known at the time and that other features are not started until the important ones are finished.

A Case Study

COMPANY PROFILE: Large software product company

CHALLENGES: Tightly coupled, complex product enhancements being built at the same time. Not clear of the exact scope of features.

INSIGHT: During a planning session where all related features were put on a wall and all interested parties were present, one of our consultants asked the question—"how many people here are 100% certain that all of these features will be built in the time frame we have?" To no one's surprise, no one raised their hand. Then the consultant asked—"which of these features must be done by the deadline or you don't have a product?" There was actually fairly consistent agreement on this question. These were the features selected for the first release.

Lean suggests doing the essential things first in the fastest time possible by building quality in. By de-scoping early, we focus on the Pareto Rule of 20% of the work providing 80% of the value. By time-boxing our development, we minimize the affect of Parkinson's Law that "work expands so as to fill the time allotted for its completion."

---

8. Plan the Elevations

There may be another degree of complexity to consider when there is more than one team involved in the software development or there is a subset of the software that can be tested but cannot yet be released.

The first case can be made more difficult if there is hardware on which to test as well. In these cases, an internal release is necessary to test the system—either its technical integrity through integration testing or its quality to customers through external system testing using alpha or beta testers. We call these pseudo/external releases "elevations." We are moving the software farther down the value stream, but not all the way to the customer. We will consider two different types of elevations.

Elevations for Integration Testing

Very often a team will build software must interact with software that other teams are building. You cannot be sure exactly how it will function until the other teams use it. Or teams are creating multiple products that must be used on a hardware platform. Until the software is actually on the hardware, you cannot know for sure how it will function.

One type of elevation planning is to look at the milestones the software must reach prior to true release. In a situation like this it could be

- Software passes a team's functional test.
- Software passes several teams' functional test.
- Software works on a specified hardware platform.
- Software has been alpha-tested by a set of customers.

This example would require three elevations prior to the final release:

1. Move the software to the other teams that will use it.
2. Load and test the software on the hardware platform using internal testers.
3. Enable external users to try out the software.

These elevations are shown graphically in Figure 7.9.

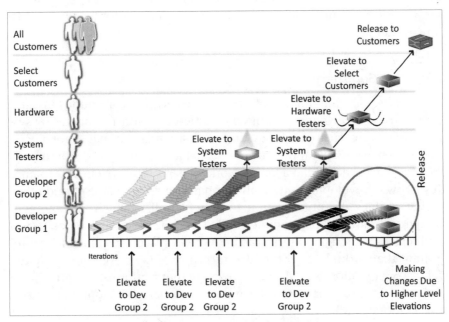

Figure 7.9   Elevations across teams and testing platforms

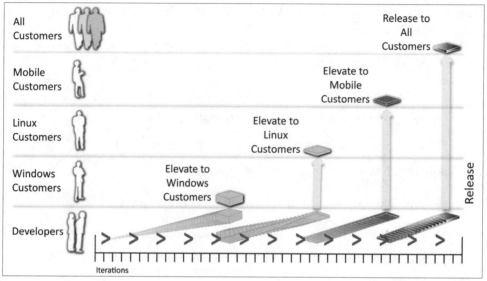

Figure 7.10   Elevations to different operating systems

Elevations to Different Platforms

A different elevation pattern exists when the software you are writing must work on different operating systems. For example, suppose you are writing software for Windows, Linux, and mobile platforms. Figure 7.10 illustrates that elevation plan.

Elevation Summary

There are no set rules for elevations. The ideal case is continuous integration across all development. But when different platforms, operating systems, hardware, customer bases, and so on are present, that is not always possible. Elevation planning, however, enables you to investigate the best way to get feedback about a larger, working part of the system. Acceptance Test-Driven Development with an emphasis on design patterns and refactoring enables the organization to benefit holistically from emergent design techniques. For example, skilled organizations that mock to test and refactor to design patterns can do more in-place and continuous integration than would be required to incorporate Lean-Agile in complex-release organizations that deliver across different platforms. Chapter 9, The Role of Quality Assurance in Lean-Agile Software Development, covers this in more detail.

A Few Notes

We end this chapter with a few more release-planning thoughts on estimation and risk—and Pareto versus Parkinson.

On Estimation and Risk

Many people think that there is risk attached to missing your estimate. At worst it might be embarrassing; however, the real risk is in missing your *delivery dates*. It is not important to be able to predict at the level of the story; what is important is predicting at the release level.

Risk also plays a role in prioritizing features. Usually, we prioritize by the business value each feature represents—possibly offset by the cost of creating it. However, sometimes prioritization is affected by the potential cost of delay. For example, let's say we have Feature A and Feature B. Feature A may be twice as important as Feature B, but we need Feature B for a conference coming up in three months. We may actually do Feature B first to ensure its completion before the conference if delaying Feature A is not too costly.

Pareto versus Parkinson

We have heard Lean software development likened to following Pareto's Law: 80 percent of the value comes from 20 percent of the work. In other words, find that 20 percent of features that will provide your customers with 80 percent of their value; then, find the next features that will provide the greatest value to your customers.

The problem with this is that if there is no time-boxing—no end-date—Parkinson's Law may apply: "Work expands so as to fill its time for completion." Parkinson's Law is particularly dangerous when multiple product managers are competing for a team's resources. Manager A is focusing the team on one thing and Manager B is concerned about when she will have the team's availability. You can counteract the effect of Parkinson's Law, by having the team follow Pareto's Law in the shortest amount of time they can. In other words, have the team always focus on building the smallest things as quickly as they can, end to end, while ensuring quality.

Add the most value possible in the least amount of time possible with the right level of quality.

Summary

An organization that maintains visible release plans that are driven by continuous validation of velocity have a powerfully competitive weapon—key tactical and strategic moves can be analyzed continuously for maximum value. Enterprise Agility is achieved when the delivery organization is actively engaged in the release planning activity, through estimation and the discovery of options based on effort.

Try This

These exercises are best done as a conversation with someone in your organization. After each exercise, ask each other if there are any actions either of you can take to improve your situation.

Consider a few typical past projects.

- Most successful Waterfall projects require de-scoping in order to reach target dates. If this was the case for any of your past projects, when did de-scoping occur?

- What would have happened if de-scoping would have occurred *before* the development team started implementation?

- How does release planning (with visible velocity) aid in the discovery of right-sized, high-value work?

Recommended Reading

The following works offer helpful insights into the topics of this chapter.

Denne and Cleland-Huang. 2003. *Software by Numbers: Low-Risk, High-Return Development*. Upper Saddle River, NJ: Prentice Hall.

Reinertsen. 1997. *Managing the Design Factory*. New York: Free Press.

CHAPTER 8

Visual Controls and Information Radiators for Enterprise Teams

"If you can't measure it, you can't improve it." —Anonymous

"If you can't see it, you really can't improve it." —Alan Shalloway

"If it ain't visible, we ain't working on it." —Guy Beaver

IN THIS CHAPTER

This chapter discusses several of the most important visual controls in the Lean-Agile toolkit. A visual control is used by teams and management to make progress visible to all, to help identify impediments to progress, and to keep everyone focused on delivering value. The purpose of each visual control is described in this chapter; however, the specifics about how to create and implement them are left to other resources. After exploring each visual control, we conclude with a thought about what makes a good control.

Takeaways

Key insights to take away from this chapter include

- Visual controls help teams see what is happening and help management assist teams.

- Visual controls should exist for all levels of the organization.

- If a visual control doesn't feel right to the team, they should modify it until it does.

Visual Controls and Information Radiators

Many Agile methods, such as Scrum, use what are known as "information radiators" to convey information about the status of development to the team and management. Alastair Cockburn says an information radiator "displays information in a place where passersby can see it. With information radiators, the passersby don't need to ask questions, the information simply hits them as they pass." (Cockburn 2001)

Common information radiators used in Scrum environments include

- The product vision
- The product backlog/release plan
- The iteration backlog
- Burn-down and burn-up charts
- The impediment list

These are often organized on a team project board, a kind of "super" information radiator.

Information radiators are a specialized type of what Lean calls a "visual control." In Lean environments, visual controls are used to make it easier to control an activity or process through a variety of visual signals or cues. The visual control:

- Conveys its information visually
- Mirrors (at least some part of) the process the team is using
- Describes the state of the work-in-process
- Is used to control the work-in-process
- Can be viewed by anyone

Note

Have a conversation within your organization about whether to use "information radiator" or "visual control." What you call it is not that important as long as both teams and management clearly understand the intent: two-way communication, controlling processes, appropriate discussions.

We prefer the term "visual control" to "information radiator" because it communicates more effectively the attitude and behavior we want. "Information radiator" indicates a one-way direction of information from the team to passersby, including management. It subtly reflects a belief that some Scrum practitioners (incorrectly) hold that the team needs to provide only information about results to management but does not need to provide management with information about how they work. Such an attitude hinders implementing Scrum at the enterprise level when such information is needed.

In Lean thinking, "visual control" is more inclusive. In addition to communicating information to all passersby (so that they don't have to ask for status reports, which are disruptive to generate), it also reflects the intent that management is a participant in the team's processes. Visual control invites management to help detect early when there are problems impeding progress toward the team's goals. That is exactly when the team needs to be interrupted—so that they can stop and adjust while it still matters. Visual control increases the likelihood that management's "interruptions" actually *add* value to the process.

Lean-Agile Visual Controls

Visual controls should be present at all levels: business, management, and team. That is, they should help the business see how value is being created as well as assist management and the team in building software as effectively and efficiently as possible.

Let's go into a little more detail about the visual controls used in Lean-Agile. The controls include

- Product Vision
- Product Backlog/Release Plan/Lean Portfolio
- Iteration Backlog—simple team, multiple teams
- Story Point Burn-Up Chart
- Iteration Burn-Down Chart
- Business Value Delivered Chart
- Impediment List

Product Vision: Providing the Big Picture

Every Agile team should have a product vision. This provides the big picture for the product: what is motivating the development effort, what the current objectives are, and the key features. We have seen teams who were flailing about, trying to figure out what they were supposed to be doing, suddenly gain focus when the product champion produced a product-vision statement. Creating a poster of the product vision, such as the one in Figure 8.1, helps the team stay focused.

Product Vision Example

Geoffrey Moore's *Crossing the Chasm* (1999) suggests a template for creating product visions, as follows:

FOR *<target customer>*
WHO *<statement of the need>*,
THE *<product name>* **is a** *<product category>*
THAT *<product key benefit, compelling reason to buy>*.

UNLIKE *< primary competitive alternative>*,
OUR PRODUCT *<final statement of primary differentiation>*

The Net Objectives course, *Agile Planning and Estimation with User Stories*, involves a project for a coffee shop with the following product vision:

For frequent customers
who need to get in and out of our coffee shop quickly,
the Coffee Kiosk **is an** ordering and payment system
that allows customers to order their drinks quickly and easily.

Unlike any other coffee shop,
our product provides superior and faster service than our competitors.

Of course, there are other ways to write a product vision, as shown in Figure 8.1.

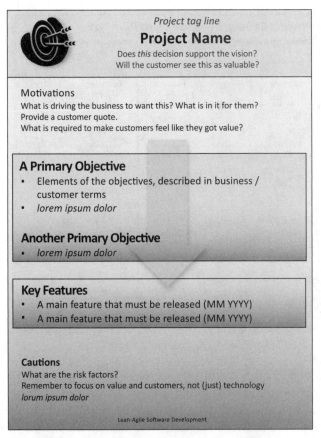

Figure 8.1   Example of a product-vision poster

Product Backlog with Release Plan

A backlog is the accumulation of work that has to be done over time. In Lean-Agile, the product backlog describes that part of the product that is still to be developed. Before the first iteration, it shows every piece of information that is known about the product at that time, represented in terms of features and stories. As each iteration begins, some of these stories move from the product backlog to the iteration backlog. At the end of each iteration, the completed features move off of both backlogs.

During "Iteration 0," the features in the product backlog are organized to reflect the priorities of the business: higher-priority features on the left and lower-priority features on the right, as described in chapter 4, Lean Portfolio Management.

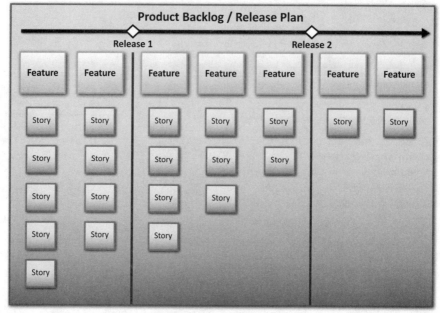

Figure 8.2   Example of a product backlog with release plan: Releases align with team velocity.

Using this arrangement, it is straightforward to lay out the tentative release plan. The team has already estimated the size of features and stories. With experience, the team learns its capacity—the number of points it can sustainably deliver in a release (also known as the team's velocity). Working left to right, the release points come when that capacity is met. Ideally, we never want to go beyond their capacity. Figure 8.2 shows release points based on team velocity.

Iteration Backlog

As noted previously, iterations also have backlogs that need to be tracked.

The Basic Visual Control for Individual Teams

Iterations are managed with visual controls as well. Figure 8.3 illustrates a basic iteration backlog visual control. It is equivalent to a Scrum story board. The larger rectangles in the build column represent stories to be completed. The smaller rectangles under each of those are tasks. The stories are prioritized from left to right.

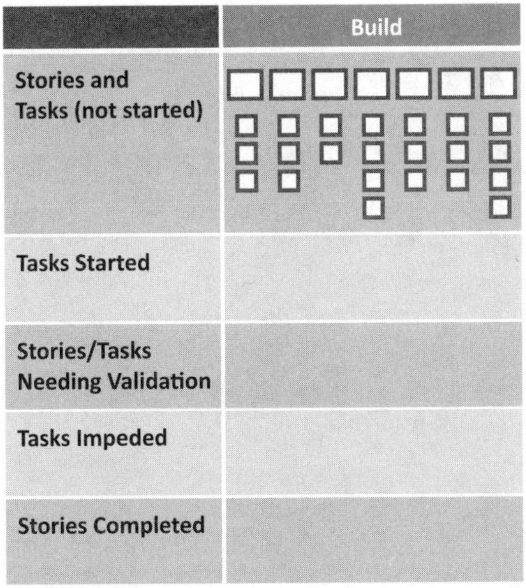

Figure 8.3   A basic iteration backlog visual control

As the team starts working on stories, they move tasks down to the Tasks Started row, as shown in Figure 8.4. The team must monitor how many stories are open and try to minimize that number (that is, keep

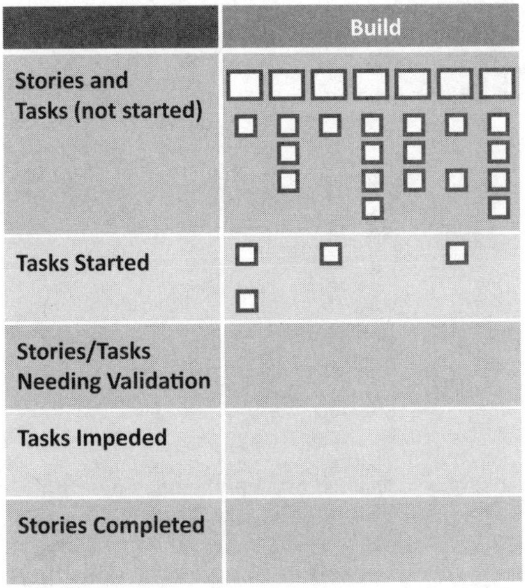

Figure 8.4   An iteration backlog that shows tasks started

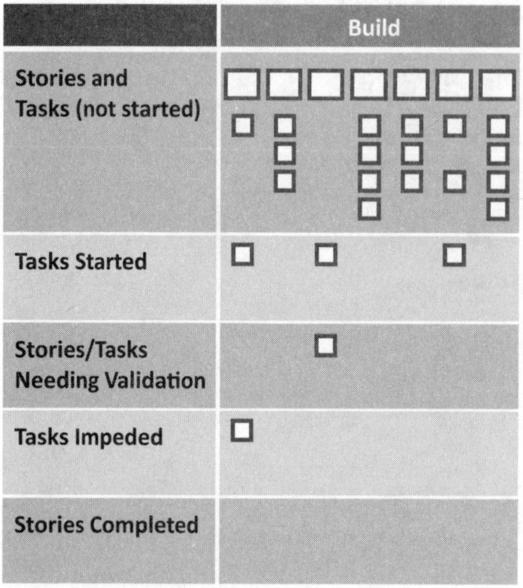

Figure 8.5   An iteration backlog that shows tasks started, completed (awaiting validation), and impeded

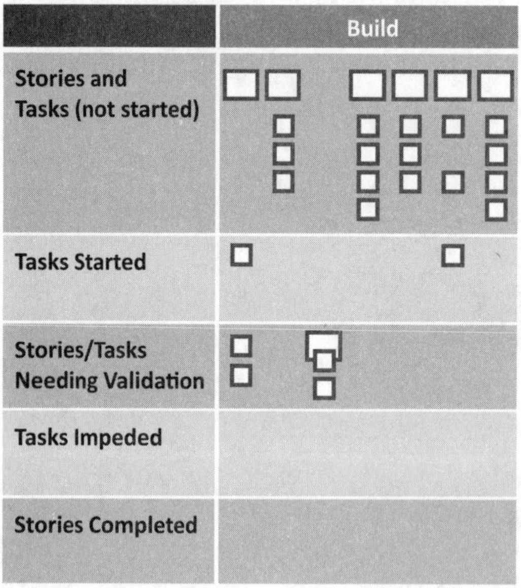

Figure 8.6   An iteration backlog that shows finished tasks and stories needing validation

WIP to a minimum). Since the stories themselves have an agreed-upon priority, the visual control clearly shows focus on that priority, since, as

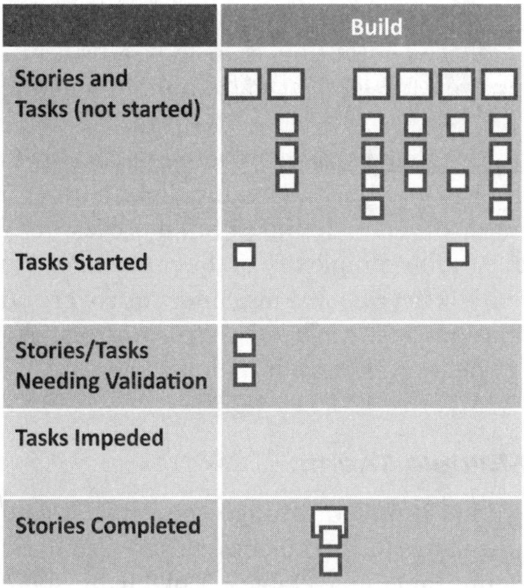

Figure 8.7   An iteration backlog that shows a competed story

much as is reasonably possible, they open the stories in priority order. A good rule of thumb is that there should be fewer tasks open than there are people, which emphasizes collaboration and teamwork. There are three open stories in Figure 8.4. For each task, a separate, more detailed control shows who is working on it, an estimate to completion, and a verification statement.

Once a task is completed, it is moved to the Stories/Tasks Needing Validation row, as shown in Figure 8.5. Alternatively, if a task becomes impeded, it is moved to the Tasks Impeded row.

When tasks and stories are done, but not yet validated, they are moved down into the Stories/Tasks Needing Validation row, as shown in Figure 8.6.

Once a story has been validated, it is moved to the bottom row, signifying its completion, as shown in Figure 8.7.

The Limitations of the Basic Visual Control

The basic iteration backlog visual control works well for individual teams on small projects; however, it has a serious limitation. It assumes that the analysis and estimation required for an iteration is accomplished at the beginning of each iteration. That is, it offers no support for looking a little bit ahead. Even when building in small pieces, it is still important to do a little pre-work analysis to facilitate building the next iteration.

Keep in mind, though, if you take this to an extreme, you get a Waterfall model. *So don't do that!* The intention is to look ahead just enough and no more. In other words, follow the Defer Commitment and Just-In-Time principles.

To build software that returns the greatest value to both our customers and the business, we must discover the business value, define how to create it, and then build it. This discover → define → build process may take more than one iteration due to the complexity of the problem or the limited availability of people with the necessary skills. Since "discover and define" is very much part of the process, we need visual controls (the iteration backlog in this case) to help us manage it.

The Visual Control for Multiple Teams

In Lean-Agile, the work to be done is pulled through the value stream based on what delivers the most value to the business. There are three phases in this work: discover, define, and build. Table 8.1 highlights some of the important points from each phase.

The basic iteration backlog visual control can easily accommodate this richer understanding of the workflow simply by adding two columns: Discover and Define Stories. This is shown in Figure 8.8.

Table 8.1.   Three Phases in Product Development

Phase	Question Considered	Answers Pulled from . . .
Discover	What features does the business consider valuable? How can we release those incrementally? What are the priorities for those features?	The business, based on business needs and objectives
Define	What is the minimum set of features we need to build in the next release?	The backlog of features that has been discovered and prioritized
Build	How should we build those features?	The prioritized set of features that have been defined for this release

How to create it.   *Business value*

	Build		Define	Discover
Stories and Tasks (not started)	☐☐☐☐☐☐☐ ☐ ☐ ☐ ☐ ☐ ☐ ☐ ☐ ☐ ☐ ☐ ☐ ☐		☐☐ ☐ ☐ ☐	☐ ☐
Tasks Started				
Stories/Tasks Needing Validation				
Tasks Impeded				
Stories Completed				

Figure 8.8   A visual control for discovery, definition, and building

- The Discover column holds stories and tasks while we analyze them. The goal is to discover and establish what is needed to implement the story so that it achieves the business goal. As a story is being worked on, it is placed in the Story row; the task—such as analysis work required to get a better understanding of the story so we can work on it—is placed under it. This task will likely generate other stories as we break down the initial one. These will migrate over to the Define column, although it is possible that more discovery work will still be needed in the next iteration.

- The Define column contains stories and their associated tasks that require clearer definitions before they can be built. These tasks may include analysis, spikes,[1] and creating test cases. Tasks completed here ultimately generate stories and tasks in the Build column.

The advantage of this visual control is that it gives full visibility on the build process. In addition, it gives a brief look ahead to the build. Clearly, the Define and Discover sections should contain no more than needed to avoid having too much WIP.

---

1. A spike is a short exploration into some aspect of the system. A developer typically writes code that will be discarded just to help understand the problem at hand.

One challenge with this control is showing priorities across the three columns. Although each column is prioritized from left to right, the relative priority of stories in the different columns is not clear. In practice, this is generally not a problem since people typically work on stories in different columns. But if it is, the control can be adapted easily by merging the Build, Define, and Discover columns into one section, denoting "define" and "discover" stories as distinct from our regular "build" stories.

As Lean-Agile extends up through the enterprise, a visual control of the Lean Portfolio should emerge as the focus point for business decisions and planning. Ideally, Lean organizations are able to decouple business value from technical effort (cost) so that business decisions can be made at the minimum-marketable-feature level. This is typically an emergent trait that results when organizations learn the value of identifying minimum marketable features instead of the batch-and-queue approach of large requirement-gathering efforts.

Establishing Clear Line of Sight

The Lean-Agile flow from product backlog to iteration backlog works best when the product team has clear sight of what the development team is implementing and the development team can see what is coming. This is illustrated in Figure 8.9.

The product- and iteration backlogs are two halves of the communication loop between the two teams. Manage them together and the result is continuous alignment between different teams: They will begin to act as one team! Following is an explanation of how this works.

The product backlog keeps the development team aware of what is coming from the product team. The product backlog shows estimates for features and stories, as described in chapter 4, Lean Portfolio Management. Since the development team is the source of these estimates, the size of the estimates helps reveal the story's readiness to be implemented. And the lack of an estimate is a cue that the development team has not yet seen a feature or story.

The iteration backlog keeps the product team aware of what is done. Stories in the iteration backlog are not closed—not done—until the product champion accepts them. Closed stories help the product team see the progress being made.

Managers should pay attention to visual controls—how they are organized and what they are saying. Consistency is critical. In fact, this is an area in Lean-Agile where absolute conformity is required. *Anyone, any-*

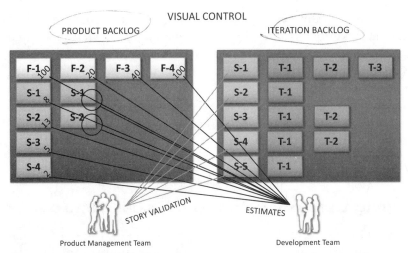

Figure 8.9   Visual controls give line of sight between the product-management and development teams.

where in the organization, should be able to understand the status and progress for any team at *any* time.

The entire enterprise (business, management, and development teams) also need line of sight to velocity (points/time), which, after the first few stories are done, should begin to represent the velocity of business solutions delivered. This is a clear representation of the value stream (from flow of ideas to completed work) and is mapped to the number of points that teams can sustainably deliver in a release. We use two visual controls, working as a pair, to give management a dashboard-type view of work (see Figure 8.10). The *release* burn-up chart tracks cumulative points

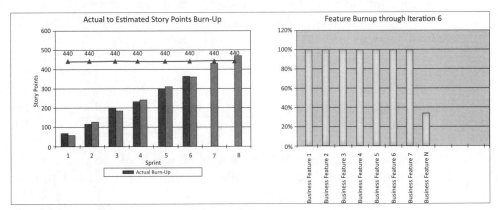

Figure 8.10   The release- and feature burn-up charts together provide a business-driven view of enterprise WIP.

delivered with each iteration. This can be broken out or rolled up based on program, stakeholder, and so on. The *feature* burn-up chart is created by using the initial high-level estimate to calculate the percent complete after each iteration and then plotting this for all features currently identified in the release plan.

This view gives the enterprise a clear visual control of current priorities, along with what work is actually in process. A Lean enterprise continuously watches out for too many features being worked on at any time— this indicates process problems and potential thrashing.

Managing Dependencies with Visual Controls

As discussed in chapter 4, Lean Portfolio Management, the release plan lays out the priorities and sequence of implementation planned by the team. The approach has been to sequence rows of estimated features and divide them into potential iterations derived from the team's velocity (story points per iteration). Not only is this visual presentation a great approach for seeing the sequence, it facilitates discussions between multiple dependent teams (for example, enterprise data, ETL, UI Design, mid-tier services, and so on), as are typically found in large enterprises.

It is easy to adapt this visual presentation to illustrate dependencies by using simple colored dots. For example, a team can use yellow dots on features and stories to indicate a known future dependency on the enterprise data team; green, some other team. The colors chosen to represent dependencies don't matter; however, we highly urge consistency, particularly across the enterprise. Teach those who are represented by the dots how to read the color-coded release plan. Once managers in those dependent organizations can do that, they should be able to break down the work and deliver incremental pieces (best case) into iterations leading up to the release plan or (worst case) deliver complete pieces when needed.[2]

Imagine the insight this simple visual control provides to the enterprise. It brings multiple release plans together, with colors indicating shared service dependencies required to make each planned release. For example, if yellow dots with "ED" represent dependencies on every backlog for enterprise data to deliver something, we should be able to recognize quickly whether that organization has the capacity to keep multiple

---

2. Another approach is to use one color for the dependent item and another color for the item it is dependent on (using the same number for each to show the relationship).

release plans on track. The mature Lean enterprise has a corresponding visual control for the development team to ensure that they do indeed have the velocity to keep up with the demands of their internal clients.

The key to this dependency management is being able to give enough lead time to support or service groups so that the Agile release plan can successfully accept and integrate the deliveries by those organizations. We track those deliveries with stories that capture the impact on our team and the effort required to integrate the dependent deliveries.

One approach is to use stories that "look ahead" to future features. These are sometimes referred to by the number of iterations required to complete the dependent delivery. For example, if we have to lead enterprise data's delivery by two iterations, we would call its stories "N-2," indicating the dependent data team needs a two-iteration lead time to deliver our requested data change. Figure 8.11 shows what these dependencies might look like in a large organization.

A Lean-Agile best practice for dependency management is to include dependent representatives in release-planning discussions and then encourage the same representatives to begin attending daily stand-up sessions as their delivery date approaches. This way they can update status and work with the team to test and validate the integration of the dependent delivery piece.

User Story 1		User Story 2		User Story 3	
N, N-1	Requirements	N, N-1	Requirements	N, N-1	Requirements
N-1	UXG	N-1	UXG	N-1	UXG
N, N-1	UCD/Web Services	N, N-1	UCD/Web Services	N, N-1	UCD/Web Services
N	UI Dev/MT	N	UI Dev/MT	N	UI Dev/MT
N	MT Dev	N	MT Dev	N	MT Dev
N	Data Development	N	Data Development	N	Data Development
N	SAT	N	SAT	N	SAT
N	CAT	N	CAT	N	CAT
N-1	Batch/Heat	N-1	Batch/Heat	N-1	Batch/Heat
N-2	Data Discovery	N-2	Data Discovery	N-2	Data Discovery
N-1	Data Design	N-1	Data Design	N-1	Data Design
N-1	Data Define/Deploy	N-1	Data Define/Deploy	N-1	Data Define/Deploy

Figure 8.11   Example of dependency management (N-1 means the story requires lead time of one iteration)

Burn-Down and Burn-Up Charts

The purpose of the task burn-down chart (Figure 8.12) is to illustrate the effort spent to date and the expected effort remaining. The story point burn-up chart (Figure 8.13) shows the amount of work-in-process and the amount of completed work; it gives credit for a complete story only after it has been validated. They both report effort expended.

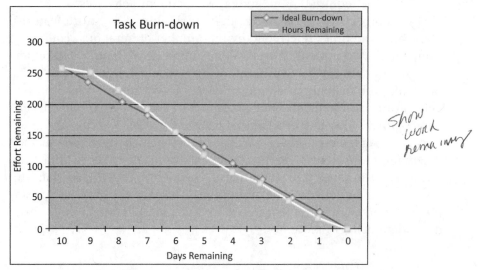

show work remaining

Figure 8.12   Example of a task burn-down chart for an iteration

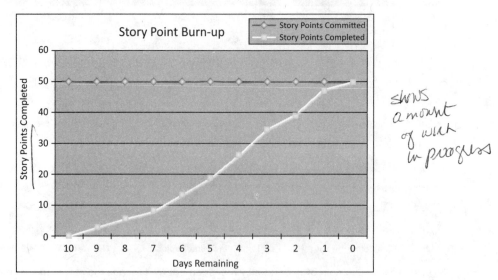

shows amount of work in progress

Figure 8.13   Example of a story burn-up chart for an iteration

The Impediment List

The Impediment List is the final visual control we will consider here. A foundation of both Scrum and Lean-Agile is that continuous improvement includes continually removing impediments. One of the purposes of the daily meeting is to expose impediments, to make them explicit. The Scrum Master or Agile project manager must maintain a list of current impediments so that progress on resolving them can be visible to all. Entries on this list should include

- Date entered on list

- Description of impediment

- Severity of impediment (what its impact is)

- Who it affects

- Actions being taken to remove it

The impediment list should be maintained on an ongoing basis as impediments are removed, added, or modified in some way.

How to Tell If You Have a Good Visual Control

In general, there is no right visual control to use. However, a particular visual control can be more or less suited to a particular team. Good visual controls have the following characteristics:

- Require little overhead work to use

- Illustrate to the team what to do next

- Illustrate to management how and what the team is doing

If the visual control a team is using does not have these characteristics, then it needs to be improved. In particular, teams should assess whether they like their visual controls. Do they help them get their work done? Are the controls themselves an impediment? If the visual controls do not indicate clearly what the team needs to do next, they should look for ways to improve their controls.

> **No Complaints**
>
> If a team complains about the visual controls they are using, then *something is wrong*. Either the team doesn't understand the purpose of visual controls or the visual control itself needs to be improved.

Summary

Visual controls are a key component for managing Lean-Agile software development efforts. They provide a low-cost method for the team to see where they are. Just as important, they create visibility so that management and customers can see the progress of the development efforts. By providing status information to all of these parties, the visual controls enable them to work together to solve whatever problems the team faces in getting the highest value, highest quality products out the door.

Visual controls provide a mechanism for teams and management to work together. They help management monitor the team's progress on the outcomes that management has corrected. Command and control is replaced with visibility, support, and direction.

The visual controls in this chapter are not intended to be a complete list. They are rather a description of some of the more fundamental ones required for a project. Teams should add additional visual controls as they see fit.

Try This

These exercises are best done as a conversation with someone in your organization. After each exercise, ask each other if there are any actions either of you can take to improve your situation.

- What visual controls do you have that don't seem to add value?
- What aspect of work are you not measuring that you think would be valuable to measure?
- What is management asking for that is not in a visual control?
  - What would the cost be to put it in a visual control?
  - Would this help you?

Recommended Reading

The following works offer helpful insights into the topics of this chapter.

Cockburn. 2006. *Agile Software Development: The Cooperative Game*. 2d ed. Boston: Addison-Wesley.

Mann. 2005. *Creating a Lean Culture: Tools to Sustain Lean Conversions*. New York: Productivity Press.

Moore. 1999. *Crossing the Chasm*. New York: Harper Business.

Reinertsen. 1997. *Managing the Design Factory*. New York: Free Press.

CHAPTER 9

The Role of Quality Assurance in Lean-Agile Software Development

"When you are up to your ass in alligators, it's hard to remember your original intention was to drain the swamp." —Author unknown

IN THIS CHAPTER

This chapter covers several critical issues surrounding the role of quality assurance in Lean-Agile software development.

- The role of testers must be one of preventing defects, not finding them.

- How moving the specification of acceptance test to the start of the development cycle can greatly reduce waste—both the waste of building the wrong thing and the waste of building the thing wrong.

- What to do when it is not easy to test early.

The terms "Quality Assurance" (QA) and "Quality Control" (QC) are used in a variety of ways in our industry. IT organizations and product organizations, in particular, seem to have different meanings for the same term. For purposes of this chapter . . .

- Quality Control is the practice of ensuring products or services are designed and produced to meet or exceed customer requirements and

- Quality Assurance refers to planned and systematic production processes that provide confidence in a product's suitability for its intended purpose.

We recognize that, in some organizations, QA refers to ensuring that people are following the process they are supposed to. That is not what we mean in this chapter. Here, QA focuses on ensuring that the product is both suitable for the customer and that it is built correctly.

Takeaways

Key insights to take away from this chapter include

- Testers should seek to avoid problems, not fix them.

- Moving testing up front can improve quality at little, if any, extra cost.

- Developers should always ask the question, "How will I know I've done that?" before writing code.

- We strongly endorse up-front testing, but if you are not going to do it, we feel you should at least consider testing before writing code.

Introduction

Two Lean principles factor prominently in quality assurance: *build quality in* and *eliminate waste*. Defects indicate that quality is not being built in to the product. And a lack of quality causes a lot of waste in the form of rework and added complexity.

This goes beyond simply bugs in code. Since Lean looks across the entire development process, all of the following symptoms indicate problems with quality:

- Building something with insufficient quality (bugs)

- Building something the customer did not ask for because a requirement was misunderstood

- Building something the customer did ask for, but later realized it was not what they meant and they do not want it now

- Building something the customer described properly but once they saw it realized that they had asked for the wrong thing

- Building something the customer did ask for and it was what they meant but now they want something different

---

Removing Bugs Is Waste

Lean would say that there is no value in taking bugs out of systems. Why? One reason is that putting a bug into code and then taking it out adds no value. No customer has ever asked any development team to do this. Ever! Let's make this personal to drive home the point: Suppose you take your car in to the dealership for a $50 oil change. When you pick up your car, the bill is $550. When you complain, "The oil change was supposed to be only $50!" they respond, "Well, it was $50, but we charged you $500 to take the dent out of your fender." "But there was no dent in the fender when I brought it in!" "True, but we dented it when we changed your oil!" Did you receive value from their taking the dent out?

From the customer's point of view, all of these are defects in the product. Whether a bug, a lack, or an excess, they do not consider these valuable. And building anything that the customer does not find valuable is waste. We want to reduce or eliminate waste and so improve quality. The responsibility for eliminating waste lies with the team.

Where to start? Lean thinking says to look at the system within which a defect arises rather than seeking someone to blame. In other words, look to systemic causes rather than to problems with individual performance. In software development, one typical systemic problem is the separation of the development team from the test team. Developers create code and the test team tries to detect errors and help fix the code. Yes, the testing team is addressing the defect problems, but the system as a whole allows the defects to arise in the first place.

The practice of testing bugs (defects) out of a system is akin to Deming's famous quip, "Let's make toast American style. You burn, I'll scrape!" How can this be improved? Can we reduce the occurrence of defects? Wouldn't that be a better use for quality assurance rather than having them try to intercept defects after the fact?

Yes! In Lean-Agile,

The primary role of QA is not to find defects but to prevent them.

Quality assurance provides an opportunity to discover why bugs occur. QA's role should be to improve the process so as to prevent defects and to use found defects to improve the process from which they sprang. In other words, when errors occur, take that as an indication that something about the process could be improved—and find an improvement that will prevent the error from occurring again.

QA at the End of the Cycle Is Inherently Wasteful

Placing quality assurance at the end of the development cycle contributes significant waste to the process. Let's see why.

Consider the typical development process where QA is done at the end of the cycle.

1. The analyst and the developer discuss the requirement to be implemented.

2. The developer goes off to develop it and

   a. Writes some code,
   b. Considers how she will know she has implemented it properly,
   c. Runs her own tests to confirm it is correct (often, this is done by hand), and then
   d. Hands off her code to QA for testing.

3. QA discusses the requirement with the analyst and determines what a good test case would be.

4. QA implements this test.

5. If (when) an error is found,

   a. QA tells the developer there is a bug,
   b. The developer investigates by looking at the QA's test case, and then may

      • Discover her bug and go on to fix it,
      • Discover her bug and put it in a queue, or
      • Believe she has the correct test case and that the QA person has done the wrong thing and then get into a dispute over how to resolve the error.

At best, this approach has a lot of redundancy built in. In addition, there are numerous opportunities for miscommunication. And when an error occurs, there will likely be a significant delay until it is discovered.

Misunderstanding Is More Natural than Understanding

It is always dangerous to assume that what you heard is what was said. Communication requires work and is built on common understanding between those communicating. English is an ambiguous language. Many words are actually their own antonyms. For example, "clip" can mean "to put together" (as in "clip the coupon to the paper") or "to take away" (as in "clip the coupon from the paper"). Thus, "clip the coupon" is ambiguous.

However, trying to avoid this ambiguity by writing everything down can lead to something enormous, like the requirements document for a tank Winston Churchill once described by saying, "This paper, by its very length, defends itself against the chance of being read."

Improve Results by Moving QA Up Front

Moving QA closer to the front of the value stream can reduce or eliminate redundancy, miscommunication, and delay. One way to do this is to ensure that whenever a requirement is stated, the team asks the question, "How will I know I've done that?" The answer should be in the form of specific inputs and outputs. Because they are specific examples, they can be used as tests. These answers need either to come from the customer or to be validated by her. The answers should be in the form of an acceptance test of the code produced.

Getting this question asked and answered before a developer starts working has several advantages. First, it avoids the redundancy of asking and answering multiple times by different people. Second, it gives the developer something to shoot for: guidance to get the job done. Finally, if the test is automated, it can be run any time the code is altered and thereby verify that the code still works—or give warning that it does not.

It creates a context for a better and more reliable conversation between developer and analyst.[1]

Let's consider an example. Suppose you are given the following requirement:

> **Basic Employee Compensation** For each week, hourly employees are paid a standard wage per hour for the first 40 hours worked, one-and-a-half times their wage for each hour after the first 40 hours, and two times their wage for each hour worked on Sundays and holidays.

Since we have moved QA up front, the team starts by asking, "And how will I know I have done that?" They might come up with the tests shown in Table 9.1.

The developer starts reviewing these tests: Looking at the first row, he says, "Okay, I see this; 40 hours times $20/hour gives me $800. That makes sense. But 45 hours times $20 should give me $900, not $950. Oh, but I see, I forgot the time-and-a-half, so it's really 40 times $20 plus 5 times $30 so $950 is correct. But let's see, 48 standard hours means 40 times $20 plus 8 times $30 plus the holiday hours at double-time should give me $800 + $240 + $320 or $1360. Not $1520."

This is confusing! So the developer talks to the customer/analyst and the tester to clear it up. One of them explains, "Well, the 48 standard

Table 9.1   Examples Describe Tests for the Requirement

StandardHours	HolidayHours	Wage	Pay()
40	0	20	$800
45	0	20	$950
48	8	20	$1520

---

1. We got this insight by reading Rick Mugridge's fabulous book *FIT For Developing Software* (Mugridge 2005). The beginning of this book is a must-read even if you are not going to use FIT.

hours gives you $1040 but the 8 holiday hours, since they are overtime, are paid at time-and-a-half of double-time or $480 for a total of $1520." Ah! Things become clearer!

Notice how having the test specified with the requirements changes the conversation between the developer and the analyst? Moving the testing process to the start of the creation process—before coding—makes it more likely that the developer will build what the customer intends.[2]

In the previous example, the team gets the benefit whether or not the tests are automated. They benefit simply by better communication. While some arguments can be offered against automating testing, it is hard to argue against at least specifying the tests up front. It adds no extra work and it creates great value. This should always be done.

The first task in implementing any story should be to answer the question, "How will I know I've done that?" Often, this must done in the iteration before the team does the story (or in the planning on the day of the iteration in which they intend to do the story), since it may take considerable time as well as be required in order to size the story.[3]

QA Is Responsible, but So Is Development

We do not mean to imply that QA's responsibility to improve the process makes developers any less responsible. The entire team is responsible. Both developers and QA must work to avoid buggy code in the first place. If testers are removing bugs from the developers' code, developers are not doing *their* jobs correctly.

When the Product Champion Will Not Answer Your Questions

Specifying tests up front is powerful, as long as you can do it. What if the analyst, product champion, or customer representative cannot or will not answer the question, "How will I know I've done that?" What do you do

---

2. In our classes, before we specify the test, we ask people to name all of the different possibilities for misunderstanding the stated requirement. Usually another half-dozen not mentioned here are stated. When we ask, "How do you know you've got them all?" people realize it is impossible to know what you don't know.

3. This may seem contrary to some Agile concepts; however, in real-world large projects, standard Scrum practices are often overly simplistic.

then? In our classes and consulting, we have heard so many teams complain that their "customer" (meaning whomever is representing the customer) just wants the team to figure things out for them. The customer does not want to help, does not want to be bothered, or simply wants to leave it to the "professionals," who probably know better how to do things in software projects (right?). Should the developers just go ahead and do the work for the customer? No! Help the customer, but don't do it all for them.

The team can develop preliminary answers to the question, "How will I know I've done that?" and then take the tests to the customer to ask, "If we do this, will we have met your needs?" Giving them something concrete to work with makes it easier for the customer to answer the question. In virtually every case where we have seen teams take this approach, the customer makes the time to get the specifications completed. And if they don't, you probably should not proceed.

As Jeff Sutherland says (2003):

> The task then is to refine the code base to better meet customer need. If that is not clear, the programmers should not write a line of code. Every line of code costs money to write and more money to support. It is better for the developers to be surfing than writing code that won't be needed. If they write code that ultimately is not used, I will be paying for that code for the life of the system, which is typically longer than my professional life. If they went surfing, they would have fun, and I would have a less expensive system and fewer headaches to maintain.

If you cannot get verification of what is needed, you will almost certainly build something that is not useful. And, even worse, you will be adding complexity to your code base. That is waste. And waste is an enemy.

If the customer cannot or will not confirm that you have delivered what they want, you should simply state that you believe that the customer does not value the feature; that it is not a high priority. If it were valuable, they would make the effort to specify the tests. Moreover, you should tell your management team that you recommend *not* building the functionality. If you are required to build it anyway, go ahead, but know that it could well turn out to be a waste of time.

There is an exercise at the end of this chapter that you should do with another team member. It helps make apparent that when the "customer" won't help clarify their needs, the functionality that is delivered is almost always not what was needed.

Executable Specifications and Magic Documentation

Tests represent documentation for the requirement. They describe very specifically how the system behaves. Even better, when tests are made this explicit, they can be put into a testing framework, such as Framework for Integrated Test (FIT), and these tests can actually be written by non-developers. This makes it relatively easy to tie the tests to the code. At any time, the tests can be run to ensure that the code is giving the desired results.

In the previous example, a test run might produce results such as those shown in Table 9.2. The rows for which the tests have run successfully are green while those that have failed are red (with both the expected and actual results shown). If the tests are not connected to the code they would be shown in yellow.

This is powerful. Such automation provides "magic" documentation. Most documentation just sits there when the system doesn't correspond to what is stated. But automated test specifications represent executable specifications and turn red (magic!) when they break. Besides the improvement to documenting requirements, these automated tests provide a safety net when the code is changed, and they allow shorter iterations with lower costs for the accompanying regression testing.

Table 9.2.   Example of FIT Tests When Executed

StandardHours	HolidayHours	Wage	Pay()	Result (Color)
40	0	20	$800	Green
45	0	20	$950	Green
48	8	20	$1360	Red (expected $1520 but got $1360)

Acceptance Test-Driven Development

Test-Driven Development (TDD) began as a coding method based on writing unit tests for functions prior to writing the functions themselves. The main drivers behind TDD were to 1) ensure an understanding of what the functions were to do, 2) verify that the code was doing it, and 3) take advantage of the fact that this kind of design process (defining tests before writing code) improved the quality of the code written. Classic TDD, however, is primarily a developer function. It is about reducing technical risk—the risk that the software implementation won't match what is being asked for.

Once we bring together the customer, quality assurance, and developer roles, a new perspective on test-driven development emerges: the concept that test-driven development should seek to reduce both technical and market risk. Reducing market risk means both identifying properly the needs of the marketplace and accurately conveying them to the development team. Reducing technical risk requires ensuring that the code works as it is designed to.

By driving code development from acceptance tests, both of these risks should be reduced. The conversations described previously in this chapter reduce market risk because they assist the customer, tester, and developer in understanding one another. Once acceptance tests have been defined, creating smaller tests that implement aspects of the acceptance ensure that the code works properly. This is called Acceptance Test-Driven Development (ATDD).

Perspective again is a big contributor to effectiveness here. Classic TDD is often about writing unit tests for functions. It is not uncommon to see acceptance written as a combination of unit tests. But we're strongly suggesting that going the other way makes much more sense—writing unit tests based on acceptance tests. This extends TDD into a process of ensuring an understanding that the tests are complete. In other words, start at the top (acceptance) tests and break them down instead of starting at the bottom (unit) tests and putting them together.

This top-down approach can be used to ensure test coverage of the needed behavior is complete. This is not unlike starting with a jigsaw puzzle that is put together—to make sure that you have all of the pieces—and then breaking it up so you can put it together. If you start with all of the individual pieces, you can't be sure you have it all right until you've put the entire puzzle together.

Perspective Can Make All of the Difference

To best understand the power of perspective, consider this conversation we once had with someone who was considering Agile methods for his company, which built instruments for the health care industry. He asked how he could verify that he had complete test coverage if he built up his test cases on small stories. Since he knew that we were Agile consultants, he expected some fancy answer that would allay his concern. But instead we told him that you couldn't—at least not easily and not with great certainty. We said that instead of creating stories and putting them together—and therefore starting with test cases and putting them together—you need to start with acceptance tests and break the stories down.

Summary

Quality Assurance should be responsible for *preventing* defects, not merely for finding them. To achieve this, QA should be moved up to the front of the development cycle. This helps teams avoid many of the communication errors that often result in delays, defects, and waste. Before each story is implemented, the team and the customer should ask and answer the question, "How will I know I've done that?" If possible, tests should be implemented before code is written, thereby assisting the developers in both seeing how their code behaves and ensuring that high-quality code is produced with minimal waste.

Try This

This exercise is best done as a conversation with someone in your organization. After the exercise, ask each other if there are any actions either of you can take to improve your situation.

The purpose of this exercise is to help you and your group understand the value of asking the question, "How will I know I've done that?"

Do this exercise with someone else if you can.

1. Consider a time when you developed code, only to discover later from the customer that what was developed was not what they

meant when they asked for it. Make sure this was a time you did not asked the question, "How will I know that I've done that?"

2. How would the result have been different if you had asked that question?

An Anecdote about this Exercise

We run this exercise in all of our Lean and Agile/Scrum classes. In one class, the dialogue was particularly animated. People discussed how they had tried to get this question answered but could not get the product manager (their customer rep) to answer it. This was mostly because the product manager didn't know himself. They went ahead and built things as best they could but later ended up essentially having to redo the system. We had the group reflect on all the times that this had occurred in the last couple of years for any of the projects that the teams had worked on. They realized that *every* time this had occurred they had had to redo the code. Not only had they wasted much effort, they had also made their system much more complex than it should have been. They resolved *never* to write code unless they could answer the question, "How will I know I've done that?" We've often said there are not any best practices that all teams should follow, but if there is one—this is it!

Recommended Reading

The following works offer helpful insights into the topics of this chapter.

Mugridge. 2005. *Fit for Developing Software: Framework for Integrated Tests*. Upper Saddle River, NJ: Prentice Hall.

Sutherland, Jeff. 2003. "Get Your Requirements Straight." *Jeff Sutherland*. http://jeffsutherland.com/scrum/2003/03/scrum-get-your-requirements-straight.html (accessed March 13, 2009).

CHAPTER 10

Becoming an Agile Enterprise

"Continuous improvement is not about the things you do well—that's work. Continuous improvement is about removing the things that get in the way of your work. The headaches, the things that slow you down, that's what continuous improvement is all about." —Author Unknown

IN THIS CHAPTER

This chapter discusses the challenge of becoming an Agile enterprise. This involves thinking clearly about where you are, where you want to go, and what is in the way. We consider three different organization types, based on what we have seen in helping companies transition to Agile. Fundamentally, the transition involves continuous process improvement.

Takeaways

Key insights to take away from this chapter include

- There are many ways to achieve Agility throughout the enterprise.

- If you have well-established development teams, start by making them Agile; then improve the portfolio-management team, all the while improving both how your teams work together and their technical skills.

- If you don't have well-established teams, reduce the number of projects underway so you can create teams focused on completing prioritized requests that can be validated by the product champion.

Where Do You Want to Go?

Before you can decide on your path, you must know where you are and where you want to go. Where you want to go is probably clear: It is where most other companies also want to go. These include being able to do the following.

- Identify the needs of the market.

- Respond quickly to market changes.

- Create software that is tuned to the market: high quality and focused on providing the most valuable features.

- Create products (internal and external) that are long-lived, easily extended, and easily maintained.

To achieve this, Lean-Agile suggests enterprises do the following.

- Identify and define minimum marketable features to build.

- Manage their development organization so that it maximizes throughput, minimizes cycle time, and produces high-quality software in the process.

- Ensure their teams follow Lean principles to the best of their capabilities within their constraints.

- Employ teams that are highly skilled in the engineering practices needed to sustainably build high-quality software, including test-driven development and design patterns.

- Adopt continuous process-improvement practices and become a learning organization.

All of this is based on the need for the organization to be business-driven. It is not enough for the teams to become Agile; the business must structure and lead teams to where they can add the most value for their customers. We call this "Business-Driven Software Development."

What Gets in the Way?

Working with dozens of companies that have adopted Lean-Agile, we have seen a number of common impediments to making the transition. These include

- **Teams are not well formed**. A project is done by a collection of people assigned to work on it. Problems arise when these people are assigned to work on many other things as well.

- **Teams are not co-located**. Studies have shown that situating people more than 30 feet away from each other greatly reduces their ability to communicate and work together. As this is a reality today, we have to learn to deal with it effectively.

- **Annual planning cycles result in longer-than-necessary projects**. In addition, failing to focus on Minimum Marketable Features results in larger-than-necessary projects, which take longer to complete.

- **Large batches of unprioritized requirements are pushed through the organization**. There is no mechanism to limit work to resource capacity.

- **Program managers and business sponsors compete for resources rather than working together to maximize the return on them**. The preponderance of large projects means that different product lines compete with each other for budgets. This competition does not promote delivering the best value enterprise-wide.

- **Automated acceptance testing is not being done**. Test-driven development also is not being done. Testing is initiated too late in the development cycle.

- **Integration is done at project's end**. Integration costs are high because teams work independently of each other for too long, resulting in waste.

- **Code quality is left up to programmers' personal beliefs**. There is much known about what constitutes quality code. Unfortunately, most companies still allow developers to code based on their own preferences and have not set standards for what constitutes quality code.

- **Finding and removing the root causes of problems is not pursued aggressively**. Bugs are tolerated as a way of life in the software world. In fact, many organizations utilize bug tracking as status for release readiness.

- **Continuous process improvement is not practiced or valued**. Most companies are so busy trying to fix the latest crisis that there is no time to focus on process improvement to avoid causing the next one.

To become Agile, an organization must overcome these challenges.

Trim Tabs

We have always admired and been inspired by R. Buckminster Fuller, author of the ground-breaking book, *Critical Path*. Among other things, he coined the term "Spaceship Earth" and invented the geodesic dome.

He reflected on trim tabs, which are used in aviation and shipping. They are attached to large control surfaces (e.g., flaps and rudders) that would otherwise be difficult to move.

Bucky once wrote about standing on a dock reflecting on how difficult it was to change society when he saw a large ship go by. He considered the effort it would take to change its direction. Pushing on the bow (front) of the ship was one way but it was not very efficient. Using the rudder is not as easy as it might appear. When the large surface area of the rudder is pushed against the water, the effort required and the stress on the rudder itself is very great. Just as Bucky was thinking, "It's very difficult indeed to change the course of a great ship," the stern (tail) of the ship went by and Bucky noticed what's called a trim tab on the rudder.

A trim tab is like a miniature rudder. When you move it, it creates a low-pressure area that allows the rudder to turn much more easily. Bucky realized that with the trim tab, it took relatively little effort to move a great, big ship. If one is to make a difference in the world, Bucky realized, one had to look for the trim tabs in life, that is, those things that require little effort to produce a large effect.

Guidelines for the Transition

When companies transition to Agile, they must always consider the following three questions.

1. What are the pain points that can be most easily eliminated?

2. What cultural attitudes are in the way of the transition?

3. What metrics are in the way of the transition?

In addition, it also helps to remember these points:

- Trying to do too many things at the start can be counterproductive, even if all of them are useful.

- People undergoing transitions have a certain degree of fear.

- People must always understand what is in it for them.

- Adding significant work to the team about to make a transition may cause people to abandon the transition.

- We should look for the "trim tabs" that will help smooth the transition.

You don't have to find everything that will help you, but you do need to find the few, most critical things that will make the transition work in your organization. You must also focus on the proper things, on the things you can change. Some people call this "picking the low-hanging fruit." We prefer "finding the trim tabs" because it implies more than a little effort, it also implies high return for that effort.

Where Do You Start?

So where do we start? That depends on where you are.

To help you think about it, we will consider three examples that are based on our experience helping companies become Agile. Most of the companies we have worked with fall into one of three general categories:

- Product companies making software that is sold to those outside of their company

- IT organizations that have reasonably well-defined teams creating software that is used directly by their own staff, their agents, or their customers in support of their company's services

- IT-product companies (a hybrid of the first two) making software that is used in an administrative role of other companies; for example, a company that makes hospital-administrative software

Do not be concerned if your company does not exactly fit one of the following descriptions. Instead, look at the issues and structures present and how we recommend the transition take place. See which issues are most important for your company. In all of the examples that follow, the organizations are comprised of 300 to 4,000 people and each product/ service line has 50 to 500 people dedicated to it.

The Product Company

Product companies build software that individuals or other companies use. These products might be in the gaming industry (e.g., a PC game), in the business arena (e.g., a word processor), in the defense arena (e.g., missile-guidance software) or really almost anything. The biggest differentiator of product companies is usually whether or not they are writing embedded software (i.e., software running on dedicated hardware such as a car's controller).

Product companies typically have well-defined teams but usually have people on more than one team. Very often people are on one team, building a new product or enhancement, while also on another team that supports legacy products. The company's biggest challenges are generally improving product quality and increasing team efficiency. Although they typically don't have the yearly planning cycles that plague IT organizations, they often have long-range plans for their products that result in building excess features.

The most common place to start in product companies is with improving their teams' efficiencies, as shown in Figure 10.1. This is frequently achieved by implementing Scrum or Kanban (whichever is more appropriate for the type of work they are doing). By learning how to build software in stages, it puts pressure on the program managers to select better product-enhancement definitions. When implementing Scrum, it is advisable to move quality assurance up to the front of the process. This improves team organization and communication.

In a team's adoption of Scrum or Kanban, they will encounter many challenges that they can fix or improve directly. We have found frequently that a useful change is moving quality assurance up to the front of the development process (see chapter 9, The Role of Quality Assurance in Lean-Agile Software Development). After doing so, teams find that they can make significant improvements to their process and to the quality of code they develop. However, after some period, they find that they are impeded by things outside their control. For example, the requested

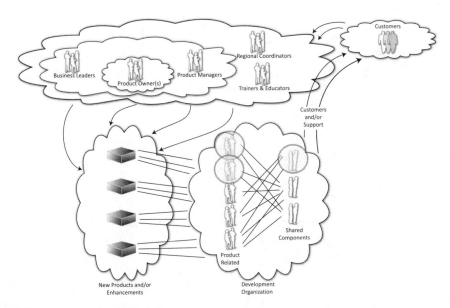

Figure 10.1   Create Agile teams

product enhancements may be over-defined and/or contain too many features (i.e., be bigger than necessary). This may require them to work on several product teams, causing thrashing.

While team training can be limited to the Scrum and Kanban methods required, once it becomes clear that the issues affecting the team are beyond the team's control, it is time for the next step. This is also a good time to train the teams in the wider principles of Lean—because at this point, one must look beyond the team.

The next step is coaching program managers on how to select smaller enhancements to build. That is, it's time to start building minimum marketable features (MMFs). This is shown in Figure 10.2.

These two steps can actually be done at the same time but it is often difficult to get program managers to see the viability of it until after teams are able to shorten their development cycles. Once that is done, teams can make a case for more time with product managers or their proxies because they can demonstrate that doing without this contact impedes the team's ability to deliver high-quality code quickly.

Once an organization is building MMFs quickly, it should become possible for the product portfolio-management team to select MMFs based on maximizing ROI for the entire organization, not merely each product line. In other words, once program managers see smaller product

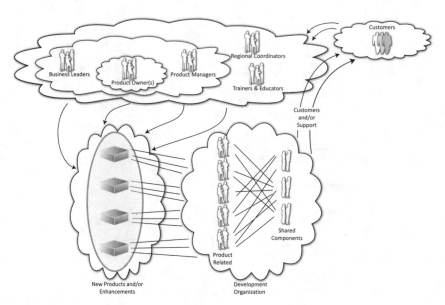

Figure 10.2   Improve the way product enhancements are selected

enhancements implemented by the development teams, they will realize they are competing with each other for resources in a very direct way. As program managers clearly see the value of having fewer product enhancements in the delivery pipeline at any one time (to ensure maximizing development teams' efficiency), they understand the need to select product enhancements that align with the needs of the entire organization. This collaboration—rather than competition—among program managers is illustrated in Figure 10.3.

Throughout this process, the development side of the organization should be improving itself in two ways:

- Teams should be adopting engineering best practices, including test-driven development and design patterns tailored for their particular situation.

- Teams should be organized to work with other teams to lower integration costs and improve cycle time.

This "last" step, to reorganize the way teams work with each other, is actually an ongoing step. It often starts after the others because it takes an understanding of flow to guide it. The process of improving how teams

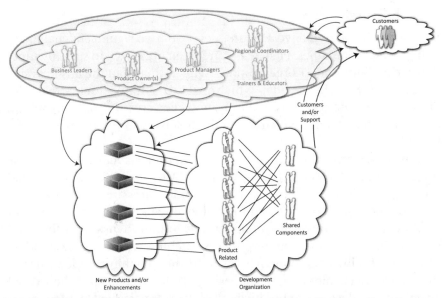

Figure 10.3   Program managers collaborating to pick MMFs that will "optimize the whole" of the development organization's efforts

interact with each other is discussed further in chapter 12, The Product Coordination Team.

When the Product Company Writes Embedded Software

When embedded software is being written, the transition becomes quite a bit more complex due to the added cost of integrating across both the software and hardware teams. Value stream mapping early on can illuminate many issues. Lean's focus on flow and minimizing cycle time provides insight on how to better integrate these teams. We discuss a method of coordinating different product teams in chapter 12, The Product Coordination Team.

The Product Company's Transition Path

Essentially, this is a path that often starts with the teams at the bottom and, guided by Lean, works its way to the top. The previously described path is not meant to be the specific way to do it as much as it is a guide on how one aspect of the transition leads to another.

The IT Company

IT organizations often have a greater degree of two significant challenges than product companies. First, teams are often organized in silos (by function); in addition, the IT organization itself—rather than the business side of the organization—decides which product enhancements to build. These are separate concerns. Typically, however, creating well-organized, cross-functional teams, which solves the first issue, often helps guide the second.

Ironically, starting Scrum on selected pilot projects may improve those projects while adversely affecting the rest of the organization. If the total number of projects does not change, and some teams are selected to work on only one at a time using Scrum, the result will be that the people not on these Scrum teams will end up with even more work than they had before. This causes even more project switching with its corresponding thrashing and lowers productivity even further. Looking at the results of the pilot projects alone often makes Agility look great, but the overall effect can be a decrease in productivity of the software development organization as a whole. If one mistakenly thinks that Scrum is helping (because of the success of the pilot projects), "scaling" Scrum may prove difficult and even counterproductive. In IT organizations, a combination of lowering the number of active projects and creating well-defined teams to work on them must be done simultaneously to avoid causing some teams to thrash (non-Scrum) while others succeed (Scrum).

IT organizations, however, tend to be more driven by the development (IT) side of the business than product organizations are. They also have a greater stake in building software that end users can actually consume. In product companies, releasing a product is often all that is needed to make it available to the business's customers. But in IT organizations, the software is tightly tied to the processes of the organization. Adding a capability that the service group is not prepared to implement adds no value to the company because the mere availability of the software is not sufficient for the service organization to use it.

The IT Product Company

The IT product company, although it looks like other IT companies, is actually a product company—it sells services to other companies. However, since it provides services that its customers' IT departments would otherwise provide, it is often organized like an IT organization.

And as we have seen in many IT organizations, it may not have real teams at all. Instead, when a product needs to be enhanced, people who can take on the appropriate roles are selected to do it. The annual project budget life cycle is very much alive in organizations of this type: Learning how to create smaller projects is key.

We have found that the best way for these organizations to transition to Agile is to educate the program managers right from the start. The first step is to identify the possible MMFs to build, then prioritize them according to ROI. Once that is done, teams must be created and assigned MMFs to build. This should be done for the entire product line—so that several teams will transition to Agile right from the start. Teams working on the same MMF can pull from a common product backlog.

minimum marketable features

By selecting smaller product enhancements, it is more likely that each team will have all of the roles necessary to develop the features they are assigned. Co-locating teams will increase productivity even more. While this is a major transition for many companies, the creation of cross-functional teams will create immediate productivity gains which will more than offset any confusion the transition itself may cause.

The Importance of Continuous Process Improvement

Lean is not about transitioning to a specific place; rather, it is more about learning that transitioning should be an ongoing process. However, transitioning for the sake of transitioning is not the goal; improving productivity and ROI is. Teams need to look at how to improve their own process and the dependencies they have with other teams. Management needs to continuously seek ways to reduce cycle time and increase quality. This requires both coaching their teams to improve and discovering how the organization's structure impedes teams so that they can fix it.

Summary

How a company transitions to Agile Software Development depends upon the where it is and what challenges it has to overcome. A combination of improving the teams, the structure within which they exist, and their ability to drive from business need will help it get there.

Try This

These exercises are best done as a conversation with someone in your organization. After each exercise, ask each other if there are any actions either of you can take to improve your situation.

- How many projects do the people in your company work on at any one time?

- What part of your organization is driving the business—the business/marketing side or the development side?

- How does this affect what is selected for development?

CHAPTER 11

Management's Role in Lean-Agile Development

"Management is doing things right; leadership is doing the right things."
—Peter Drucker

"You have to manage a system. The system doesn't manage itself."
—W. Edwards Deming

IN THIS CHAPTER

This chapter discusses the role of the manager in Lean-Agile to foster the proper environment that leads to highly performing teams. The manager helps teams to stay focused on results and to continuously improve their processes. Visual controls are a powerful tool for management and teams to help teams identify when there are impediments. Creating knowledge over the long term is also a key responsibility for management. Lean provides a model in which managers can avoid both micromanagement and abdication through delegation.

Takeways

Key insights to take away from this chapter include

- Lean-Agile management is the art of leading people, not directing them.

- Leading people involves creating the correct environment, keeping them focused on the right things, trusting them to do their work—and helping them when they need it.

- Lean-Agile leaders manage with visual controls that focus on maximizing the throughput of completed work that is properly prioritized by business value.

- Lean-Agile managers concentrate on minimizing the overall cycle time—from initial idea to delivered and consumed solutions.

Lean-Agile Management

How you view managing is the key to a successful transition to the Lean-Agile enterprise. In Lean-Agile, the focus is on managing the value stream and leading people. This includes the creation of knowledge about the product, the formation of an infrastructure to build the product, and the creation of the product itself. A visible workflow makes it much easier to align everyone with the goals of the business and improve the flow of value to customers. Management watches for anything in the process that impedes or blocks that flow of value. Great software can emerge from your organization when you lead with the value stream in mind.

 For example, it is common for management to track the number of unfixed bugs. It seems like natural approach to assess how a team is doing. Lean-Agile thinking uses a different approach: Instead of worrying about fixing the bugs, we should concern ourselves with what is causing them. Unfortunately, many Agile approaches don't have a well-enough defined value stream to get consistent answers. Lean's mandate for a well-defined value stream provides new opportunities for management to lead the team in discovering the source of bugs. Bugs indicate a problem in the process. What could be allowing these bugs to occur or remain? By focusing on our value stream, we can detect these problems and correct them. Perhaps it is that testing is not being done until the end. Perhaps it is that large amounts of work are batching up, which leads to delays in detecting bugs, which increases the impact when a bug is found. Fix the process and reduce bugs. The Lean-Agile manager drives the organization to fix the process by identifying and removing delays, impediments, and blockages in all of the value stream's processes.

These fixes may depend on just the team or they may rely on relationships with other teams.

Creating the Environment

Developing Agile teams that are well formed and hyper-productive requires an environment that fosters team growth, healthy group dynamics, and good team behaviors. Such an environment does not just happen. It requires a leader with good insight, focus, and understanding about what is required. Leaders set the stage for cultivating the needed behaviors rather than trying to train the behaviors "into" the team.

Lean cultures develop in the same way. They are the outcome of leadership that is focused on applying Lean principles up and down the organization and across the enterprise. It is common to hear about the need to change the culture of a company. Unfortunately, it isn't possible to change culture directly. Company culture results from the conversations that people have about how the company behaves—and these are based on their experiences with management and how managers behave.

Changing culture involves changing the system of management. Fortunately, Lean helps us here. Lean suggests that management can improve results by improving the system within which their people work. Management needs to assist teams in creating proper visual controls so that the teams can do their work better. These same controls enable management to see how they need to coach their teams. By focusing on improving management systems, people's experiences in the organization will change. And that changes the company's culture.

In Lean-Agile, the manager has two primary responsibilities:

- Setting the outcomes or goals expected of the team

- Assisting the doers in improving their processes and their workspaces to facilitate getting their jobs done

Carrying out these responsibilities involves helping the team focus on continuously improving the process, eliminating waste and delays. The result should be ever-increasing ability to deliver value to the customer.

The Lean-Agile manager should be relentless in raising awareness of the two biggest wastes in software development: delays and building what is not needed. As impediments to the value stream are uncovered, the well-formed team should be motivated to root out and fix these as part of their daily work.

Lean-Agile's Balanced Approach to Management

Many people in our industry have wondered why "Taylorism"[1] is so rampant today. Is it because that is how we were brought up in our families or schools? Perhaps. But as we mature, haven't we learned that this approach does not work? And yet, we stick with it. As risks mount, command-and-control feels safe.

Or we have read about delegation and supporting our people, trusting them to do the work. It seems democratic but it feels like abdication and certainly promotes its own set of problems.

Lean thinking provides an alternative: Delegating work and the methods to achieve it while still retaining responsibility for the outcomes. Lean suggests several methods and tools that create visibility into challenges that teams encounter. These include value stream mapping, visual controls, walking around, being involved in problem solving, and kaizens.[2] This visibility enables managers to help teams develop and improve without emotions and blame getting in the way. The manager can point to the value stream map or visual controls to spot issues, ask the developers about processes they are following, and help them investigate root causes of issues. This provides a way for a manager to support and encourage the team—without taking over—while retaining full visibility to what is going on and how she can contribute. While Lean provides many tools, visual controls are particularly useful since they provide information on what is happening now. Chapter 8, Visual Controls and Information Radiators for Enterprise Teams, discusses visual controls.

In Lean-Agile, the manager is essential in helping teams avoid waste. Teams often can't recognize waste in their own work processes (which can seem like water to a fish) or can be overwhelmed by how to address the issues (the impediments can feel insurmountable). These might occur either because the problem is outside the scope of the team's work or the team has no authority to make changes. Or the team may see the problem and, being very passionate and committed, may get so focused on solving it that they don't know when to stop trying to fix it.

---

1. "Taylorism" is the tendency toward command-and-control styles of management, as espoused by Frederick Taylor in the early twentieth century.
2. *Kaizen* is a Japanese word meaning "change for the better." A kaizen is a highly structured brainstorming session used to generate ideas for an alternative work method to solve a particular challenge.

In any of these cases, the team's ability to work is impeded. If they are kept up-to-date, the visual controls make it apparent to the outside observer when the team is impeded.

It is at this time a manager can provide a useful interruption to get the team to reflect on what's causing its lack of progress. While management should not provide a solution to the problem, getting the team to pull back and avoid going down a rat hole can be a big waste saver.

Create Knowledge within the Team

Technical product delivery requires specialists in many different technology areas. Certifications tend to create organizations that break down work and assign it to the specialist who can complete the individual task in the shortest amount of time. Lean-Agile managers must create knowledge within their organization and have a clear understanding of the harmful impact of pushing work through their teams in this manner. Tactical moves that bring short-term, sub-optimal efficiencies should always be challenged as detracting from optimizing the flow of completed work up and down the value stream. An example of good Lean-Agile leadership is to resist the logical urge to assign work based on skill set in an attempt to maximize short-term efficiency.

In other words, we can often save time by cross-training people in skill areas that are specialized or otherwise in short supply. Even though these newly trained people may not have the speed or quality of the specialist, they can alleviate the bottleneck that ensues during heavy loads. Thus, we do not have to cross-train to be able to handle each step in the best manner possible but just to remove the bottleneck that extends the cycle time during heavy loads.

The lesson from this is that "keeping people busy" is not only an administrative headache, it also creates barriers to a good team environment. Managers supporting Lean-Agile development must pay attention to creating a teaching/learning culture that values specialists but requires them to perform their work with a mentoring approach to others and to be willing to learn skills outside their immediate area of expertise. This is counter to most tactical management beliefs, which attempt to fully utilize each skilled specialist by breaking down tasks and assigning them based on which individual can most efficiently do the work. This sub-optimization results in creating large batches of unfinished work, which we know increases cycle time in a nonlinear fashion. The strategic alternative is instead to create Lean-Agile teams that can adjust and adapt to

changing business needs and whose main focus is on completing prioritized work as quickly as possible with no technical debt.

Get to the Root Cause

Adhesive bandages are great to have around the house, especially in a
household with kids. Skinned knees somehow lose their sting when
properly bandaged with a cartoon character. They also work wonders on
hikes to cover hot spots about to cause blisters (if caught early enough).
But if you are a serious hiker, you probably should not depend on bandages to prevent blisters; instead, you should attack the real problem and
buy boots that fit properly—which leads to the following example.

A large financial-services company with an impressive IT division
required both detailed weekly status reports and up-to-date project plans
for all in-flight projects. This best-in-class shop was both Waterfall and
process-centric, and it had built a software-factory model organized by
the process area (e.g. business analysts for requirements, UI developers,
mid-tier developers, database developers, architects, system testers, and
so on). Project managers had the tough role of assembling matrix teams
that had to navigate through the institutionalized Waterfall process and
specify a committed date, using a given amount of resources. To keep
control over projects underway, detailed weekly status reports and
accompanying project plans were required by upper management to track
the status of deliverables underway in each phase of each project.

I once participated in a meeting of project-management process experts
for this company. The group met regularly to share practices and to
improve the IT project-management process. Two experienced project
managers enthusiastically presented a new tool that they were about to
roll out to all project managers in the organization. These two project
managers had worked overtime to create a very impressive application
that could synch up project plans with status reports, both of which were
required by upper management on a weekly basis. There had been many
complaints about how redundant it was to have to maintain both project
plans and status reports. With this new tool, the deliverables could be
maintained in one place and standardized weekly status spreadsheets
would be created automatically. For a nice added touch, the spreadsheet
had color-coded tabs for each phase in their Waterfall methodology. The
project managers were enthusiastic about how much value this tool created. What do you think?

Lean principles would suggest that this tool, however well intended, will not fix whatever problems these well-meaning project managers face (other than producing a status report). It is merely a bandage that makes the current situation more tolerable, makes it easier to create status reports, thereby supporting a questionable process. The real question is, "What value do the reports provide to the customer?" Really, no direct value. So we should ask, "Why are we doing them?" In this particular case, it is fairly clear that we are doing them because we have a lot of work-in-process we need to manage.

Using the "Five Whys," we should continue by asking, "But why do we have all this WIP?" (Answer: Because we're doing large batches of work that require coordination.) And "Why are we doing large batches of work?" (Answer: Because we are following a Waterfall process.) We come to see that these reports are actually an accommodation of following an inefficient process and trying to reduce the pain that results.

How do we solve this? Agile methods would not require such a detailed reporting system and would make coordinating resources simpler. Agile methods also provide visual controls that remove the need for the wasted, redundant work of creating status reports in the first place.

As a manager in a Lean-Agile enterprise, you must acquire this new way of thinking—get at the root cause of the problem first, to ensure that the tool is adding value, and *not* merely bandaging over a more fundamental issue. Lean thinking guides us to look first to the value stream and commit to continuously eliminating anything that does not add value—from the flow of ideas to delivered solutions coming out of our organization.

Agile Software Development is Not Anarchy

There is a large contingent in the Agile community that has embraced Agility as a way to throw off the "tyranny" of management. We are not in this contingent. We believe that management is an essential part of any Agile transition. When undertaking an Agile transition, it is imperative that management be involved. This is what convinces us that the only viable Lean-Agile transition strategy is one with top-down leadership and bottom-up implementation. Lean management provides us with managers setting visions and outcomes while coaching teams and improving the organizational structure within which they work. Management creates the context in which the team works. This context is set according to many factors, but it must be sensitive to the team's needs.

We believe a Scrum-alone approach, even supplemented with Scrum-of-Scrums, is not sufficient. Consider managing a group of firefighters in action against an intensive blaze. Let's say we have a crew of 100 firefighters organized into ten teams of ten. We would assign each of these teams to attack a different area of the forest fire. Scrum would suggest that each team do the best they can and coordinate efforts with a Scrum of Scrums (probably with walkie-talkies in this instance). Lean would have a leader at the top giving objectives to the ten teams and keeping them coordinated. The manager would expect each team to organize themselves for the best way to fight the fire in their own situation—but the objectives would be set from above (the manager). No micromanagement here—rather, managers set a vision, giving direction and coaching as needed. Note the difference if one of the right things to do is let one section burn so as to work on others. The "Scrum" firefighters may feel abandoned—their part of the forest got burned. But the "Lean" firefighters are more explicitly part of a larger group and more easily identify with the bigger picture that was being managed.

There is no question that there are managers out there who are, unfortunately, somewhat similar to the pointy-haired boss in Scott Adams's *Dilbert*. Lean says we must transform these bosses, not merely get them out of the way. Compare this with the original intent of the Scrum's Daily Meeting:

> People who are not committed to the project and are not accountable for deliverables at the meeting do not get to talk. They are excess overhead for the meeting.

Management is not excluded as long as they are accountable for deliverables. Later, Ken Schwaber and Mike Beedle (Schwaber and Beedle 2002, 40) define the Daily Meeting as composed only of team members, explicitly removing management from it—and subtly implying management is not accountable for deliverables. Whether intended or not, the result we've seen is that Scrum teams tend to insulate themselves from management. This is done with both the Daily Meetings, where management is excluded or at least derided (calling them "chickens"), and by having the Scrum Master essentially play the role a good manager can play without the HR responsibilities.

Lack of Management May Equal Lack of Success

Scrum works by exposing inadequacies or dysfunctions within an organization's product and development practices. The intention of Scrum is to make them transparent so the organization can fix them. Unfortunately, this seems to happen less frequently than one would like. The Scrum community generally concedes that about three in four of organizations implementing Scrum will not succeed in getting the benefits from it that they hoped for. The explanation is that many organizations change Scrum in order to accommodate the inadequacies or dysfunctions in the organization rather than solving their organizational problems.[3] The implication is that Scrum gives them the tools to see but not to change.

It is not enough simply to expose organizational inadequacies. Even if the issue is somehow exposed, will you notice it? And if you notice it, will you feel that you can do something about it? And if you feel that you *can* do something about it, will you feel that management supports you? And will the problem actually get fixed? There is much to be done between initial awareness and ultimate resolution. The management involvement espoused by Lean-Agile methods provides insights into solving many of these challenges that standard Agile approaches don't address.

It would be like your stockbroker saying, "Here is your monthly statement. Notice how it exposes every bad decision you've made in the stock market. Now, to fix things, you need to stop making these bad decisions. You need to inspect when you bought stocks at the wrong time and adapt to make the proper purchasing decisions. What I absolutely don't suggest you do is accommodate your bad decisions by continuing to buy high and sell low." Apologies for the comparison—it is both ridiculous and not fair. But it exposes the fallacy of saying that because you see a problem you recognize it as something you can fix or that you know how to fix it.

We believe that many of the dysfunctions that Scrum teams run into are in the organizational structure of the enterprise within which they exist. For example, staff may be organized around roles, which can make it difficult to create teams that can swarm on problems. Sometimes these organizational issues are easy to see and not that hard to fix. But other times they are hard to see. Or they are accepted as "just the way things are" and not as something to be worked on.

---

3. Schwaber, AgileCollab 2008.

Many of those that can be worked on require management's involvement. Managers must see, firsthand, how the teams are being impacted by their policies. This will enable them to make necessary changes. Unfortunately, Scrum's basic practices and roles tend to insulate teams from management. Avoiding bad management by insulating yourself from it is an accommodation of the problem. Ironically, this isolation does not help first-line managers learn to avoid micromanagement. This insulation is an accommodation of an impediment—the very thing Scrum suggests you cannot do.

A Personal Story, Alan Shalloway

Some people are natural managers; I am not one of them. Historically, I have always micromanaged. Because I am good in a crisis (often creating and then solving them), when one occurred I would tend to jump in and tell my team how fix it. I knew that this behavior was inhibiting the team's growth, so I tried delegating—letting the team figure out how to do things on their own—often with very poor results.

I was really abdicating via delegation. I needed to find a way to let the team figure out the solution but remain involved enough to ensure that it would be a good one. Fortunately, Lean management provides a way to do this. With visual controls, I can see the team's process—I can see how the team is doing at any time—and I can see the team's outcomes. If the team gets into trouble, I can actively coach them to improve their results without telling them what to do. Lean gives me a way to become a better manager without resorting to old habits.

Improving Management with Lean Thinking

We all have seen how difficult it is to change habits. Tales abound about developers learning proper coding techniques only to revert to familiar, but poor, habits when crunch time occurs. This is true of people in general—when a crisis is on, we return to old habits. The same is true for managers. Many managers got to where they are by being more capable than others in a crunch. When the chips were down, they often were the ones who led the way, who surmounted the challenge and achieved the goal. Now, they are managing people who need to be able to do this. One of their jobs is to coach people, to empower their staff so they'll be able to achieve results. When things are going smoothly, most decent managers can do this. However, when crunch time comes, it is all too easy for managers to just jump in and fix the problem.

This isn't a good idea: It results in micromanagement and inhibits the team from learning and creating their own solutions. By providing visual controls, however, a Lean manager can see the team's results and work with the team to improve them. Coaching to achieve the needed outcomes provides a way for managers to keep their eye on the end result but enable the team to get there.

Summary

Lead from a belief system that always seeks to maximize the amount of completed, high-quality, value-added work coming out of your organization. Using Lean and business-driven principles, this work should always be prioritized by highest return, whether determined by profit, sales, client importance, or any other factor determined by the product champion. Resist the urge to keep people busy. Knowledge of queuing theory helps reinforce the importance of cross-functional teams that have the capacity to retool rapidly based on changing priorities.

Try This

These exercises are best done as a conversation with someone in your organization. After each exercise, ask each other if there are any actions either of you can take to improve your situation.

- Think of a time that a manager was able to provide an outside perspective that helped solve a problem that the team was mired in. Are there ways to facilitate this happening more often?

- Consider when process was added because of a failed or challenged software delivery. What was leadership's role in determining the process? Were true root causes addressed or were organizational barriers too large to overcome? Were impacts to finishing prioritized work considered? Was cycle time considered? Why or why not?

- Do layers of process make it easier or harder to minimize work-in-process?

- If a process requires traceability, do you consider it a good process? Why or why not?

- How can leadership in your organization bring visibility to completion of prioritized work?

Recommended Reading

The following works offer helpful insights into the topics of this chapter.

Kennedy, Harmon, and Minnock. 2008. *Ready, Set, Dominate: Implement Toyota's Set-based Learning for Developing Products and Nobody Can Catch You.* Richmond, VA: Oaklea Press.

Mann. 2005. *Creating a Lean Culture: Tools to Sustain Lean Conversions.* New York: Productivity Press.

Reinertsen. 1997. *Managing the Design Factory.* New York: Free Press.

Schwaber. 2008. *AgileCollab.* www.agilecollab.com/interview-with-ken-schwaber (accessed June 19, 2009).

Schwaber and Beedle. 2002. *Agile Software Development with Scrum.* Upper Saddle River, NJ: Prentice Hall.

CHAPTER 12

The Product Coordination Team

"In theory, theory and practice are the same. In practice, they are different."
—Attributed to many

IN THIS CHAPTER

This chapter describes the challenge of teams coordinating with each other. Self-interest lies at the root of this problem: Teams (rightly) focus on their immediate needs and work. The Scrum-of-Scrums is one approach that many organizations try. It can work when teams have natural affinity but when there are competing needs, it is not effective. The Product Coordination Team (PCT) is a better alternative that works in all situations. In a sense, the PCT acts as a product champion for cross-team coordination issues.

Takeaways

Key insights to take away from this chapter include

- The Scrum-of-Scrums approach does not work well when teams do not have common motivations or interests to bind them.

- The Product Coordination Team is chartered to focus on cross-team issues with the authority to place stories in individual teams' product backlogs when needed.

- PCT membership comprises both permanent and rotating members.

- The work of the PCT continues across the iteration cycles.

Getting Teams to Work Together

Many organizations attempting to scale Scrum to the enterprise ask how to get teams to work together. The standard approach is to use a Scrum technique called the "Scrum-of-Scrums." The notion of Scrum-of-Scrums is to have members of different teams meet regularly to foster collaboration, communication, and shared requirements. While we have used this technique, and seen others use it successfully to coordinate teams that were closely related, more often we have seen companies struggle with it when they were attempting to coordinate teams across an organization or teams that have disparate goals. In other words, if you have a large-project team with a common goal, Scrum-of-Scrums may work well; however, if you have several project teams with different goals, we believe the approach is fundamentally flawed.

Scrum-of-Scrums

The Scrum-of-Scrums is a coordination team that is composed of a representative (usually a technical person) from each team. They gather on a regular basis to discuss issues of collaboration across the teams. These meetings are typically held weekly but may be held more often as required. A typical agenda for these meetings is:

1. During the first 15 minutes, each participant answers four questions:

   a. What has your team done since we last met?
   b. What will your team do before we meet again?
   c. Is anything slowing down your team or in its way?
   d. Are you about to put anything in another team's way?

2. The rest of the meeting is spent resolving problems and discussing issues on the teams' backlogs.

Factors that Work against Scrum-of-Scrums

What works against the Scrum-of-Scrums? There are three factors: team perspective, team motivation, and human nature.[1] Teams usually take a

---

1. We are very much pragmatists. Theoretically, there is no reason that Scrum-of-Scrums can't work in many of the places it is attempted. But we are more concerned with what happens when teams actually use it. These factors get in the way enough of the time to make it a poor practice.

local perspective—their work is somehow more important or otherwise different from the work of the other teams. A common expression is "can't see the forest for the trees." Certainly, they are motivated to focus on their own work because most companies measure and reward people based on the work they do directly or, possibly, based on the success of their own projects. Rarely are rewards based on how their department—or how the company as a whole—operates. This tends to focus them on their own needs, not on the needs of other teams that may need their help. Thus, when a Scrum-of-Scrums is just about sharing information, it may work well because there is no conflict of interest. But when it comes to coordinating work—when one team has to help another at the expense of its own work—the Scrum-of-Scrums does not work.

Why can't teams overcome this bias? Why don't team members recognize that when they help each other, they are impacting the company as a whole to do better? Why can't they see the big picture? Is it mostly the fault of how they are measured? Very often, but that is not the only reason. People tend to identify more closely with the people they work directly with than they do with others in the company. This is readily observable. If you have ever been a member of a large organization, you can easily see this. People are most interested in how their immediate coworkers are doing, then how their department is doing, then their division, and finally their company. This is just human nature.

Scrum-of-Scrums fights against this basic trait. It assumes that putting individuals from various teams together in a loose confederation creates a bigger view of the organization across all of the teams. There is little evidence that this works in practice, particularly when self-interest is involved.

A different approach is usually needed. A team comprised of members with the same perspectives, motivations and purposes must be formed. You should not expect a person to be effective when they are drawn by two sets of loyalties. People just don't work that way.

The Challenge of Coordinating Teams

Consider the four teams in Figure 12.1. The two teams at the bottom of the diagram are pulling from exactly the same product backlog. While they might share some common interests, as a whole the four teams won't have the same vested interest in the bigger picture. For example, let's consider how multiple teams working together may view these issues:

- Progress across teams

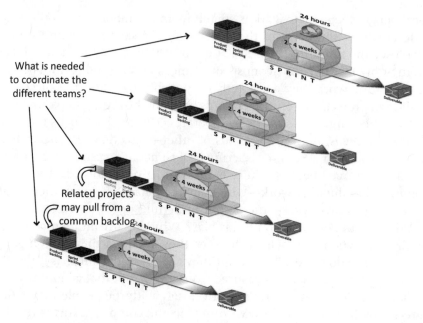

Figure 12.1   Several teams working together

- Requirements that need multiple teams to implement them
- Technical dependencies between teams
- Common components that are used by several teams
- The need for one team to modify their code to assist another team
- Code shared by the teams
- Knowledge one team has that another team needs

Their views on these issues are addressed as follows:

- **Progress across teams.** Management needs to see the progress that teams are making as a whole. Consolidated burn-down and burn-up charts present most of this needed information. However, management often looks for a more comprehensive and aligned view of the entire operation. A meeting of teams can be a good approach for this combined view. A Scrum-of-Scrums works well here because no conflict exists among the team members.

- **Requirements that involve multiple teams to implement them.** Very often, multiple teams are required in order to implement a particular story. For example, consider a development organization that has a database team. Stories requiring changes to the database may require both the team writing the story and the team responsible for maintaining the database. A Scrum-of-Scrums often works well here because the teams are coming together to solve a shared problem.

- **Technical dependencies between teams.** Frequently, teams use software that is developed by other teams. The APIs for these service classes need to be discussed by both teams. The teams need to coordinate with each other while the modules are being developed. Teams need to warn one another when they are about to change a component or function that another group needs to use. This avoids what we call "clobberation."[2] The Scrum-of-Scrums approach has a mixed track record here. If the team providing the code to be used functions as a service organization to the teams that are using their code, Scrum-of-Scrums works well because it is a good method for both groups to get their jobs done. However, a conflict of interest may arise if what one team wants adversely impacts the team that is writing the code. The Scrum-of-Scrums does not help resolve such conflicts.

- **Common components that are used by several teams.** Large organizations require common components for several different teams. Some sort of collaboration to identify and define these is necessary. When a component team is set up to meet this need, Scrum-of-Scrums can be a good way to communicate between the component team and the others since it helps all of them get their jobs done.

- **The need for one team to modify their code to assist another team.** Teams often build software that is similar, if not exact duplicates. Collaboration between teams is necessary to avoid duplication. This is particularly important in Agile environments because software evolves over time. This means teams must collaborate as software is developed so that they notice when duplication (or almost duplication) is being produced. The challenge comes when

---

2. "Clobberation" is a term coined by Alan Shalloway to describe the effect one team has on another team with which it is collaborating when the first team does not communicate changes it is making that will adversely affect the second team.

one team ("Team A") writes something that another team ("Team B") could use if only Team A's code were modified just a little. If Team A is too busy with other things, Team B often resorts to copying and pasting the code or rewriting the code completely. Scrum-of-Scrums may find this a potential case for re-use, but even if it does, there is no guarantee that the people on Team A will modify the code since they may be under pressure to do their own work.

- **Code shared by the teams.** Sometimes duplication happens when one team builds something and another team could use a variant of it. If an up-front design approach were being used, a common interface might be settled on early. But with emergent design, these interfaces must be discovered when the second variant is needed. Collaboration among different teams is necessary to see this. This results in the same situation as the previous case: One group needs to update their code for another's use.

- **One team has knowledge that another team needs.** Very often, one team needs knowledge that another team has. Unfortunately, they do not always know which information it is. Frequent communication across teams can assist with this. While Scrum-of-Scrums may work here, it is often hit or miss.·

In theory, Scrum-of-Scrums should work because it provides teams a way to communicate with each other and all members want overall success. But the reality is that Scrum-of-Scrums does not create a bigger view and requires people to step outside their immediate concerns and look at the bigger picture—one they may not agree with across the teams. Something more is needed.

The Product Coordination Team

In all of this, the root cause for teams not collaborating is that their perspective is too narrow, focused on their own local needs. To achieve collaboration, they need a perspective that works with their self-interest.

What is needed is a coordination structure that is fundamentally focused on the larger organization's perspective. Rather than a loose confederation, like the Scrum-of-Scrums, it is chartered to look more broadly: It identifies and prioritizes stories involving cross-team issues and assigns stories to other teams to do the work when it is most appropriate for them. We call this the "Product Coordination Team" (PCT).

In a sense, the Product Coordination Team becomes another product champion for the team, one that prioritizes those stories that involve not the product the teams are building, but the way teams are working together.

While there are many similarities between the PCT and the Scrum-of-Scrums, the dynamics are quite different. The PCT is focused on a higher view: "optimizing the whole." The PCT is a true team, composed of members from different teams, unified to reach a common goal. Scrum-of-Scrums tends to devolve into individual teams representing their own team's issues in the bigger picture.

Case Study: Product Coordination Team

GROUP PROFILE: Web Applications for large healthcare insurance company

CHALLENGES: Multiple scrum teams unable to coordinate using Scrum-of-Scrums

INSIGHT: Multiple cross-functional teams were having coordination challenges. As they pulled work from merged backlogs, teams began to step on one another as they touched the same code baseline. A Product Coordination Team was created, using architects and technical leads. The multiple teams synchronized their iterations to start and stop on the same schedule. This enabled the teams to demonstrate, plan, and retrospect together. Putting the multiple teams together (with the PCT present), enabled the teams to present their upcoming iteration plans to each other. It was much easier to identify opportunities for encapsulating effort when the teams presented their committed stories. As the PCT identified these duplicate efforts, they created stories that were distributed to the appropriate teams so that each group could safely focus on implementing code with minimum overlap. This model also enabled the teams to recognize when they were potentially duplicating effort, so the PCT was able to guide effective abstraction so that duplicate code was avoided.

Product Coordination Team Membership

The PCT is composed of both permanent and rotating members.

- **Permanent Members.** Permanent members are useful to maintain consistency as well as to ensure the team's purpose is understood.

- **Rotating Members.** Including rotating members from development teams helps keep the PCT from becoming too removed from the needs of the development teams; it also means it has members who readily identify with the development teams. The PCT is first and foremost a service team. Although it will be creating stories for the teams to work on, its purpose is really to improve how the development teams function as a whole. These members stay for a certain number of iterations or one to two months.

- **Planning Members.** Planning members come from the development teams and participate on the PCT only during the iteration planning sessions.

Product Coordination Team Guidelines

First and foremost, the Product Coordination Team is about maximizing business value. This comes from:

- Determining and then coordinating how the company can maximize the technical synergy among the development teams. In particular, it is looking for shared components, avoiding redundancy, assisting emergent design, and avoiding "clobberation."
- Validating elevation plans (see chapter 7, Lean-Agile Release Planning).

The activities of the PCT vary during the iteration. Tables 12.1 and 12.2 offer some basic guidelines for a Product Coordination Team.

Table 12.1   Activities of the Product Coordination Team

Time Period	Activities
Day before iteration planning *or* Before the first planning day (if the teams being coordinated plan on different days)	The PCT meets with the product champions of each team to discuss possible coordinating stories. This meeting is attended by all members of the PCT, including at least one person from each development team that doesn't have a permanent or rotating PCT member.
	Discuss the stories that each team needs to do. If any one of these stories is directly associated with a story already on the backlog, it can be made dependent upon that story's being done.
	Note that although the next iteration's stories are not certain, just before the iteration it is reasonably clear what the team will do next.

Table 12.1   Activities of the Product Coordination Team, *continued*

Time Period	Activities
During iteration planning	Each PCT member now goes to their corresponding team's planning session. At this point they present the stories the PCT has created to their associated team. New PCT stories may also be created at this time.
After iteration planning	The members of the PCT get together to review what has taken place and see if any new stories are needed or if any stories can be removed or deferred.
During the iterations	Permanent and rotating members meet with teams on an as needed basis to look ahead for future coordinating stories.

Table 12.2   Guidelines for the PCT

Topic	Guidelines
Authority	The PCT does not have any command-and-control authority over the teams it is coordinating; however, they can place stories on any team's product backlog at any place on the backlog. In many ways the PCT and the product champions fill similar roles—both determine what needs to happen next. The PCT acts to prioritize the work required between teams while the product champion prioritizes work for a team.
Architecture	The PCT is not an architecture team, although it is often composed of many people from an architecture team if one exists. The PCT is not a vehicle for forcing particular design approaches onto teams.
Over-committing teams	The PCT can only place stories on teams' product backlogs. They cannot tell the teams they have to do "just one more story."
Doing the work themselves	The PCT typically should not do the work themselves. Instead, they write stories that one team needs another team to do.

Mentoring

The PCT can also provide the framework for a mentoring organization. Typically, the people on the PCT are of personality types that would make good mentors. They can also become the basis for a community of practice and other knowledge management/sharing methods.

Summary

This chapter describes the challenge of teams coordinating with each other. Self-interest lies at the root of this problem: Teams (rightly) focus on their immediate needs and work. It is hard for them to look at larger issues. This is not a bad thing, it is a human thing. The product coordinating team (PCT) is a true team-of-teams that has the proper perspective and charter to focus on cross-team issues. Membership involves both permanent and rotating positions. In a sense, the PCT becomes a product champion for cross-team coordination issues. While it is similar to a Scrum-of-Scrums, the dynamics are very different.

Try This

These exercises are best done as a conversation with someone in your organization. After each exercise, ask each other if there are any actions either of you can take to improve your situation.

- What are some challenges you have seen in getting teams to coordinate with each other?

- Who would be likely candidates for a PCT for our projects?

- Discuss how metrics in your organization assist team collaboration or hurt it.

CHAPTER 13

Software Architecture and Design's Role in Lean-Agile Software Development

"If builders built buildings the way programmers wrote programs, the first woodpecker that came along would destroy civilization." —Gerald Weinberg

"Prediction is very difficult, especially about the future." —Niels Bohr

IN THIS CHAPTER

At the beginning of the Agile movement, software architecture and design was often considered irrelevant. Most Agile advocates have since recanted this notion; however, the damage still lingers. In Agile development, proper software architecture and design is still not well understood. This chapter discusses the changing role of software architecture and design, from a framework that holds pieces together to a framework that enables change as requirements evolve. We also discuss the need for design patterns and test-driven development.

Software architecture and design is somewhat of a technical issue and this is not a technical book. Nevertheless, it is important to touch on the topic because it is an essential aspect of Lean-Agile software development. There are a number of excellent books that cover software design in more detail, such as *Design Patterns Explained: A New Perspective on Object-Oriented Design* (Shalloway and Trott 2004), *Emergent Design: The Evolutionary Nature of Professional Software Development* (Bain 2008), *Agile Software Development: Principles, Patterns and Practices*

(Martin 2002), and the forthcoming *Essential Skills for the Agile Developer: A Guide to Better Programming and Design* (Shalloway and Bain 2010).

Note: In this chapter, we will refer to software architecture and design simply as "software design."

Takeaways

Key insights from this chapter include

- Software design is not static; it must evolve as our understanding evolves.

- Developers must attend to both design quality and automated testing in order to provide software systems that can change quickly when needed.

Avoiding Over- and Under-Design

None of us is very good at anticipating future needs.[1] This leads to a common concern among developers: how to avoid over-designing and under-designing the system. That is, while you know that you don't want to overbuild your system, you don't want to be hacking in your solutions either. The remedy is

> Build only what you need at the moment and build it in a way that allows for it to be changed readily as you discover new issues.

Most developers have had an experience in which they were given some unexpected requirements that were difficult for the system to accommodate. The pain of going through this once or twice leads most of us to try to anticipate what will be needed in the future, which invariably leads to building more than is truly necessary. That leads to systems that are more complex than they need to be. And over the long term, complexity slows teams down.

---

1. Alan likes to say that "we are all pre-cognitively impaired." Every one of us is limited in our ability to predict the future.

To handle this problem, developers need to be able to do the following:

- Write code quickly.

- Make changes to code without breaking it.

- Be able to change code safely; that is, if you break it, know you've broken it.

Doing this enables developers to add functionality to systems in a fast, safe, efficient manner. Following are three questions you can use to self-assess whether your team can safely and efficiently change code.

- Can you easily change your code?

- If you change it, are you likely to break it?

- If you break it, can you automatically detect the break?

People who are new to Agile might think that Agile compounds the problem of modifying code because it is geared toward making quick changes. But in truth, changing code has become a way of life no matter how you do development. Requirements come at development teams much faster than they used to. The speed of change in the software industry has accelerated so much that a continuously evolving system is a way of life. If we aren't improving our system continuously, we are already falling behind.

Agile highlights the problem because of its emphasis on effectiveness. It has become common practice in Agile approaches to require automated regression tests so as to detect the consequences of changes. This is good practice for safety and for efficiency.

But automated acceptance tests are only part of the answer to changing code quickly. Accommodating change also requires good design. This is why design patterns have become an essential part of any competent developer's toolbox. Unfortunately, design patterns are little understood (or, more correctly, largely misunderstood).[2]

From what we've seen in working with dozens of clients, we fear our industry does not measure up to the test. We say this because of the almost universal answer we get to the following question:

---

2. Improving legacy code to handle change is also essential to consider but that is beyond the scope of this book. *Working Effectively with Legacy Code* (Feathers 2004) provides an excellent treatment of this important topic.

Imagine you are working on a well established system and you need to add some new functionality. Where will you spend most of your time—in writing the new functionality or in integrating the functionality into your existing system?

For the past ten years, we've been asking this question; consistently—95 percent of the time—the answer is, "integrating it in."

Most organizations will not pass this test. By and large, developers do not write their code to be changeable. Instead, they focus on implementing the task at hand and don't recognize when they should put in a design layer, or when they shouldn't. Putting layers in your code whenever possible is a path to overly complex code; but not putting in layers when you need to is a path to code that is both difficult to change and brittle.

Designing for Change

So how do you build for change?

One approach is to use the simple question, "How would I design this if I found out later that however I designed it now was not the best way?" Our experience in design-patterns training leads us to believe that most developers do not like to think abstractly. Combine that with the pressure they are under and it isn't surprising that often they just deal with the task at hand instead of reflecting on what a general solution might be. Given time to reflect, they unfortunately often go the other way—and overbuild to handle anything that might come up. The trick is to realize at the beginning that it is unlikely you'll make the right decision—that is, you must write your code so that it is able to handle change, but it is unlikely you'll know how it will change. There is too much unknown and too much to learn—not only by the developers, but also by the users or whoever is speaking for them. As the system progresses through the development process, more ideas will come to the fore. The key is to write high-quality code so that the system is changeable, and full acceptance tests so that it is *safely* changeable. Management needs to support and encourage teams to do this.

This attitude is based on a characteristic of programming that most developers have come to understand:

Other than for exceptionally complex functions, more effort is typically required in handling the coupling of a function to other elements in the code than in writing the function itself.

Doing Just Enough Up Front

A (fortunately dying) myth in Agile software is that it is bad to do any sort of design work up front. While Agile grew up partly as a counter to over-design (big design up front—BDUF), no design is going too far. From a design point of view, what we need early on is the big picture so that we can identify the main concepts in the problem domain and determine how they relate to each other. This gives us "just enough" detail to create a conceptual framework within which to think of the problem domain. Then, as we become aware of new concepts, we can see how to add them, how they fit in. In contrast, BDUF can actually obscure the big-picture view by giving us too many details and too much complexity.

If you are interested in how to create a high-level design that identifies the concepts in a problem domain, see the chapters on Commonality and Variability Analysis and the Analysis Matrix in *Design Patterns Explained: A New Perspective on Object-Oriented Design* by two of this book's authors (Shalloway and Trott). These chapters cover some of the basics of identifying the essential application architecture that should be discovered prior to actually writing code.

The Role of Design in Software

The role of design in software is to make it easy to change code, to minimize the effect of changes in the system. This can be done through a combination of decoupling (isolation), encapsulation, and avoiding redundancy. In other words, the purpose of software architecture is not to define a place for each of the pieces as much as it is to handle properly the dependencies of the pieces.

Software design needs to evolve as more is learned about what the program is supposed to do. We inject better designs as needed, following what we call "Just-in-Time Design." This avoids over-building designs in anticipation of what may be needed later, because developers often over-anticipate what is needed.

The Role of Management in Software Design

Management's role is mostly to support the software development team while providing a vision of what needs to be built. Part of this support is to help the team focus on what they need to do without overly pressuring them to cut corners, especially when it comes to creating automated tests. This does not mean that management should just quietly accept everything development teams want to do. Management needs to ensure that there is a cost justification for development's efforts. However, they should trust the development team's judgment when it comes to how to build quality.

Summary

The purpose of software design is not to build a framework within which all things can fit nicely. It is to define the relationships between the major concepts of the system so that when they change or new requirements emerge, the impact of the changes required is limited to local modifications.

Try This

These exercises are best done as a conversation with someone in your organization. After each exercise, ask each other if there are any actions either of you can take to improve your situation.

- As a manager:
  - Ask yourself, "What is the business value of having a flexible system?
  - Do you trust your team to build only what they need?
  - Why or why not?

- As a developer:
  - Ask yourself what basis you use for deciding to improve the infrastructure of your system.

- Do you feel supported by management to build in the right amount of quality to your software?
- Do you feel management understands the value of quality in software?

Recommended Reading

The following works offer helpful insights into the topics of this chapter.

Bain. 2008. *Emergent Design: The Evolutionary Nature of Professional Software Development*. Boston: Addison-Wesley.

Feathers. 2004. *Working Effectively with Legacy Code*. Upper Saddle River, NJ: Prentice Hall.

Martin. 2002. *Agile Software Development: Principles, Patterns and Practices*. Upper Saddle River, NJ: Prentice Hall.

Shalloway and Bain. Forthcoming, 2010. *Essential Skills for the Agile Developer: A Guide to Better Programming and Design*. Boston: Addison-Wesley.

Shalloway and Trott. 2004. *Design Patterns Explained: A New Perspective on Object-Oriented Design*. Boston: Addison-Wesley.

PART III

Looking Back,
Looking Forward

"I can't change the direction of the wind, but I can adjust my sails to always reach my destination." —Jimmy Dean

---

IN THIS PART

To offer a more holistic view of Lean-Agile thinking, this part offers some of the key insights we have gathered while coaching and training Lean-Agile. These stories are based on the principles we have talked about throughout the book. With any new way of thinking, it is always good to see that it is grounded in the real world; this is especially important with Lean-Agile. The bottom line for Lean-Agile is to build the most important items as quickly as you can and with high quality. This will result in quicker time to market, more value to customers, and lower cost.

This part also offers suggestions about where to go next.

CHAPTER 14

Seeing Lean

"What's in a name? That which we call a rose by any other name would smell as sweet." —William Shakespeare

IN THIS CHAPTER

This chapter summarizes the ideas of this book—where we have been and where Lean and Agile fit in the context of software development. Lean may have its origins in manufacturing—Toyota is the greatest example—but it applies much more widely. We approach Lean by viewing it as a combination of three bodies of knowledge:

- Lean "science" (principles of pull, theory of constraints, flow)

- Lean management (management and teams can work together)

- Lean knowledge stewardship (how we can learn, coach, and keep our knowledge alive)

It is this approach that lets us apply Lean so powerfully to software product development. We include several descriptions of cases from our consulting experience that illustrate this.

This chapter shows how Lean's mantra of fast-flexible-flow helps to create a better development organization; then it concludes with suggestions for the next steps you can take to apply it to your organization.

Takeaways

Key insights to take away from this chapter include

- Delivering smaller, well-defined features faster results in greater efficiency for teams.

- Fast delivery forces product managers to cooperate with each other.

- Lean is based on a century of practical application in a variety of contexts, and it continues to evolve.

- Lean combines many levels of thinking.

- Factors that improve flow include

  - Working on smaller, well-defined, high-value features
  - Limiting the amount of work-in-process to the capacity of the teams
  - Removing delays wherever possible
  - Looking to the system for causes of waste and continuously improving the process

Toyota: The First Great Example of Lean

In the 1950s, several forces combined to help Toyota create Lean. Toyota faced a difficult situation. They didn't have a lot of experience in making cars. They were competing against the United States—the powerhouse of mass production at the time. Rather than competing directly, Toyota was forced to look closer to home at niche markets, which meant they could not build many units at any one time. This required making small runs of several models instead of huge runs of a few models. Impediments to this were enormous. For example, the turnover time for die-cast equipment took weeks. To compete, these times had to be reduced.

They did not know exactly what to do.

Ironically, this lack of knowledge was an advantage. They knew they had to rethink everything; and because they didn't have a large investment in what they knew, they could invent knowledge from the ground up.

One more force was at work: The U.S. Army brought W. Edwards Deming—one of the great pioneers of quality improvement—to Japan to help with reindustrialization. The Toyota production system (TPS) was built on his ideas.

Taiichi Ohno, the implementer of Lean at Toyota, says[1]

> The basis of the Toyota production system (TPS) is the absolute elimination of waste. The two pillars needed to support the system are:
> - Just-in-Time
> - Autonomation, or automation with a human touch

Just-in-Time means that, in a flow process, the right parts needed for assembly reach the assembly line at exactly the time they are needed and only in the required amounts.

Autonomation requires processes to run smoothly. When they don't, don't just fix the symptom, but fix the root cause of the problem. Whenever there is an impediment, remove it. This is why management must be involved in autonomation: Almost always, root causes touch multiple systems or cross organizational barriers. This does not mean that managers fix the problems themselves or tell their staffs what to do, but, rather, managers lead and coach their teams in implementing change.

As it evolved, the TPS, founded on Deming's philosophy, was composed of three parts: Lean practices, quality management, and continuous learning and improvement. This is shown in Figure 14.1.

Lean is focused on customer value; however, what that means depends on the context. In manufacturing, you more or less know what product the customer wants; the focus is on delivering that value (the product) to the customer as the customer expects it. On the other hand, in product development, you do not necessarily know what the customer wants; your focus is on learning, on improving your understanding of what the customer wants and needs. One of the brilliant insights at Toyota was that Lean principles are implemented differently in manufacturing than they are in product development.

This gave rise to another great example of Lean: the Toyota Product Development System, which is a better example for us in software development.

Let's consider Toyota as one of the classic examples of Lean thinking. What is important is not exactly *what they did* but *how they applied Lean principles to their context*. Looking at what they did in the Toyota Product Development System will give better insight to our sort of work.

---

1. (Ohno 1988, page 4)

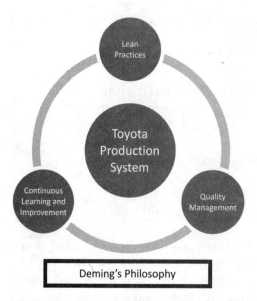

Figure 14.1   The Toyota Production System, built on the Deming foundation

For example, one of the practices frequently mentioned in the Toyota Product Development System is "Set-Based Concurrent Engineering" (SBCE), which is a very good risk-mitigation practice. In building physical products, establishing the right approach is often critical and difficult. What about in software development? Don't ask, "How can we apply SBCE to software?" Instead, ask, "What is the best *risk management strategy* we can apply to building software products?" (Risk mitigation is the objective behind the SBCE practice.) This may lead you to a different approach; you may decide that SBCE still makes sense, but you may choose to rely on proper encapsulation of unknown issues or other means.

Three Bodies of Lean

Over the last 60 years, Lean has been applied in many organizations and contexts including, lately, software development. We have learned to view Lean not as a collection of specific practices, but as a combination of three important bodies of knowledge (see Figure 14.2):

- Lean science (principles of pull, theory of constraints, flow)

- Lean management (management and teams can work together)

- Lean knowledge stewardship (how we can learn, coach, and keep alive our knowledge)

Lean Science

Lean Science lays out the rules that Lean tells us to follow in product development, including:

- Just-in-Time
- Utilization theory
  - Small queues and batch sizes
  - Limit WIP
  - Little's law[2]
  - Causes of thrashing
- Pull management
- Real options

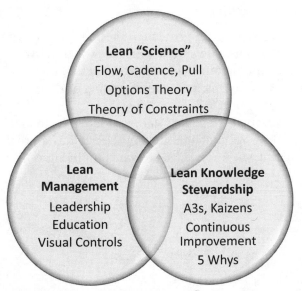

Figure 14.2   Lean thinking is based on science, management, and knowledge stewardship

---

2. Little's law establishes the relationship between cycle time, WIP, and throughput: Cycle time = WIP/throughput, and the key insight is that to reduce cycle time, start by reducing WIP.

We call it Lean science to underscore that there are rules (like gravity), and we violate them at our own peril. Learning these rules increases our ability to accomplish what we want. And, like the scientific method, we can make hypotheses about how our work relates to these rules and then test those hypotheses by seeing the results of our work.

Lean Management

Lean Management emphasizes the responsibility managers have for their team's performance. Far from being a micromanager, the manager teaches the team to implement a new process, which includes helping the team discover the specific work-flow they need to follow. Managers become leaders, coaches, and trainers. They are not "servant leaders," in that they have to take a proactive approach to helping their teams. Perhaps it is best to say that they are fellow workers who are responsible to lead.

Because Lean has a science we can build on, it provides an opportunity for management to help their staff both learn this science and apply it.

Lean Knowledge Stewardship

Lean's focus on continuous process improvement touches on many aspects of development, including understanding how product/software development works; understanding our own problem domain, our own challenges, and how they relate to this; and understanding our customers' (either internal or external) needs.

There is clearly a lot of learning taking place here—a lot of information that must be transferred. How we manage this knowledge has a great impact on our effectiveness. Lean knowledge stewardship includes the proper use of:

- A3s

- Kaizens

- After Action Reviews (AARs) and retrospections

- Practice of the Five Whys, getting to root cause

- Value stream mapping

We won't go into more detail, as there are a great many resources already available. However, it should be clear that obtaining, retaining, and moving knowledge around is critical. Teaching people how to learn is just as critical.

Insights from Lean-Agile Coaches

It is perhaps helpful to have a higher-level perspective. Let's turn to real life. During our courses and coaching engagements, we have had some "Aha!" moments that have given us significantly deeper insights into Lean-Agile thinking. We hope the illustrations in this section will help you, too.

The stories are real but, of course, names have been left out to protect confidentiality.

Focusing on One Project at a Time

The context and insight include the following:

- **Company profile**: Develops software used by insurance companies

- **Challenges**: Lots of projects, sometimes little clarity on requirements, looming deadlines, overworked development team

- **Insight**: One software development director said, "I have two projects. One is for a key client who knows what they want, and the enhancements we are working on will make a big difference to them. The other client is not as big, but more importantly, aren't as clear about what they want. I see that instead of having my team working on both projects at the same time, I should have them work on the project for the client who has clarity, but keep the work focused on the Minimal Marketable Features so that I will get it done quickly. In the meantime, our product managers can be talking to the other client to get better clarity. Then we can focus on them. At the least we'll get value to our more important client quicker while being more efficient."

Initiating Fewer Projects Instead of Imploring Teams to Work Better

The context and insight include the following:

- **Company profile**: Health insurance company

- **Challenges**: Lots of projects, non-co-located, non-matrixed teams

- **Insight**: After a presentation on Lean's view of software development as fast-flexible-flow, and underscoring how much waste results from pushing too many products through the development pipeline, a vice president of the company declared, "Oh, I see, I should be giving my development teams fewer things to work on instead of imploring them to work harder."

Shortening Batch Times

The context and insight include the following:

- **Company profile**: Large software-development company

- **Challenges**: Lots of bugs with long cycle times to fix them.

- **Insight**: The truly Lean approach is to get to the root cause of the bugs. Two directors were trying to determine how to address and prioritize the great number of bugs facing them. Finding a root cause on all of them felt overwhelming. They realized that if all they did was work in three-month batches instead of six-month batches, they would get many more high-priority bugs fixed and released sooner. Although it didn't get to root cause, improvement was available by simply changing batch size. Sometimes it's worth getting what you can when that is virtually free.

Getting to the Root Cause

The context and insight include the following:

- **Group profile**: Support group for a large IT organization

- **Challenges**: Lots of internal-customer calls

- **Insight**: Once he understood that more problems are of a systemic nature than due to the person using the system, one member of the team reconsidered how they handled support. Instead of just answering questions, he started asking, "What is the root cause of this question?" Since he was not able to change the computer system that the users were having troubles with, he answered that question in terms of the support system that was available to the users who had questions. He realized that he could improve the support system by getting to the root cause—why was manual intervention required? After one year of doing this, and improving the automated support, he found it took half the time to handle twice the number of users—a fourfold increase in value added by his group.

Knowing Where You Are: Minimum Releasable Features

The context and insight include the following:

- **Group profile**: Makes administrative software used by large healthcare organizations

- **Challenges**: After committing to deliver a large program (two-plus years, several million dollars), the organization was not confident about their progress after five months

- **Insight**: The organization was focused only on the end date, which was two years away. There was no sense of priority for any of the work that was underway, as it "all had to be done." Without having set this priority (sequence of business features), the teams had no control over how much work was started, and no visible work was completed. Once the organization came together and visibly sequenced features, the teams began to utilize iterations to deliver the features one by one. The key insight gained by the organization was that by working this way, they did *not* have to wait until the far-off date to release. Instead, they prioritized and sequenced the features so that smaller releases could begin, which enabled them to keep key customers happy without having to wait two years to deliver the program.

Priorities and Work-in-Process

The context and insight include the following:

- **Group profile**: Creates reporting software used by large healthcare organizations

- **Challenges**: Integrating across functional areas and technical debt

- **Insight**: After struggling with integrating different functional areas, the organization was seeing a lot of delay-related waste. Toward the end of each development life-cycle, they usually discovered a large number of defects (bugs, or what we call "technical debt"). In part, this was because they did not integrate and test until it was too late to do anything except manage the bugs that were found. Their goal was to get the bugs to some sort of acceptable level.

The group's next release was organized into a Lean Portfolio of prioritized features, which they scheduled using Agile release planning. The organization got huge insight when they discovered that the teams had only focused on the lowest priority features. The functional silos were reorganized into cross-functional teams, and much shorter cycles of integration were achieved. For the first time, the organization was able to do a full regression test and complete the User Acceptance Test cycle prior to releasing the software to their clients.

Productivity and Quality

The context and insight include the following:

- **Group profile**: Administrative software for large enterprise storage array networks

- **Challenges**: Seeking productivity and quality gains in releases that must deliver features into a complex matrix of different operating systems, databases, and hardware environments

- **Insight**: After reorganizing into cross-functional teams that pulled work from a well-managed product portfolio, the teams began to focus on incrementally completing features in the order defined by the user's view of the system (administrator). The product team could easily validate specific flows for their clients and give the team quick feedback. With ten-day iterations, the team completed its release commitments three months ahead of the regular time allotment for releases of this size, and with a third of the defects.

Cross-functional Teams

The context and insight include the following:

- **Group profile**: Software for healthcare data and intelligence

- **Challenges**: Growing business made it difficult to scale

- **Insight**: Increasingly larger releases were creating a disproportionate number of defects. The development teams had grown significantly beyond a core group of developers, and yet deep knowledge of their code base had not kept pace. The individual developers were very comfortable in their silos, but the increasingly complex system was becoming unwieldy. Big-batch thinking seemed to be as basic as breathing air.

We selected a Minimum Releasable Feature and then defined the stories and tasks required to accomplish that one feature. The team rallied around this concept. They aggressively distributed their knowledge and discovered blind spots among the silos that were contributing to the higher defect count.

The Mantra of Lean: Fast-Flexible-Flow

Before concluding with next steps, we want to offer one more perspective on Lean thinking, using Womack and Jones's characterization of Lean as "Fast, Flexible, Flow" (Womack and Jones 1996).

Think of the software-development value stream as a pipeline. At the beginning of the pipeline, there is a variety of items to work on. We have to select the right items to work on in order to provide the greatest value. And to have good flow through the pipeline, we need them to be the right size and the right number. Our goal is to reach the greatest possible flow by maximizing our efficiency in the two main tasks: discovering how to build work items and then building them.

To accomplish both of these activities we need to optimize the entire value stream. The focus is not on productivity at each step, but rather the time for ideas to go from beginning to end, from initial concept to consumption. This includes

- **Short queues**   Imagine a bank where, from the outside, you see lots of people going in and out each hour. This looks good, but if you see huge lines inside, the cycle time (waiting time) is long, even though the throughput (people exiting over time) is high. Items should have cycle times that are as short as possible.

- **Eliminating waste**   This is accomplished by building things in the right sequence and with a just-in-time approach. When things go wrong, we look at our systems and get to the root cause of the errors.

While this description is simple, in real life it is usually hard. Often, it requires structural change with both top-down guidance (leadership) and bottom-up implementation. The focus is on continuously refining the system while working on delivering value faster, better, with less waste—and at lower cost.

To do this, *we must rely on utilization theory* to guide our decisions aimed at improving the process.

An Example of Fast-Flexible-Flow

Here is an example of how proper planning and a focus on fast-flexible-flow helped a small development organization become effective again. As you read through this story, you can probably remember a time when you went through this yourself. Or maybe you are still there!

Let's Try Specialization

This organization starts out with one stakeholder and one team of 12 people. The stakeholder asks the team to do a month's work (240 person-days), with a schedule something like the one shown in Figure 14.3.

The organization grows to include three stakeholders but is still supported by the same 12-person team. Each stakeholder asks for one month (again, 240 person-days) of work. The team works on these simultaneously. At best, they might get by with a three month schedule like the one in Figure 14.4.

The original stakeholder wonders why something that used to take one month now takes three! This causes a lot of problems. He now has to forecast his needs three months in advance instead of only one.

The team tries to gain productivity by creating specialized subteams: UI, mid-tier, data flow, and enterprise data. This helps a little: Figure 14.5 shows the work for each stakeholder by subteam and Figure 14.6 shows what happens when they schedule the work by subteam. They shorten the flow by a few weeks.

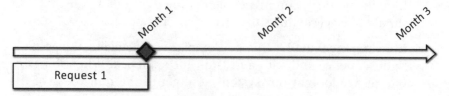

Figure 14.3   One stakeholder, one request, one month

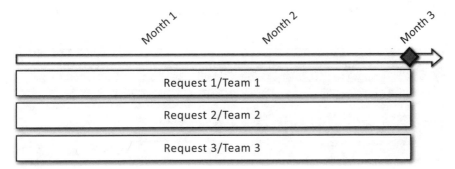

Figure 14.4   Three stakeholders, three requests, three months

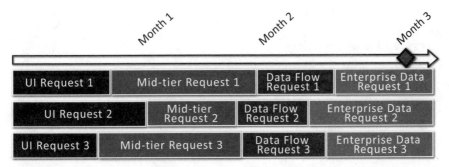

Figure 14.5   Specialized team working on three requirements simultaneously

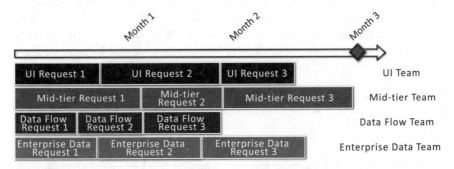

Figure 14.6   Specialized team working on three requirements in sequence

Unfortunately, it is not that easy. They find that subteams cannot simply do their work in sequence. There are interactions. Now, they have to plan ahead and figure out how to integrate the results. So the result looks like Figure 14.7. It takes even longer!

Hmm. Maybe specialization isn't the right approach after all.

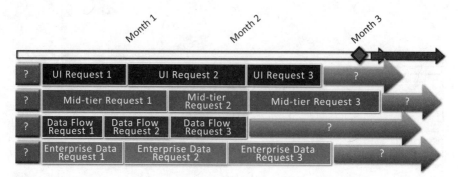

Figure 14.7   Now, extra planning and integration is needed

Let's Try Lean Thinking

Lean thinking says to do the following:

- Minimize cycle time.

- Do things Just-in-Time.

- Complete one task before going on to the next task.

This can best be accomplished by addressing one request at a time, with a team swarm, as we did in the beginning. This is illustrated in Figure 14.8.

This is clearly better than what we had before. In Figure 14.7, the average cycle time is three-plus months whereas in Figure 14.8, the average cycle time is only two months (that is, Request 1 took one month, Request

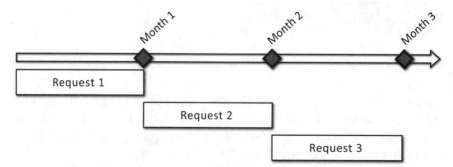

Figure 14.8   One team doing multiple jobs, each in sequence

2 took two months, and Request 3 took three months). This shows good improvement.[3]

However, as you can easily imagine, the stakeholder of Request 3 is not very happy. What happens if things don't go so well and the first two requests take all of the time available? Her request will never happen!

Stakeholders are nothing if not creative at getting what they want. When the three stakeholders get together to talk about the plan, they decide to compromise. Each stakeholder agrees to build the smallest functionality required to satisfy immediate needs and then work on more. Of course, this is exactly what should be done: When product champions start talking to each other about the smallest functionality that is actually needed, it is more likely that the most valuable features for the enterprise will be built.

This seems like a simple example. We have seen the application of these principles work again and again to help organizations become highly effective.

Next Steps

How do you learn more? There are many ways available. First, you have, we hope, learned a few principles here that you can see are true from your own experience. Start applying these when you have challenges. Understanding principles by way of your own experience can be powerful. They should help you when you need to solve a problem that you haven't solved before. If you are currently using an Agile process, but not using Lean, we suggest doing a value stream map of your entire process—from customer request to deployment. Identify where your problems are. Don't assume that creating an Agile team makes you an Agile enterprise. You may need to start out with your product-management team. Notice where your problems are coming from—don't just jump in with the popular Agile methodology of the moment.

There are many ways to gain more knowledge as well: user groups, books, and web sites. We have put together a portal of Lean-Agile information at our own web site for the book:

www.netobjectives.com/lasd

---

3. Note that the benefit actually scales. For example, if we tried to work on ten concurrent requests, the average cycle time would increase to ten months, but if we worked them in sequence, the average cycle time would be only five months.

We've included a few examples of those resources here, but please refer to the site, as things change quickly in this industry.

User Groups of Interest

- **Lean-Agile User Group**   This list is moderated by Alan Shalloway and lurked on by many Lean dignitaries. Discussions regarding any aspects of Lean and/or Agile methods are welcome. http://tech. groups.yahoo.com/group/leanagile.

- **Lean Development**   This list, moderated by the Poppendiecks, focuses on Lean Software Development. It is similar to the Lean-Agile list. http://tech.groups.yahoo.com/group/leandevelopment

- **Kanban Dev**   This list focuses on Kanban Software Development, moderated by David Anderson. Many Kanban practitioners lurk here as do many others just trying to understand Kanban. http://finance.groups.yahoo.com/group/kanbandev

Books to Read

Table 14.1 lists some essential books you should read, based on your role in the organization. Also, check the resources section of the Net Objectives web site (following, in Other Resources) for more up-to-date sources.

Table 14.1   Essential Reading

If you are...	These are essential books...
Mid-level Manager or above	*Lean Thinking: Banish Waste and Create Wealth in Your Corporation* (Womack and Jones 2003)
	Implementing Lean Software Development: From Concept to Cash (Poppendieck and Poppendieck 2006)
	Product Development for the Lean Enterprise: Why Toyota's System Is Four Times More Productive and How You Can Implement It (Kennedy 2003)
	Ready, Set, Dominate: Implement Toyota's Set-based Learning for Developing Products and Nobody Can Catch You (Kennedy, Harmon, and Minnock 2008)

Table 14.1   Essential Reading, *continued*

If you are...	These are essential books...
Team Director or Lead	*Lean Thinking: Banish Waste and Create Wealth in Your Corporation* (Womack and Jones 2003) *Managing the Design Factory* (Reinertsen 1997) *Implementing Lean Software Development: From Concept to Cash* (Poppendieck and Poppendieck 2006)
Product Manager	*Software by Numbers: Low-Risk, High-Return Development* (Denne and Cleland-Huang 2003) *Managing the Design Factory* (Reinertsen 1997)
Team Lead, or Interested in Kanban	*Scrumban: Essays on Kanban Systems for Lean Software Development* (Ladas 2009) *Kanban: Successful Change Management for Technology Organizations* (Anderson, Forthcoming 2010)
Interested in Lean Knowledge Stewardship	*Learning to Fly: Practical Lessons from one of the World's Leading Knowledge Companies* (Collison and Parcell 2004) *Managing to Learn: Using the A3 Management Process to Solve Problems, Gain Agreement, Mentor, and Lead* (Shook 2008)
Interested in Lean Science	*Managing the Design Factory* (Reinertsen 1997) *Lean Thinking: Banish Waste and Create Wealth in Your Corporation* (Womack and Jones 2003) *The Principles of Product Development Flow: Second Generation Lean Product Development* (Reinertsen 2009)
Interested in Lean Management	*Creating a Lean Culture: Tools to Sustain Lean Conversions* (Mann 2005) *The Leader's Handbook: Making Things Happen, Getting Things Done* (Scholtes 1997)
Involved in Transitioning Teams	*Managing Transitions: Making the Most of Change* (Bridges 2003)

Other Resources

All three authors of this book work for Net Objectives. At Net Objectives, we provide services including assessments, consulting, and training. We have had many experiences with many different companies. We help businesses realize value faster from their software-development investment. Our typical clients are trying to extend their Agile endeavors from the team to include management concerns and business priorities. Our range includes Lean, Agile, Kanban, Scrum, acceptance-test-driven development, test-driven development, design patterns, and more. All of our trainers and consultants are seasoned practitioners, authors, and thought leaders.

In our attempts to help our clients, we have collected and maintained a set of resources that span virtually all Lean-Agile disciplines and provide information and value for all roles that are involved. You can get access to this information by going to www.netobjectives.com/resources. This site offers days of free online training in the form of recorded webinar sessions, as well as dozens of articles to read.

Summary

Lean-Agile software development is about building software faster, better, and with less waste and cost than ever before. It requires a different mindset than many of us have had. Lean principles are based on a combination of science, management, and knowledge stewardship. Our journey doesn't end with Lean. It is an ongoing process. Our goal of continuous process improvement means always being in transition to better methods.

Lean-Agile thinking is grounded in the day-to-day realities of creating software. It is a way of thinking more than a fixed prescription to follow. Using its principles, you can apply Lean-Agile to address your own local conditions. Over time, you will realize the benefits— building the most important items as quickly as you can with high quality, getting products to the market quicker, adding value for the customer, and lowering costs.

Try This

These exercises are best done as a conversation with someone in your organization. After each exercise, ask each other if there are any actions either of you can take to improve your situation.

- As a manager: Identify some delays that affect your work. Why are they there? What purpose do they serve? Would eliminating them add any value?

- As a developer: Identify some delays in your development process that you can eliminate without asking management's permission. Would doing so help your process?

- What principles of Lean thinking can you apply throughout your organization?

- Do you see any counter-productive delays that you could eliminate or that someone else could eliminate by changing something?

- What are some examples of waste in your organization that you could decrease?

APPENDIX A

Team Estimation Game

The Team Estimation Game (created by Steve Bockman) helps teams size features and stories based on *relative* complexity. It works because people find it easier to compare the complexity of one feature or story with another even if they do not yet know all aspects of that story. This game is fast, easy, and fun. It helps people avoid getting bogged down in too many details, which is always a risk during estimation exercises. Relative ranking gives the team the information they need to decide what to work on and how much to commit to in the current planning horizon.

Remember, estimates represent our best guesses about the effort required based on what we currently know. As we gain more experience, we will have more information and can then refine the estimates.

One good way to think of feature or story complexity is the degree of connectedness the feature or story has. This can indicate either how interconnected it is with itself or the number of connections to other features or stories.

Traditionally, this game is played at the iteration planning session to size stories for the next iteration. The game details are presented in Table A.1.

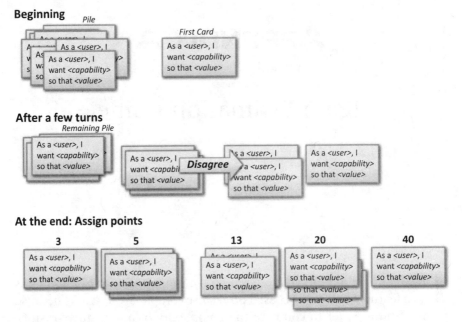

Figure A.1   Moving cards in the team estimation game

Notes about the Game

When a story is going to be placed on the playing surface, and it is being compared to another story, ask, "Will this take about the same effort, significantly less effort, or significantly more effort?" In other words, don't be too precise. If the effort is about same, just put it in the same column as the story you are comparing it to. If it is significantly less effort, put it to the left—significantly more effort, put it to the right. After all of the columns are done, you can then use the pseudo-Fibonacci sequence described in the table to size the effort. We chose these because each number in the sequence is significantly greater than the one before it without being so great that there is no continuum. The precision of these differences goes down as the numbers get larger.

We have found that Team Estimation is easier to learn, faster to do, and causes less bickering than Planning Poker for most teams who are new to Agile. We highly recommend trying it whether you've used other estimation methods or not.

Table A.1   Team Estimation Game

Step	Do this
Set up	Place story cards in a pile on the table. Select the top card in the pile and place it on the playing surface, a foot or so away from the pile.
First play	A player takes the top card off the pile and places it somewhere on the playing surface, indicating the size of its effort relative to the first card: to the left if it is easier, underneath it if is the same size, to the right if it is more complex.
Relative estimation of the rest of the deck	Each person plays in turn, doing one of the following: 1. Play the top card from the pile as described above. 2. Move a card already on the playing surface, declaring disagreement about its relative size. 3. Pass. Play ends when there are no more cards in the pile and there are no more adjustments needed. **Note:** During play, anyone may talk about why they are moving cards or about what they think about size of the stories. The goal is to get clarification and not to get too hung up on the exact sizes of the estimates. Remember that these are just estimates!
Assign points	The team works together to assign points to each stack to indicate the size (level of effort) of stories that are in that stack. Use the sequence: 0, 1, 2, 3, 5, 8, 13, 20, 40, 100, 200, 400, and 800. When done, write the assigned points on each card.

APPENDIX B

A Model of Lean-Agile Software Development

"As far as the laws of mathematics refer to reality, they are not certain; and as far as they are certain, they do not refer to reality." —Albert Einstein

We have always found it useful to create a model of our thinking. This both sharpens our understanding of things as well as gives us frequent opportunities to check its validity. While one should not work off a model as truth without understanding it, very often, the extra awareness that a model brings is useful—it allows us to take advantage of our intuitive knowledge by bringing it to the surface. As with all models, this one will change. Please refer to the book's web site (www.net-objectives.com/lasd) to get the latest version.

Something as complex as Lean thinking can be viewed in many different ways, and each of these may have several levels of understanding. These perspectives are not orthogonal, but rather build on each other. Figure B.1 illustrates how practices build on knowledge, which builds on attitudes, which build on perspectives and principles, which builds on foundational thinking.

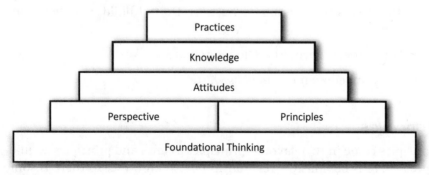

Figure B.1   *The building blocks of the model*

Foundational Thinking of Lean

This is the underlying belief system that Lean is based on. Much of this work comes from W. Edwards Deming.

- Most errors are systemic in nature.

- People are basically good and want to do a good job (therefore, respect people).

- Businesses will do best when they maximize the value they give to their customers.

These create the possibility and goal of achieving continuous process improvement through a combination of people doing the work while being coached and led by management.

Perspectives

You can think of perspective as how to look at things. Perspectives in themselves don't tell you how things work. But if you don't attend to the right things you can lose a lot of power. We often see things but don't understand how important they are, or we otherwise misinterpret them. The perspectives of Lean are a combination of Deming's system of profound knowledge, blended with Toyota's focus on Just In Time (JIT).

- Look at time, not resource utilization.

- Think of the development process as fast-flexible-flow.

- Lowering buffers between steps increases visibility into the process.

- The best way to eliminate waste is: Do not build what you don't need.

- Your process is your baseline for change.

- View impediments to flow as waste.

Principles

Principles come in two flavors—principles as laws and principles as guidance. There is obviously a relationship between these, so there is some redundancy in the listings.

Principles (Laws)

The following are what we think of as laws of development. Break these at your own peril and incur waste. That does not mean you never break them. There are times where emergencies call for action that is not optimal. But understand that a cost is being incurred.

- Shortening cycle time reduces waste and increases quality.
- You tend to get waste and lower quality when you increase the time between:
  - When you need information and when you get it
  - When you make an error and when you discover the error
- Making decisions too early increases the risk of waste.
- Excess work-in-process (WIP) increases both risk and waste.
- Impediments to flow cause waste.
- Increasing the number of concurrent projects without increasing resources working them increases the length of the projects.
- Working on more than one project at a time decreases a person's efficiency.
- Large batches cause waste.
- Switching from one task to another such that thrashing occurs causes waste.
- Ignoring risk may cause waste.
- Delivering value quickly increases ROI.

Principles (Guidance)

These are principles to follow. That is, these give us guidance. Those that are in bold are the seven principles detailed in *Implementing Lean Software Development: From Concept to Cash* (Poppendieck and Poppendieck 2003).

- **Optimize the whole.**
  - Look to shorten cycle time from concept to consumption.
  - Do not make local improvements at the expense of total cycle time.

- **Eliminate waste.**
  - Limit work to capacity.
  - Eliminate delays waiting for people or information.
  - Eliminate the delay from making an error until detecting it.
  - Focus on eliminating the cause of errors.
  - When something impedes the team, find a way to eliminate it.
  - Have teams work on one project at a time.

- **Create knowledge.**
  - Look to the system for errors.
  - Follow the scientific method to see how to improve your process.
  - Select the most important things to work on.
  - Define your workflow as much as feasible so that it can be used as the baseline for change. This also creates visibility to management.

- **Build quality in.**
  - Quality problems are often caused by delays in the work flow. Removing such delays improves quality and increases speed of delivery while decreasing cost.

- **Defer commitment.**
  - Make decisions at the appropriate time.
  - Make decisions reversible if possible.

- **Deliver Fast.**
  - Organize product enhancements into Minimal Marketable Features.
  - Follow the guidance for "eliminate waste" to remove delays.

- **Respect people.**
  - Have the people with the greatest knowledge of the problem at hand make the decisions regarding it.
  - Improve your culture by improving your management systems.
  - Set a goal of continuous process improvement where the people doing the work improve the process of the work being done.

Attitudes

Attitudes are important. They help define how we look at things and whether we consider something valuable. Attitudes are a result of our belief system and affect how we view many things.

- Management is important. Management needs to set outcomes for teams, allowing the teams to figure out the best way to achieve them.

- Have a goal of delivering as much value as possible in as short a period of time.

- Focusing on removing delays by eliminating waste will raise quality and lower costs.

- Always go to root cause to find and solve impediments.

- Do not let errors go by without fixing them, or at least noting them, so the root cause can be fixed later.

Knowledge

This is knowledge based from experience. We could also call this lessons learned.

- If you have long test and fix cycles, you are not testing early enough.

- If you have requirements churn, you are doing too much of requirements early.

- Optimizing components of your process without attending to the whole may result in waste.

- Focusing on lower costs typically results in lower quality and longer cycle times.

- Focusing only on quality may result in longer cycle times with little value to the customer.

- Focusing on achieving speed through eliminating delays will shorten delivery time, raise quality, and lower costs.

- People doing the work have a greater appreciation of it than those managing it.

- A high level of work-in-process (WIP) often indicates lots of thrashing.

Practices

There are, of course, many practices that Lean suggests doing. However, you have to be very careful about following practices. Practices make sense only within a particular context; always ensure that the practices being followed are sensible for the context at hand. Knowing practices, however, is a good starting point. Using principles to guide practices in unfamiliar contexts is often a good way to create new practices.

- Use value stream maps to see delays.
- Manage with visual controls.
- Build software in stages (iterations).
- Do continuous process improvement.
- Move testing up to the start of the development process.
- Select stories to work on to minimize risk (note, the biggest risk is often building what you don't need).
- Use Minimum Marketable Features to manage release cycles.
- Have cross-functional teams take on projects until they are completed and then move on to another.
- Go to the "gemba" (that is, go to where the work is being done).

Just a Beginning

The model presented here is just a beginning. Lean product development is not new. As our understanding of Lean unfolds, this model will be refined. There is already much more available. We are very excited about Don Reinertsen's book, *Principles of Product Development Flow: Second Generation Lean Product Development* (2009), in which he lays out 175 principles of Lean product development, organized into the following areas:

- Economic
- Queuing
- Variability
- Batch Size
- WIP Constraint
- Flow Control
- Fast Feedback
- Decentralization

This work presents a extensive model that Don began with his excellent book, *Managing the Design Factory* (1997), which is a must-read for any Lean product developer.
We will continue to post what we learn on the web site for this book. You can find it at www.netobjectives.com/lasd.

References

Poppendieck and Poppendieck. 2003. *Lean Software Development: An Agile Toolkit*. Boston: Addison-Wesley.

Reinertsen. 1997. *Managing the Design Factory*. New York: Free Press.

———. 2009. *The Principles of Product Development Flow: Second Generation Lean Product Development*. Redondo Beach, CA: Celeritas Publishing.

Bibliography

Alexander, Christopher. *The Timeless Way of Building.* New York: Oxford University Press, 1979.

Agile Alliance. www.agilealliance.org.

Anderson, David J. *Agile Management Blog: Thoughts on Software, Management, Constraints and Agility,* posted June 8, 2009, www.agileman-agement.net/Articles/Weblog/KanbanBlogosphereRoundupJ.html (accessed June 8, 2009).

———. *Kanban: Successful Change Management for Technology Organizations.* Seattle: Blue Hole Press, Forthcoming, 2010.

Aral, Sinan, Erik Brynjolfsson, and Marshall W. Van Alstyne. *What Makes Information Workers Productive.* December 2008. http://sloanreview.mit.edu/smr/issue/2008/winter/12/ (accessed October 2008).

Bain, Scott L. *Emergent Design: The Evolutionary Nature of Professional Software Development.* Boston: Addison-Wesley, 2008.

Beaver, Guy. *Knocking Down Silos: Transitioning the Enterprise to Agile.* February 11, 2008. www.agilejournal.com/content/view/753/76/ (accessed February 9, 2009).

Beck, Kent, and Cynthia Andres. *Extreme Programming Explained: Embrace Change.* 2d ed. Boston: Addison-Wesley, 2004.

Beck, Kent, Mike Beedle, Robert C. Martin, and James Grenning. *Manifesto for Agile Software Development.* 2001. www.agilemanifesto.org (accessed October 1, 2008).

Bridges, William. *Managing Transitions: Making the Most of Change.* Cambridge, MA: Da Capo, 2003.

Johnson, Thomas, and Broms, Anders. *Profit Beyond Measure: Extraordinary Results Through Attention to Work and People.* New York: Free Press, 2000.

Cockburn, Alistair. *Agile Software Development: The Cooperative Game.* 2d ed. Boston: Addison-Wesley, 2006.

Cohn, Mike. *Agile Estimating and Planning.* Upper Saddle River, NJ: Prentice Hall, 2005.

Collison, Chris, and Geoff Parcell. *Learning to Fly: Practical Lessons from One of the World's Leading Knowledge Companies.* Milford, CT: Capstone, 2004.

Denne, Mark, and Jane Cleland-Huang. *Software by Numbers: Low-Risk, High-Return Development.* Upper Saddle River, NJ: Prentice Hall, 2003. Feathers, Michael. *Working Effectively with Legacy Code.* Upper Saddle River, NJ: Prentice Hall, 2004.

Gamma, Erich, Richard Helm, Ralph Johnson, and John Vlissides. *Design Patterns: Elements of Reusable Object-Oriented Software.* Reading, MA: Addison-Wesley, 1994.

Kennedy, Michael. *Product Development for the Lean Enterprise: Why Toyota's System Is Four Times More Productive and How You Can Implement It.* Richmond, VA: Oaklea Press, 2003.

Kennedy, Michael, Kent Harmon, and Ed Minnock. *Ready, Set, Dominate: Implement Toyota's Set-based Learning for Developing Products and Nobody Can Catch You.* Richmond, VA: Oaklea Press, 2008.

Ladas, Corey. *Scrumban: Essays on Kanban Systems for Lean Software Development.* Seattle, WA: Modus Cooperandi Press, 2009.

Liker, Jeffrey. *The Toyota Way.* New York: McGraw-Hill, 2003.

Mann, David. *Creating a Lean Culture: Tools to Sustain Lean Conversions.* New York: Productivity Press, 2005.

Martin, Robert C. *Agile Software Development: Principles, Patterns and Practices.* Upper Saddle River, NJ: Prentice Hall, 2002.

Mascitelli, Ronald. *Building a Project-Driven Enterprise: How to Slash Waste and Boost Profits through Lean Project Management.* Northridge, CA: Technology Perspectives, 2002.

Meszaros, Gerard. *xUnit Test Patterns: Refactoring Test Code*. Upper Saddle River, NJ: Addison-Wesley Signature Series, 2007.

Mugridge, Rick. *Fit for Developing Software: Framework for Integrated Tests*. Upper Saddle River, NJ: Prentice Hall, 2005.

Ohno, Taiichi. *Toyota Production System: Beyond Large-Scale Production*. New York: Productivity Press, 1988.

Poppendieck, Mary, and Tom Poppendieck. *Implementing Lean Software Development: From Concept to Cash*. Boston: Addison-Wesley, 2006.

———. *Lean Software Development: An Agile Toolkit*. Boston: Addison-Wesley, 2003.

Reinertsen, Donald G. *Managing the Design Factory*. New York: Free Press, 1997.

———. *The Principles of Product Development Flow: Second Generation Lean Product Development*. Redondo Beach, CA: Celeritas Publishing, 2009.

Scholtes, Peter R. *The Leader's Handbook: Making Things Happen, Getting Things Done*. New York: McGraw-Hill, 1997.

Schwaber, Ken. *AgileCollab*. February 2, 2008. www.agilecollab.com/interview-with-ken-schwaber (accessed June 19, 2009).

Shalloway, Alan. "Lean Anti-Patterns and What to Do About Them." *Agile Journal*. 2008. www.agilejournal.com/content/view/553/39/ (accessed February 2, 2009).

Shalloway, Alan, and Scott L. Bain. *Essential Skills for the Agile Developer: A Guide Object-Oriented Design*. Boston: Addison-Wesley, 2010.

Shalloway, Alan, and James R. Trott. *Design Patterns Explained: A New Perspective on Object-Oriented Design*. 2d ed. Boston: Addison-Wesley, 2004.

Shalloway, Alan, and James R. Trott. *Lean-Agile Pocket Guide for Scrum Teams*. Seattle: Net Objectives Press, 2009.

Shook, John. *Managing to Learn: Using the A3 Management Process to Solve Problems, Gain Agreement, Mentor, and Lead*. Cambridge, MA: Lean Enterprise Institute, 2008.

Sourceforge. *Junit: A Cook's Tour*. January 10, 2009. http://junit.source-forge.net/doc/cookstour/cookstour.htm (accessed January 10, 2009).

Sutherland, Jeff. "Get Your Requirements Straight." *Jeff Sutherland*. March 11, 2003. http://jeffsutherland.com/scrum/2003/03/scrum-get-your-requirements-straight.html (accessed March 13, 2009).

Townsend, Patrick L., and Joan E. Gebhardt. *How Organizations Learn: Investigate, Identify, Institutionalize*. Milwaukee, WI: ASQ Quality Press, 2007.

Womack, James P., and Daniel T. Jones. *Lean Thinking: Banish Waste and Create Wealth in Your Corporation*. 2d ed. New York: Simon & Schuster, 2003.

Womack, James P., and John Shook. "Lean Management and the Role of Lean Leadership Webinar." *Lean Enterprise Institute*. October 19, 2006. www.lean.org/Events/LeanManagementWebinar.cfm (accessed October 23, 2007).

Index

Architecture, *continued*
    Product Coordination Team guide-
        lines, 201
    in Scrum, 85
    software. *See* Software design and
        development
As-is value stream maps, 18–19
ATDD (Acceptance Test-Driven
    Development), 134, 166
Attitudes in Lean-Agile model,
    240–241
Authority guidelines for Product
    Coordination Teams, 201
Automated acceptance testing
    Agile process, 171
    Scrum, 91
    specifications, 165
Autonomation, 215

B

Backlogs
    clear line of sight for, 148
    Iteration 0, 113
    with visual controls, 141–146
Backward-looking experiments, xxxv
Bain, Scott L.
    *Agile Developer: A Guide to Better
        Programming and Design*, 203
    *Emergent Design: The Evolutionary
        Nature of Professional Software
        Development*, 38, 91, 203
Balanced management, 184–185
Batch times in Lean, 220
Batching project analysis, 57–58
BDUF (big design up front), 207
Beaver, Guy, xxx, 137
Beck, Kent, 91
Beedle, Mike, 188
Berra, Yogi, xxxv
Bias issues in Scrum-of-Scrums, 195
Big design up front (BDUF), 207
Blame, 8–9

Bockman, Steve, 233
Bohr, Niels, 203
Books on Lean, 228–229
Bridges, William, 229
Bugs, preventing vs. finding, 158–160
Build phase
    components, 31–32
    visual controls for, 146–148
Building in quality, 158, 240
Burn-down charts, 152
Burn-up charts, 149–150, 152
Business role in Lean, 7
Business value
    Agile for, 26–31
    Product Coordination Team for, 200
    in release planning, 127

C

Capability Maturity Model (CMM), xxxii
Case studies
    building components, 31–32
    financial services, 49
    process control, 105
    Product Coordination Teams, 199
    release planning, 132
    Scrum vs. Kanban, 101–103
CFDs (cumulative flow diagrams), 99
Change, design for, 206–207
Charts, burn-down and burn-up, 149–
    150, 152
Chickens and pigs story, 87
Churchill, Winston, 161
Clear line of sight, visual controls for,
    148–150
Cleland-Huang, Jane, 28, 31, 229
Clobberation, 197
CMM (Capability Maturity Model),
    xxxii
Co-location of teams, 171
Cockburn, Alastair, 138
Code issues
    Agile process, 171

W

Waste
  delays as, 15
  eliminating, 10, 158
  Lean, 223
  Lean-Agile model, 240
  managing, 184
  from quality assurance at end of
      development cycle, 160–161
Waterfall projects
  core beliefs, xxxvi
  emergence of, xxxii
  hidden impediments in, 60
  vs. iterative development, 34–35
  steps and risks, 16–17
Weinberg, Gerald, 203
"What" question in Agile process,
      170–171
"Where" question in Agile process, 170
Whys technique, 19–20, 187
Womack, James P.
  on fast-flexible-flow goal, 15, 223
  *Lean Thinking: Banish Waste and
      Create Wealth in Your
      Corporation*, 228–229

management roles, 89
*Managing to Learn: Using the A3
    Management Process to Solve
    Problems, Gain Agreement,
    Mentor, and Lead*, 229
Work-in-process (WIP)
  Lean, 221–222
  Lean portfolio management, 62–63
  in Little's law, 217
  minimizing, 16, 59
  project ideas as, 57
Working Effectively with Legacy Code
    (Feathers), 91, 205
Wring-able necks in Scrum, 87

X

XP (eXtreme Programming), xxix, 11
  principles, 80
  vs. Scrum, Kanban, and Lean,
      103–104

FREE Online Edition

Your purchase of **Lean-Agile Software Development** includes access to a free online edition for 45 days through the Safari Books Online subscription service. Nearly every Addison-Wesley Professional book is available online through Safari Books Online, along with more than 5,000 other technical books and videos from publishers such as Cisco Press, Exam Cram, IBM Press, O'Reilly, Prentice Hall, Que, and Sams.

SAFARI BOOKS ONLINE allows you to search for a specific answer, cut and paste code, download chapters, and stay current with emerging technologies.

Activate your FREE Online Edition at
www.informit.com/safarifree

> **STEP 1:** Enter the coupon code: XCVTPVH.

> **STEP 2:** New Safari users, complete the brief registration form.
> Safari subscribers, just log in.

If you have difficulty registering on Safari or accessing the online edition, please e-mail customer-service@safaribooksonline.com